On Camera

On Camera

How to Report, Anchor & Interview

Nancy Reardon
with Tom Flynn

ELSEVIER

AMSTERDAM • BOSTON • HEIDELBERG • LONDON
NEW YORK • OXFORD • PARIS • SAN DIEGO
SAN FRANCISCO • SINGAPORE • SYDNEY • TOKYO

Focal Press is an imprint of Elsevier

Focal
Press

Acquisitions Editor: Amy Jollymore
Project Manager: Brandy Lilly
Assistant Editor: Doug Shultz
Marketing Manager: Christine Degon Veroulis
Cover Design: Alisa Andreola
Interior Design: Julio Esperas

Focal Press is an imprint of Elsevier
30 Corporate Drive, Suite 400, Burlington, MA 01803, USA
Linacre House, Jordan Hill, Oxford OX2 8DP, UK

Library of Congress Cataloging-in-Publication Data
Reardon, Nancy.
    On-camera presentation : reporting, anchoring & interviewing for TV / by Nancy Reardon.
    p. cm.
    ISBN-13: 978-0-240-80809-3 (pbk. : alk. paper)
    ISBN-10: 0-240-80809-6 (pbk. : alk. paper) 1. Television broadcasting of
news–Vocational guidance. 2. Interviewing on television–Vocational guidance. I. Title.
    PN4784.T4R43 2006
    070.1'95–dc22

                                                                              2006011122

British Library Cataloguing-in-Publication Data
A catalogue record for this book is available from the British Library.

ISBN 13: 978-0-240-80809-3
ISBN 10: 0-240-80809-6

For information on all Focal Press publications
visit our website at www.books.elsevier.com

05 06 07 08 09 10   10 9 8 7 6 5 4 3 2 1

Printed in the United States of America

Dedication

To my mother who always supported me . . . in the past
My husband . . . in the ever present
My daughter . . . now and in the future . . .
And all my dogs in the toughest times.

Contents at a Glance

Contents

3 The Interviewee

14 Anchoring II

18 Physical Techniques   277

19 Looking Good   283

Getting the Job 301

20 Preparing Your Reel 303

A Few Words to Grow By. . .

21 How to Land A Job in Television

Epilogue

Index

Foreword

As it was with so many reporters of my generation, I was a news-paperman before I got into TV and my first newspaper job was working the night police beat on my hometown newspaper, The Fort Worth Star-Telegram.

In those days, the police reporters at most newspapers did not write much. They went to the scene of the crime, or the accident, or some other untoward event, gathered the facts and called them in by telephone to a city desk rewrite man who put it all into story form and passed it on to the city editor or his deputy who decided if it was good enough to deserve a by-line.

That was not the way our City Editor Bill Hitch wanted it done. Bill insisted that no matter where we were—on a nursing station phone in a hospital emergency room, or a phone booth a block from a three-alarm fire or on a cop's phone at the police station—when we called in he wanted us to dictate a lead to the story we were covering. Once you get the lead to a newspaper story written, the rest of the story takes care of itself. You tell the important facts in the lead, generally follow that with a direct quote that adds color and sets the tone for the story and then flesh it out with the details that back up what you have stated in that first paragraph. Bill believed only the reporter on the scene knew the real flavor of what was going on there, and so he made us dictate the story to the rewrite man.

I digress to explain that I used the word "man" deliberately because there were almost no women on the city side of the paper. In those days, they were seldom allowed to venture very far from the "society" department.

The rewrite man was there to help us get the story in readable order, but it was up to the reporter to dictate that lead. Bill was right in his belief that only the reporter on the scene can convey what's happening there. That is, after all, the core of what journalism is all about. But I would later come to understand he had a larger purpose. He was teaching us to think like reporters and that meant that the moment we arrived on the scene, the first thought that went through our minds was, "what's the lead here? What's the most important thing to say about all this?" It became automatic. When you know that's going to be the first question that rewrite man is going to ask when you call in your story, that thought is constantly going through your mind as you gather the facts for your story.

I always had a fairly good reputation for finding the lead and I believe that can be traced to what Hitch taught us in those days. Years later, when I would take notes at presidential news conferences, I would always put a star beside an important quote from the President. If he later said something I considered more important, I would place two stars beside it, and then three if he later said something I considered an even better quote. What I was doing was prioritizing what he had said, just as I had done those many years ago on the police beat. Subconsciously I was asking myself the question that Hitch always asked, "What's the lead here? What should people care about?"

When the news conference broke up and I rushed to the White House lawn to do a post news conference analysis with Water Cronkite, I just looked at my note book, found the quote with the most stars and said, "Walter, what I think is important here is when the President said..." To this day, nothing annoys me more than to ask a reporter returning from a news story what happened and to have that reporter say, "Well, first he said such and such and then he said such and such..." Editors are not interested in what someone said first, they want to know what he said that was important. Bill Hitch taught us how to do that. His way was not the only way but it worked for me.

The communications landscape has changed dramatically since those long ago days, but the basics of journalism have not and all of us had to learn those basics from someone. Journalism is best learned by the apprentice method. In your early years as a professional journalist, you will attach yourself to someone who knows more about it than you do, and you will learn from them. But this book will give you a head start. Between them, Nancy Reardon and Tom Flynn have been journalists and teachers all of their adult lives and they know what works. This book reflects what they have learned, not just from textbooks but on the job-in the trenches as they describe it. They lay out the basics of covering television stories, tell you how to go about it and then use real life experiences to demonstrate why their methods really work.

This is a real "how to" book by two people who really know how. But it is more than just a fine manual on broadcast journalism, journalists and non-journalists alike will find it good reading, a treasure chest of anecdotes, stories and a tall tale or two from the most exciting profession of all—reporting the news.

- Bob Schieffer

Acknowledgments

I always laugh at the acceptance speeches when the Emmys and Oscars are awarded. What are all those gratuitous thank yous for anyway? Now that I've written a book, I see it takes a small village of support from beginning idea to final publication. So don't play the music yet...

I want to thank: Dr. Amit Das from N.Y.U, now University of Pennsylvania, for telling me to write this. To Sarah Crichton for viewing the initial proposal and making super suggestions. To my editor: savvy, creative Amy Eden Jollymore for believing in this from proposal to completion. She and amazingly attentive project manager, Brandy Lilly, have guided me every step of the way. To the following friends, who took the time to read the completed proposal and offer suggestions and comments: Jim Stewart (CBS News), Meredith Wagner (Lifetime), Dr. Peter Haratonic, (New School), and Roseanne Seelen (The Drama Bookshop).

There are friends who were so necessary on this journey: To Rolland Smith, who years ago when he was at CBS, took the time to teach me. To Dana Tyler at WCBS, New York, who has been a friend of mine and supporter of my students for years. I am grateful for the help and photography from my dear friend, Marie Wallace. To Lucy Martin for her perceptive comments, and to the brilliant ad-man, Bob Sauer. Bruce Torbet, who has been my cameraman from the beginning, when I was so technically challenged, and Steve Reilly who shot the video you will see on the CD-Rom.

And speaking of the CD-Rom, I'm so lucky to have Peter Moser on this project. He has not only created the spectacular CD-Rom for this book, he has helped me in so many other ways to finesse the finished product. And thanks to Dr. Alisa Roost, who has constructed the Instructor's Manual.

To Warren Miller, the legendary New Yorker cartoonist, for his drawings and his dear friendship. His genius and wit continually awe me, and to Joanna, his wife, for encouraging this project.

I am beyond fortunate to have Tom Flynn (writer/producer CBS News) to walk hand in hand with me for the distance. And to Katie Flynn, who took time from a busy acting career to do a grueling edit of the manuscript. Wait, I hear the music...I'm not finished yet!

Now...The sign off...If I've left anyone out, forgive me. I'll remedy that in the next edition...that is, if the second edition doesn't become the rare book.

- N.R.

Introduction

My name is Nancy Reardon. Usually at this point, I go around the class and ask your name, ask who you are and why you are interested in taking this class. Since we are doing this class differently, you will have to answer that question to yourself. Be honest. I am here to help you learn, you are there to do the learning. In this book, I've tried to anticipate some of your questions and some of your fears. If you follow along and do your part, I can also anticipate your success, can't I? Yes, you say? I agree.

Television is a very competitive business. But as you can see by turning on your local news every night, someone got the job. You have to be smart and interested: interested in people, interested in what goes on in your neighborhood and interested in the world. The one thing this book can't give you is the caring, the curiosity and the passion. Nor can I give you the courage to follow your dreams. But, as a Broadway show song says, "The best of times is now." This is true if you are a novice with no experience in front of the camera, or if you are working in a small market on your way to bigger stations.

This book will also help those who feel they simply need to brush up on their skills, which includes anyone who could use some work in the interview process: authors, artists, businessmen and women, anyone who will be facing the camera.

Now is the time to get to work if you have an interest in being on camera in any field: entertainment, sports, legal, business, weather, music or food. The fact is, putting it off is as easy as finding another excuse. You will never have fewer things to do; you will always be busy. You are not getting any younger. And speaking of younger, although television has always been a young person's business, the areas of age are loosening up these days. There is a market for all ages, genders and races.

I've written this book because if you look around, you won't find one that tells you the basic nuts and bolts of how to do the job of anchoring, reporting and interviewing once you get in front of the camera in the studio, or out on location. There are plenty of books you can find that talk about journalism. There are lectures you can find on morals, ethics and the politics of television reporting. But you might as well be a top-flight investigator to dig up a book that tells you how to report on camera. This is your simple, straightforward HOW TO DO IT book.

So let's get to work. Good luck. 3-2-1 Roll.

Writers' Biographies

Nancy Reardon created the first On-Camera course at the New School in 1982 and has been teaching there, at NYU and in her Greenwich Village studio ever since. As a teacher and coach, she has trained many network and local reporters and anchors and has taken her teaching on the road throughout the United States and as far as Helsinki, Finland. She is a veteran New York actress, having appeared in more than 10 Broadway shows as well as roles in film and television.

Tom Flynn Writer and producer at CBS News for more than a quarter century at the CBS Evening News and 60 MINUTES, he was a founding members of 48 HOURS. He is the recipient of the prestigious George Foster Peabody Award, has been honored by the National Academy of Television Arts and Sciences with six Emmy's and many other honors including the IRE (Investigative Reporters/Editors), Robert F. Kennedy Award, National Society of Black Journalists Award and Edward R. Murrow Fellowship Award.

Warren Miller has been a contract cartoonist with The New Yorker magazine since 1961. His work has been published in two collections and in collections of The New Yorker, Playboy and the Cartoonist Guild. He has illustrated children's books and also paints in oils and any other medium he gets his hands on. He lives in New York with his wife, a former bio-chemistry teacher, has three children and a granddaughter.

Bob Schieffer has been a reporter for more than 40 years, most of that time at CBS News where he served as anchor of the CBS Evening News. Before his time in television, he was at the Fort Worth, Texas Star-Telegram. In 2005, his alma mater TCU named its journalism school in his honor and made him a distinguished professor of journalism.

On Camera

When you walk into the studio for the first time to face a TV camera, you'll want to be as prepared as possible so that you are able to communicate to your viewers with elegance, tact and confidence. Your job description or title may vary: reporter or anchor, CEO or entrepreneur, press officer or politician, or the latest, on-camera bloggers, vloggers and podcasters. No matter what the delivery system, no matter what the audience, you are on camera and should do it well in order to make your point.

Being on camera is not just confined to television anymore, it's video conferences and live video messages to the clients, potential clients or employees and it's video messaging and podcasting. Never before have we lived in such a world of video communication and this requires that you be as advanced as the technology. You have to be as at ease on camera as you are in life. For one and all, this book should help you feel at ease whether doing an interview or reporting in the field, reading copy from a teleprompter or giving a presentation.

No matter what your job is, when you face that camera, you must be natural in an unnatural setting. There are lights and cameras and producers talking to you. The trick will be to make this artificial situation appear as if it is real life.

If you take this course seriously, you will be well prepared when that day comes. We will have some fun as we go, but this is a serious business and I aim to make sure you know everything you need to know to do it well.

My plan is to give to you the techniques, the exercises, the tricks of the trade and some true stories from the business ... we'll call them:

Report from the Trenches

Some of you will be by yourself on camera, such as in giving a video presentation. You will learn those tricks in the chapters on anchoring and on hosting. But you will also gain skills by studying the reporting chapters. In those reporting chapters are some valuable lessons and tools on writing skills for television and how to write your own script. Hosts, anchors and reporters, all of you are on-camera presenters. The point is: Each chapter is relevant for all of you.

For example, in the anchoring chapter, you will find one of NANCY'S RULES.

NANCY'S
RULES

The rules will be peppered throughout the book. Be on the lookout for Nancy's Rules. They offer you tricks of the trade known only to the most experienced hands in television that I am now sharing with you. The one in that chapter is simple: Room Service. But you'll have to read the chapter to learn what that means. Many of you are looking at someday having a beat such as a legal or medical reporter or sports, business or weather. There are chapters for you too. You should all read the beat reporter chapters. Almost all of you will be interviewing someone on camera. There are many tricks to learn here and they are presented in the interviewing chapters.

Tucked inside each chapter are pointers with terrific advice from some of the best in the business.

Looking good in the office and looking good on television require different make up — both for women and for men. There is a chapter on this as well.

And when the time comes for you to prepare your reel there is a chapter on what you should include and, just as important, what you should leave out. And a special treat, there is a chapter with advice from a correspondent Melinda Murphy, who was a student of mine.

On a different note, I want to say something to you that I think is important. Public opinion on the press runs in cycles. Sometimes the press is well regarded, while at other times respect runs pretty low. I believe the professionals who communicate the news of the day or information to their employees or stockholders are doing a professional job and should not be criticized or evaluated merely as performers. You are not a dancing bear. You should not feel that you have been put in a box simply to entertain. Do not degrade yourself with a demeaning concept to help (or hype) the ratings. You are a professional. You should be proud of your work and proud of your decisions.

Now learn how to do the best you are capable of by reading and exercising. I am your guide, but you must do your part. Together we will accomplish our goal — to get you on camera.

Interviewing

Interviewing

Not all interviews are the same. There are different styles of interviews and you will approach them differently. We are talking here about in-depth interviews, not on-street reporting interviews. We'll discuss that in detail in the chapter on Reporting.

Interviewing for television should appear to be a terrific and revealing conversation between you and your guest. It might be a cheerful conversation, an argumentative conversation, or even a tender conversation. There are all sorts of conversations you can have. And just as there are all sorts of conversations, there are all sorts of interviews you will conduct. They fall into two basic categories: Hard News Interviews and Soft Interviews.

The Hard News Interviews tend to be direct, informational and almost always done on tape. Soft Interviews are done with live guests or features on tape. These tend to be nonconfrontational, emotional and comfortable. More on this in a bit.

All interviews are conversations with some basic rules. In order to make your interviews conversations, you need to follow some simple rules. We'll call them Nancy's rules. So let's get started with our first set.

Prepare, Communicate, Listen.

Prepare

In all cases, you must prepare. You must do your homework and be prepared to discuss any aspect of your subject's interest or life. If he or she wrote a book, read it. If someone wrote a book or article about your guest, read that too. Then you will be ready if the conversation takes an unexpected, and often very interesting, turn.

It's not enough to breeze through the research. Read it to understand it. As you work through the information, questions will start to form in your mind. Have a notebook handy to jot your thoughts and questions down as you have them. I guarantee you will not remember all those thoughts later. And even more important,

Fig. 2-1 Prepare.

by writing down the questions when reading your research, you will remember the WAY to ask them.

Someday, you may have the luxury of having a staff to gather your research. But until you get to that exalted position of having a staff, you must do your own. It is vital. You will understand the subject and will be comfortable with your guest. The guest will also be more comfortable with you. Of course, all of that leads to a better conversation.

Your confidence will show through, not only to your interviewee but also to your audience. Think of interviews you have watched as a viewer. You can tell when someone is prepared and when they are not. You have questions in your mind that seem so obvious but aren't asked, right? That is a situation you want to avoid.

On the other hand, you have seen interviews where the reporter zaps just the right question at the right time — something the guest hadn't expected — and takes the interview to another level. That's the preparation showing through.

Rarely are *60 Minutes* correspondents tripped up by the guest. They have done their homework. They are not responsible for the primary research — the producers do that. The correspondents are given "the bible": a huge binder of notes, quotes and background material. It's prepared by the producer and includes a paragraph on each person to be interviewed and questions for the interview. So until you have a producer to do that for you, it would be a good idea for you to prepare your own bible.

Unprepared interviewers can have embarrassing moments, or worse. They can lose interviews completely.

 ## Report from the Trenches

There is one story floating around the networks that tells of the time that a young Bill Gates of Microsoft had consented to a rare TV interview. This was a big coup at the time. It was to be a taped, two-camera shoot (one on Gates, one on the interviewer). As the

Fig. 2-2 "Who is this Miss Dose?"

crew put the final touches on the set, Mr. Gates was seated in his chair across from the reporter who was just then looking at the questions for the first time. The interviewer scowled, looked around and shouted to the producer, "Who is this Miss Dose?"

The producer approached and began whispering in the interviewer's ear as Mr. Gates stared at them. The interviewer, sensing there was a problem, snapped at the producer. Gates pulled off his microphone and left it carefully on his chair. As Gates started to leave, he said, "It's not Miss Dose, it's MS Dos . . . it's my invention. That's the operating system behind Microsoft." Because the interviewer didn't know that, Gates assumed, correctly, this interview couldn't be of any value.

The story illustrates the value of research and preparation.

Research

Where do you do your research? Where do you dig up the information you need? There are the obvious places: Written research can be found on the Internet or in magazines and books. In turn, these basic sources may lead you to more obscure ones. Like a good reporter, follow through with each lead. By a close read of the magazine, book or Internet research, you might get more ideas for further contacts and consequently different ideas, stories and information.

Always read the entire article so you can understand the context. Always try to be aware of the largest possible picture. You will pick up tidbits of information that spark the guest and the listening audience. In effect, you become the source where the audience will go for information on the topics you choose.

Communicate

In all cases, whether a live interview or taped, whether hard news or soft, communication must take place. You must connect with your subject. You should stay interested.

In our daily lives, we communicate all the time. It's called having a conversation. This does not mean a leisurely chat. Keep your energy up; your guest will also. Keep your pace up and your guest

W Miller

Fig. 2-3 Communicate.

will follow. Keep your interest up and your guest will too; and you will be able to communicate fully.

Listen

How will you become a great interviewer? By becoming a great listener. There is no greater compliment that you can give a person than to listen to what he or she is telling you. Listen with enthusiasm and interest. This is called active listening. You do it already when someone is telling you something you care about.

In all cases, listen to to your guest when he or she is talking. Listen to what your guest is saying. You can check your notes later. It's disconcerting for your guest if you are looking somewhere else. Conversation breaks down, and you will probably miss something. If it's like life in general, when you aren't listening, I mean really listening, you miss the most important thing your guest says. By paying close attention, you will catch those unexpected and most interesting items.

By listening and with proper preparation, you will pick up any new or newsworthy item. Whether it's the confession of an actor

Fig. 2-4 Really listen.

Fig. 2-5 Watch the body language.

or the admission of a businessman, when you hear it, alarm bells should go off in your head. Be sure to follow up.

Be aware also: Not all language is verbal. Not only must you listen to the guest's words, but you must also read his or her body language. It speaks volumes. And it might be giving you (and the viewers) a different and more honest answer to your question. If it becomes pronounced, address it.

For example: You have been asking the corporate officer about documents that show illegal acts.

Corporate Officer: "I can tell you honestly, no one in our company did anything of the sort."
You: "You've broken out in a sweat, sir . . ."

Eye contact has become the buzzword. You hear people say, "You must make eye contact." A more precise term that I like for interviewing is FACE contact. When you are interviewing someone, if you stare directly into the eyes of the person, either of you can lose your train of thought. It's very disconcerting for both of you.

If you focus only on their eyes, you will find it difficult to assess all of what they are saying. By looking at the whole face, the eyes included, you can read their expressions and their body language.

Intonations and Silence

The intonations of the interviewee can be as important as body language. Listen for the hesitations and silences.

Speaking of silence, it can be a very useful tool for you in an interview. This works well in both taped and live interviews. At times, you get a sense that the person you are talking to is holding something back.

Try this: Don't say anything, just listen intently. Often, the response by your guest will be to want to fill the void by starting to talk. It is usually something interesting; and it may be the thing he or she was holding back. It might be a fact — something of substance in your hard news interview. If it's an emotional moment, your silence will allow the guest to complete his or her emotion. It may be a quivering lip, tears or a thoughtful pause. That can be far more telling and compelling than what is being said.

To Pre-Interview or Not to Pre-Interview?

This is a question that many argue about. So here are the two schools of thought.

YES, you should meet and chat with the guest before the cameras roll. Here are the reasons:

❖ You will hear and know what the guest has to say. You will know what he or she will say and say with passion, with feeling, with interest. You will also know what he or she doesn't say well or won't want to talk about at all. Then, when the cameras are rolling you won't be wasting time. You will already know what questions to ask and what not to ask.

❖ You will already have a relationship with the guest. When the cameras roll, you will be able to build on that comfort zone you have built in the pre-interview. The preliminary and awkward get-to-know-you is out of the way.

❖ You have more time to cover material in a pre-interview than you ever will on camera. This gives you the opportunity to dig where it might not be fruitful and come up with anecdotes and stories that you might not otherwise have learned.

NO, you should not meet or chat with the guest about the substance of the interview beforehand. Here are these reasons:

❖ You will lose spontaneity. There is nothing like the first meeting and it cannot be recreated. There is an energy to the discovery of information and of your interaction with each other. It will seem like a fresh conversation because it is. If you have gone over all of this before, the interview can sound stale and come out like a rehash of facts.

❖ You won't always get the same answer again. Remember, most of the people you will interview are not professionals at this. Just because you heard it before does not mean you will get it again or with the same passion. Often you hear interviewers say, "You said before ..." So what you get is the interviewer telling the audience what the guest said in a pre-interview and probably said well. That's no good.

Nancy's opinion:

I acknowledge that by pre-interviewing you are vulnerable to a stale interview rather than a totally fresh one. You aren't as daring as a tightrope walker out there without a net.

But I say YES to the pre-interview, especially when you are just getting started. This way, you won't miss a point or a good story that comes up in an extended pre-interview. Plus, there will be a comfort factor with your guest that will help.

But you decide what is better for you. You decide if the risk of not pre-interviewing is worth the reward. As always, the more you do it, the more you will know which works better for you.

Be Polite

Even in the most aggressive, confrontational interview you have, be polite. Even if your guest is being rude to you or others, be polite.

Fig. 2-6 Be polite, no matter what.

You are a professional and you should conduct the interview that way. You are not the story and shouldn't become it. The focus should be on your guest and the information you draw from your guest. What if your guest becomes rude? Do not take the bait. Always stay on the point of the interview.

For example: You have just shown your guest documents that prove he has done something wrong.

> Him: "You're a jerk."
> You: "I'm not the issue sir. What can you say about . . ."
> Him: "You're full of s--t!"
> You: "Sir, may I point out these documents show your company . . ."

His bad acting will reflect badly on him. If you respond badly, it will reflect badly on you. And you haven't gotten the response to the matter at hand, have you?

That is an example of a category of Hard News Interview called a confrontational interview. There are subsets in Hard News and Soft Interviews too. Now is a good time to get more in depth with our categories.

Hard News Interviews

Confrontational Interview — A news interview that is usually a sit-down interview conducted politely but with a strong point of view. Think *60 Minutes* investigative report — almost always done on tape, rarely live.

An example of a live confrontational interview took place during the 1968 Democratic convention. It was a live broadcast that was called gavel-to-gavel coverage at the time. Many confrontations took place between the Chicago mayor's henchmen and reporters on the convention floor and outside on the street where reporters were covering antiwar demonstrations.

Ambush Interview — A confrontational interview when the subject will not agree to an interview and has been avoiding you.

Headliner Interview — Usually a live interview that tends to be longer than most Hard News Interviews. Think of the Sunday Morning news broadcasts involving politicians, or late night news broadcasts such as *Nightline* or Charlie Rose interviews on Public Broadcasting.

No joking around here. A good way to start the taped interview is to make sure the guest knows the camera is rolling then ask the guest his or her name and title. You might also ask how the person would like to be referred to in the piece. Some Jims would like the more formal James, others prefer Jim. It's a professional start and gives you useful information.

One correspondent I know always states for the record, "You know this is an on-the-record interview for XXX News." Every once in a while that statement will be handy if the guest tries to claim he or she didn't know the cameras were rolling. In all cases, it is professional and sets a hard news tone.

Soft News Interviews

Soft Newsmaker Interview — Interviews of newsworthy people not ordinarily in the news, such as a firefighter hero, or people connected with newsworthy events such as trapped miners. Think of morning news broadcasts (usually live) or prime-time magazine profiles (usually taped) interviews.

Celebrity Interview — Often conducted live. Diane Sawyer, Barbara Walters and Larry King are among the best ever at the celebrity interview. They get the guests to say things by cajoling them, teasing them or sympathizing with them. They tend to be more emotional and almost completely supportive of their guests. Also, don't forget late night comics. Think Jay Leno, Jon Stewart or David Letterman.

There are techniques you will use in a Soft Interview that would be unacceptable and bordering on the unprofessional in a Hard News Interview. The hardest thing is to put a person at ease so that they will trust you. In order to have a great interview, the interviewee must feel comfortable and must trust the interviewer. A good way to gain this trust is to talk about something at the beginning that will comfort them or something that will make them laugh. Loosening up the guest will make your job easier.

Relax Your Guest

In a Morning News interview, a celebrity interview or an author interview, you want your guest to feel you are in this together. You develop a partnership, a team. You are on his or her side and you should build a trust. Most guests will not be as comfortable as you are, so it is up to you to take control in a firm and friendly way.

To make this partnership between you and your guest work best, it is a good idea to first set your guest at ease. The more relaxed the guest, the more open he or she will be, and the stronger and more riveting your interview will be.

To begin with, you might ask a question about something physical. It tends to relax the interviewee when you ask about something they can see and touch, something that's right in front of them. For example, before the cameras roll, you might make note of their new hairdo or dress or tie. You can ask this at the start of your airtime. It's fun and both the guest and the audience tend to like it. People tend to drop their guard and to laugh a bit.

Fig. 2-7 Relax your interview guest.

This way guests will feel you are nonconfrontational and on their team and that you will help them tell their story. Viewers seem to really love this intimate peek too.

Other suggestions that you can use to open the conversation include talking about something that both of you know. Of course, you are thinking, "If I've not spoken to this person before, how can I find some common ground?" Easy. Talk about the weather outside. Is it hot, cold, snowy, rainy, windy? Weather is always relatable between two people. Is there a holiday nearby? How about Thanksgiving coming up or just past? The 4th of July or Memorial Day? Or family. Any kids? Nearly everyone likes to talk about the kids, but you must be careful about some people's privacy issues.

Chat Up Your Guest

One trick I've seen used to good effect is to chat with your guest before the cameras roll, while the crew is setting the lights or putting on the microphones. Introduce your guest to the crew by name. Tell the guest that he or she should ignore these wonderful people, they are used to it. It's an ice breaker, a friendly way to have everyone meet each other and can even get a giggle from the guest.

All of this will help to relax the guest. Furthermore, this little trick will remind the guest that you two are going to have a conversation. You want to make sure the guest talks directly to you and doesn't look at the camera.

There is one host who, it is said, refuses to allow some guests back on the show because they did not look at her during the interview but instead focused on the camera the whole time.

The All-Important First Question

The first question you ask after putting the person at ease should be a great first question: something unexpected, poignant or probing — anything but boring. If it is boring, the audience will turn to a different channel and the interviewee will turn off.

If the thrust of the interview revolves around an incident and there is a story that is needed to set up the forthcoming questions, then be smart. Let the story unfold. Don't you tell the story.

For example, don't say, "You were in the office in the morning and one of your bosses walked in and spoke rudely to you." It's always more gripping to hear it from your guest, the person who lived it. It will be much more powerful, and you won't get it wrong.

Report from the Trenches

Here is a good example. Some years back, Connie Chung was doing an interview with the Captain of the *Exxon Valdez*. You may remember this was the oil tanker that ran aground in Alaska creating a devastating oil spill for many miles.

Finally when the captain returned to his family on Long Island, Chung snagged the first interview with him. Her first question was,

"How does it feel to be home?" This was a comfort question. She opened with this to put the captain at ease, to gain his trust. The word HOME has a comforting resonance for everyone.

You could see the captain relax. After that first question he trusted her. He felt she was on his side. He felt she was on HIS TEAM. And once that trust is there, you can ask almost anything. Your guest knows that you won't throw him in. This is essential for a great interview.

Charlie Rose has this ability. He makes all his guests feel he is on their side, on their team. It is a fact that guests simply will not open their hearts to you if they don't feel you are on their side.

NANCY'S RULES

People relate to people.

Your audience wants to relate to your guest. That is a real person sitting there, so bring out the human qualities that are so relatable. The way to build this relationship is through emotion. To steal an idea from Robert Penn Warren's *All the King's Men*, "make 'em cry or make 'em laugh … pinch 'em in the soft place." In other words, go for the emotion in the interview and the audience will come back to you for more. That speech in *All the King's Men* ends with another thought that's worth repeating: "For sweet Jesus' sake, don't try to improve their minds." You can teach the viewers, but they will absorb the information better when it is riding on an emotion, the same way medicine goes down with syrup.

The Shape of an Interview

If you could put the shape of an interview into a picture what would it look like? It would look like an inverted triangle. You must ask the most specific questions at the beginning.

You don't want to ask general questions at the start of the interview. The reason for this is that the general questions take too long to answer, and are not as interesting. The more specific your questions, the more specific the answers will be. The fact is that just as in any conversation, the answers are more interesting when they are not general answers.

Examples of general questions are: "Tell us what your book is about?" "What is your day like?" or "What is Greece like?" These questions are too general. You will get general responses. You won't get the best stuff because the best stuff consists of anecdotes and stories.

Remember this: There is no reason to say, "Tell us . . ." because that's what your guest is there to do and what he or she is obviously doing.

Time Is of the Essence

. . . Especially in television. So don't waste it. If your guest answers your question with a long answer, you must find an appropriate time to cut in. Often the guest is trying to fill the airtime because of nerves. Sometimes it's because the guest is trying to find the answer, forgot the question or is preprogrammed with a message. In any case, you have to politely but firmly butt in. Get the interview back on track and back to the crisp give and take of a conversation.

Answers That Are Toooo Long

The other danger of allowing a run-on answer is you run the risk of letting the guest control the interview. Whose show is it anyway? My students ask me, "How do you cut someone off if they are talking on and on, or if they get on a band box to espouse their views?" You do it as you would in normal conversation. Some people keep talking by never completing their sentences. There are obvious clues, and you should be aware of them. These people keep saying, and . . . um . . . and . . . which . . . er . . . well . . . ah. . . . You'd better jump in fast. When you sense a slight hesitation, you should jump right in.

Fig. 2-8 Tooooo long answer.

You'll start to recognize this syndrome after only one horrible experience. Once will be enough, I guarantee it. Better, however, to avoid even one. In a real-life conversation you never think about where you interrupt the person with whom you are speaking. You do it all the time, and it's not rude, is it?

Questions That Are Toooo Long

Just as answers can be too long, so can questions.

Ask tight strong questions. People usually understand what you are asking. If you keep running off at the mouth, it's usually because you can't figure out how to end the question. Not only will the viewer be annoyed and bored, so will your guest. So, be careful of questions that go on and on, forever.

Beware of questions that don't quite finish. "Were you frightened and scared and umm uh or were you...." Finish your thought.

Also be careful of asking more than one question. Don't ask, "Did you think you would survive and how's the family doing?" Also, don't limit the question: "Were you frightened or just angry?"

W Miller

Fig. 2-9 Tooooo long question.

You are giving your interviewee only these two alternatives. On your guest's own he or she might come up with a more striking and original answer. So be aware that you don't box in your interviewee.

Yes or No Questions

Should you ask questions that will get you an answer that is "yes" or "no"?

"No."

Do you know why you shouldn't?

"Yes."

Do you agree the viewer doesn't get much out of it?

"Yes."

So don't. OK?

"OK."

"Is that a yes?"

"Yes."

Fig. 2-10 Don't ask Yes and No questions.

Anecdotes and Stories

Anecdotes and stories are of vital importance to a great interview. You must get them. Without anecdotes an interview is dull. This is what will rivet your viewer. When we are let into some of the specific stories of the subject's life, the person you are interviewing becomes fascinating and we emotionally connect with them.

A good example of this is from the movie *Schindler's List*. The entire film was shot in black and white. There was a scene where hundreds of dead bodies lay on the ground. One of them was a little girl in a red coat. The red coat was the only thing in color. It stood out. It gave us the specific. It was moving. This is what the specific anecdote does for the individual telling it.

These specific stories, told by your guest, bring the viewer to an empathetic understanding of your subject's situation. The anecdotes give the guest credibility, and the viewer can hook up with the interviewee on an emotional level. We all love stories because they make up the fabric with which we weave our lives together.

Every person is different from everyone else, but we also have many similarities. It is the sharing of these specific stories that bring us together and what keeps us breathlessly watching an interview.

Have More Questions Than You Think You Will Need

You never know when you will have time for an extra question or two. Always have a couple in your back pocket ... just in case.

Fig. 2-11 Have a lot of questions.

Report from the Trenches

There is a story about a network anchor whose job that day was to interview Prince Charles. The prince was having a jolly good time during the interview, which lasted about 10 minutes. During the commercial break, Charles said to the anchor, "I'd be happy to continue this wonderful interview with you!" Unfortunately, the anchor responded that he didn't have any more questions.

If you are a good interviewer, don't be surprised by a guest who would like to stay. Make sure you always have more questions than you need.

Where Do You Look When You Are Interviewing?

Do you look at the camera or at the interviewee? When you ask a question you should ALWAYS look at the interviewee. Do not look at the camera. If it's a two-camera shoot with one camera on you, the interviewer, and one on the guest, it should be set up like this: There will be one camera placed over the interviewee's left shoulder, shooting you, the interviewer. Another camera will be aimed over your left shoulder shooting the interviewee.

The rule is be sure to START the question directly to the interviewee, and to FINISH the question directly to the interviewee. You might need to refer to your notes to read a quote, law or regulation exactly. But if you don't pay attention to the guest, this will affect the guest's answer. Furthermore, not only will the guest lose focus, so will the viewer. If it looks as though you are not interested in the answer, why should we be?

Usually, you will have only one camera, placed next to you and shooting your guest. At times, the cameraperson should pull out to a two-shot with you in the picture asking the question. As with a two-camera shoot, you should keep your focus on your interview subject.

Your Voice

Use your voice. This is a huge part of what you have to offer. We will discuss more about the voice in our chapter on Vocal and Physical Technique. But because this is so important I want to just touch on it now.

These are things about your voice you should be working on:

Expanding your range
Articulation
Modulation
Speech impediments
Regional accents
How to talk intimately

And one more: listen quietly. By this I mean, don't make extraneous sounds: Paper rustling noises, smacking your lips or over-talking. Just listen quietly.

Whose Interview Is It Anyway?

When you're interviewing someone don't worry about showing how funny you are (unless you are Jon Stewart, Jay Leno or David Letterman). Also, don't worry about showing how smart you are. Be there for the guest. Many people feel the need to show off their brains like it's some sort of Mensa competition. You should not do this in front of the camera. Show off your guest.

 Report from the Trenches

During Phil Donahue's talk show, when there was a complicated subject or one that was very technical, Donahue did a very cool two-step. He'd be standing with the interviewee, holding the mike. The guest would be chatting and he'd start stepping a bit backwards, and

saying, "I don't quite get this. Could you explain it to me further."
Or, "What do you mean by that, I don't quite get it."

Donahue is smart. He probably understood it very well. But he
was concerned that the viewers might need more explanation.
He didn't need to prove anything to anybody. He was terrific.
He helped make the interviewee look great and he made the audience feel smart. They are thinking, "Oh yeah, I get this now, I can
follow this technical/medical stuff."

What he was doing really was listening to his guest. It shows you
once again how important listening is during an interview. Listen
actively and you will make the right choice of the millions of choices
that you need to make as the interview unfolds.

The End of the Interview

Generally, you don't want to end an interview with "We are nearly
out of time ..." or "We have 15 seconds left, how do you explain
that your company lost 12 billion dollars?" It's not fair and your
viewers will not like you for it. It is not a good idea to show the
underpinnings of an interview. Remember, this is a conversation.
Do you ever recall saying to someone at your dinner table: "Here's
my last question ..."? No. Just ask your last question.

If you are running out of time, be aware of that. Don't ask a
complex question. If you are really running out of time, don't ask
any more questions but wrap it up gracefully. In all cases, you
should end your interview with something polite like: "Thank you"
or "Good Luck."

The Difference Maker

My students ask, "What do I need to become a great interviewer?"
Curiosity. No one can give you that. It's the one quality that makes
for a great interviewer as well as a great reporter. People are interested in people. You have to want to know what makes people
tick — what makes them say what they say, and how do they say it.
(The words and intentions the interviewee chooses can lead you

to your next question.) What makes your guest tick? What drives people to make the choices they make? It may be a reason you've heard before but it's always a different story. That's what makes it interesting: the difference!

You must always be open and flexible. You must be ready to change gears in a split second. You must be ready, willing and able to throw out some or even all of your prepared questions if the interviewee gives you something unexpected or more interesting than what you prepared.

Always be specific in your thoughts, and in your choices. Becoming a great interviewer takes time. It doesn't happen all at once. It's like any skill. The more you do it the better you will get. So be patient.

Checklist

- ❏ Prepare for your interview.
- ❏ Relax your guest.
- ❏ Have a conversation.
- ❏ Listen to your guest.
- ❏ Listen quietly.
- ❏ Keep the energy level up.
- ❏ Ask a worthy first question.
- ❏ Go for stories and anecdotes.
- ❏ Make sure you ask tight questions . . . one at a time.
- ❏ Don't let the guest ramble.
- ❏ Avoid questions that get Yes or No answers.
- ❏ Always be polite.

Are There Any Exercises I Can Use?

Yes, you can practice. Take risks. Get out into your community with a camera and start doing interviews with people on the street. They can always refuse to answer you, but you might be surprised at how willing people are to talk to you.

The reason you want to practice with a video camera is that it makes it much more like a real on-camera situation. The closer you can simulate the real situation the more you will get out of your exercises.

Exercise for Interview Variety

This is a stretching exercise. Stretch your interests. You do not like baseball but one day you may have to interview a baseball player.

Choose a guest who does something you know little about. Choose a variety of fields. As practice, interview a friend who is a jock, then one in the arts. Choose a motorcycle mechanic, a grocery store stocker. They all have stories to tell if you are doing your job. Dig and draw out the specialness of each person you interview.

Use several different people to stretch your skills. Be imaginative. Get your curiosity going. Get the viewers' curiosity going.

Exercise for Questions

Choose two serious newsmakers who are in the news. Write up ten questions you would ask this guest if he or she were on your show. Try asking each question two different ways.

Ask yourself: How tight can I make the question and still keep it strong? The words you choose should fire the imagination of the interviewee. An example is: "What do you like to do?" versus "What is your passion?" Words like *passion* excite the listener and will elicit a stronger response. Another word that fires up the interviewee is: *Imagine.* As in "Imagine you just won the lottery . . ."

Choose the strongest words. Be creative. Are you teasing the interviewee? Are you trying to excite the interviewee or challenge the interviewee? Are you inviting them on a journey into the past?

Exercise for Listening

I know you know how to listen. But you need practice listening as an interviewer. For practice, go out with a friend to the park, a bar or anywhere you two can talk. Ask a question and then listen. Do not interrupt, keep on listening until you can no longer bear it. My guess is that your friend would just keep going. This exercise will give you an idea of just how much people will say to fill silence.

Another thing: As your friend is talking, you will think of things to say, things that happened to you, for example. Stifle yourself. What you want to say may be interesting, may even be more interesting than what your friend is saying, but this interview is not about you. This is not as easy as you might think.

So practice until you can control yourself. Become a secure listener.

Exercise for Flexibility

This is to help you become freer and more confident in your interviews. You have to be nimble, quick on your feet. By doing some improvisation, you can get better. Work with a friend. Have him or her be the guest and throw you a curveball. Some surprise that you don't know is coming. Then deal with it.

What would you do if someone you were interviewing said:

"No, I was just released from prison where I've been for 25 years after I killed my mother."
"Nice to meet you too, most people don't talk to me because I'm the King of Europe."
"I don't talk to strangers."
"I'd like to talk about the senator. He's an ass and corrupt. He's a thief."

One Last Exercise

Interview a friend; or perhaps, for more of a challenge, interview a family member. But really do it. Be sure to ask the daring questions. Ask them what they earn. You will be surprised to find that people are reluctant to answer this. So try to get it out of them.

Fig. 2-12 Ask about money.

Ask about that family funeral, the sibling rivalry, the difficult relationship with the daughter that no one mentions. Take
risks. People can always refuse to answer you. Sometimes you can
even ask them about subjects they have told you beforehand that
they don't wish to discuss. You have to be sensitive about this.
Sometimes things are going well and you feel this is a great interview
and you can ask anything. Even when it's harder and you keep struggling for the stories and anecdotes, keep going and try a different
approach. Go at it from a different angle.

Don't keep asking the same question in exactly the same form
with the same words. A sense of humor, a joke, teasing someone
playfully or really being sympathetic are all ways that will get a
strong and helpful response from the interviewee and can turn the
interview around. It's HOW you ask the question. Ask and ye shall
receive.

Practice, Practice, Practice

Challenge yourself.
Have fun.
Be brave and imaginative.
Naturally if you're smart, sensitive, ambitious, driven, sharp (and I know you are), you've got a lot going for you.

3

The Interviewee

If you are an author, an artist, a doctor or a politician, or in any profession that might lead you to the other side of an interview, this chapter is for you. If you are a doctor, a businessman or a lawyer, you should also turn to the beats section and look at the medical, business or legal beats.

It never hurts to know what to expect from the interviewer when you appear on camera. In today's world of technology and communications, you should plan on appearing on camera at least once in your career and probably more.

You have to hold up your end of the conversation if you want to give a great interview. Like the reporter, how you express yourself does matter. The words you choose, the stories you tell, and how you speak can make you sparkle. On the other hand, doing a poor job in the interview because you didn't have some basic skills will make you look bad, no matter how smart or knowledgeable you are about your subject.

Know How You Appear

Your first step is to answer the question: How do I come across on camera? Do I stumble around for my thoughts using lots of mmms and uuuhhs? Do I look down at my hands, or at the camera, instead of looking at the interviewer? Do I speak in a low whisper or speak too loudly for a television audience?

First, you can and should know your flaws. To do this, set up a camera and have someone you know interview you. Play that back and watch. Learn where you are weak and focus your training on those aspects.

Although some businessmen present well to a large live audience they are not comfortable or trained to present on camera. Television needs less, not more. You may need to play it BIG on stage but that will come over as too big on camera.

Prepare

You should always prepare before an on-air interview. You're going on the show for a reason. You weren't just picked off the street. You have been selected because you are an expert in your particular field. Even though you already know your subject, you should brush up on the latest information. Have the facts at hand, be prepared. You don't want to freeze up or look like you don't know the answers.

You probably can anticipate many of the questions that you will be asked. If you are not experienced at being interviewed on camera

Fig. 3-1 Don't be underprepared.

Fig. 3-2 Don't overanswer.

and if you don't prepare, then you will probably commit the cardinal sin of interviewing: the sin of omission.

By the same token, while you are asked to be an expert, don't pontificate. It's a conversation between the host or anchor and you. Don't take over with some stump speech. That does not play well on television.

Long before you arrive at the studio, you should have decided which of your anecdotes will support the points you wish to make, then practice telling those stories into a tape recorder. As you are rehearsing your stories, be aware if you are using run-on sentences or if you keep saying, "and . . . and." End your sentence. Then begin the next one.

My students sometimes worry that they might overprepare. They are concerned that this preparation, such as taping your own stories and anecdotes in a rehearsal beforehand, might make them sound rehearsed, and not appear spontaneous when on camera. If you do repeat your answers the exact same way every time, then yes, you will not sound spontaneous. However, only a robot could accomplish that kind of duplication. Furthermore, if you are relating your story in a conversation with the host, it will not sound rote and robotic.

Nerves

Everyone has had some stage fright. Practicing your material before-hand will help cut it down. During the interview, you should concentrate on telling your story. Concentrate on telling it to the interviewer. Have a conversation. By keeping your focus on your story and your host, you will keep from thinking about yourself. Here is another old trick. If your business involves some physical activity, then bring it along. As long as the host agrees, you can do your physical activity and talk at the same time. You see this on cooking shows all the time. This will reduce your nervousness because you are concentrating on the activity and you are not self-conscious. This also gives you some control over the situation which is always a good thing. You will have thought through the possibilities and you will be ready for whatever the interviewer asks you.

Monotone = Boring

If you hear yourself speaking in a monotone, try changing your pace between thoughts. Also, keep that energy up too. (If you hear that you tend to come down in pitch at the end of your sentences, turn to the chapter on vocal techniques.) If you hear, on playing your tape back, those sleep-inducing ums or uhhhs, remember: Silence is golden and silence is preferable while you are searching for your next thought.

As you listen to the playback of your stories, make sure they are not too long. Don't be afraid to let your emotions emerge. No need to hide them. But also don't ACT emotional.

Make a list of questions you think you might be asked. This will put you in the head of the host and help you avoid any surprise questions. You won't know exactly in what manner or order or even if all of them will be asked. But you can be pretty sure that you will hear some of them. That should give you confidence when you walk into a studio and an unfamiliar situation.

During the actual interview, listen to the questions. Don't be trying to remember some witty thing you had prepared at home or how smart you want to sound. Be present in the moment and stay attentive to your interviewer. Don't jump ahead, or beat yourself up for what you meant to say and didn't. Move on in the conversation, and answer the questions as asked. On this point, you should not feel tied down to the questions. As any experienced interviewee knows, there is a good bit of wiggle room in most questions. If the question goes into areas you do not know about or cannot discuss, simply say something like: "That's out of my area of expertise." But it would be good to be able to reframe the question to something that you can answer. Then answer that.

Know Your Audience

When answering, be as clear as possible. If your subject is medical or technical, try to talk about it in understandable terms for the viewer. Be sensitive to the composition of your viewership. If you are being interviewed on a high-tech science show, and you know your audience is composed of mostly science geeks, you'd explain your newest heart operation one way; but if it's the late-night talk show with a broader audience, you may need to tell it using simpler terms.

You must know exactly what you want to get across, even though your interviewer may have a different agenda. You don't want to be pushy, that is if you ever want to come on the show again. But because of your preparation and your understanding of the time allotted for your interview, which you should find out in advance, you can try to put your most important points up first. Again, preparation helps you be nimble during the interview.

NANCY'S RULES

KIHAT: Keep it honest and truthful.

Viewers have become so accustomed to half-truths and spun-truths heard on television today that it is a gush of fresh air to hear from an honest, straightforward guest. I think people are fed up with the politicians, the businessmen, even celebrities who duck and dodge direct questions. You will gain lots of credibility if you answer a difficult question directly and truthfully. Don't be a slick-Sam. If you deceive, you will be caught. A warning: Hosts see a lot of dissemblers and the camera shows a lot more than you think.

If you aren't sure about an answer, don't try to make one up on the spot. It can be refreshing to hear a guest say, "I don't know," or, "I'll try and find that out and get back to you tomorrow." You may get a bonus, another mention on the show without even being there.

If you don't like the way in which the interviewer has asked the question, you should feel absolutely free to rephrase it. Then, be sure to answer it. Of course the interviewer may have several follow-up questions, so once again, be prepared. The conversation is an open-ended game, with numerous possibilities. You want to be ready for whatever is tossed in your direction.

Watch out for the trick question that comes in several parts: "Is Smith your real name and are you divorced?"

If you get this multiple choice–type question or if the question is too long or complicated, then break it down or answer only the section you wish. "Smith is my real name."

What should you do if you are asked a very private, personal question, something you definitely don't want to talk about? Now, if it's the entire reason you have been asked on the show you have a real problem, and will obviously have to discuss it in some form. But if it's not relevant to the main subject you can get around it with grace. First be nice. Don't become angry or confrontational. The interviewer is just doing a job, working to have the most exciting and enlightening conversation possible.

The truth is you should have figured this turn of events if you did your preparation. You don't have to answer. But instead of saying, "That's none of your business" or, "No comment," you should be prepared to address it in some way. You could say that it's too personal or too difficult right now. Or you could switch the subject to something even more fascinating. For example, you could say,

"I have something even better for you." You can do this, but be sure to have one of those great anecdotes ready to share. Also, a sense of humor goes a long way.

Most interviewers appreciate that, especially if you don't leave them with egg on their face, and stuck with the "No comment" in the middle of the interview.

Don't ever forget this is a visual medium, so if you can, show your work. If you state something or make a strong assertion, support it with facts, personal experience, comparisons, expert opinions (besides your own), statistics and examples.

Have a Good Time

Be as captivating as you can be. You are on this show because you have something to say that is of interest to the viewer. You should learn to say it well. Enjoy the experience. The more you have a good time during the interview, the more the viewers will enjoy your presentation and you.

Checklist

- ❏ Prepare long before the interview.
- ❏ Practice your anecdotes and stories.
- ❏ Marshal your facts.
- ❏ Don't be boring.
- ❏ Know your audience.
- ❏ Don't talk over the head of a general audience.
- ❏ If appropriate, bring along a show-and-tell.
- ❏ Keep it honest and truthful.
- ❏ Have a good time.

On-Camera Reporting

On-camera reporting is the art of gathering a set of facts about a situation, then marshalling those facts into an understandable report and finally presenting that report so people watch it, listen to it and, of course, understand it.

Many of my students ask me, "How is on-camera reporting different from other reporting, like newspaper reporting?" The answer is: The reporting, the basic journalism, is no different. Facts are facts and you dig them up the very same way. But when you get to presenting those facts, you do it differently.

A newspaper reporter doesn't have to present his report on air — you do. Your interviews are done on camera. That makes a difference right there. And when you marshal your facts, you will write the report differently and even structure it differently than a newspaper reporter would. Part of the reason is your words and information will be seen and heard, not read. Usually, you will not have the luxury of time to gather the information or the space to tell the story that a newspaper reporter has. Think tight and bright for your work at all times.

There will be two kinds of reporting you will do as an on-camera reporter: Live reports and packaged reports done on tape. They are different and we will examine the differences and you will learn how to do both equally well.

So let's start with the three elements of reporting and go through them one by one. *Gathering the facts* is dicussed in Chapter 4. *Writing the script* and *Presenting the report on camera* are discussed in Chapters 5 and 6.

Gathering the Facts

Reporters gather facts by asking questions. In some cases, you will do this on the phone or over a meal. Later, at some point, on camera you will ask questions of several people involved in your report. The interview techniques are similar to those in the interview chapter. Some rules here repeat those, but keep in mind that generally you are a reporter on the scene gathering facts that are new. For an on-camera reporter, an interview is both research and video material for your story.

You will ultimately want to tell the story with as much "sound" as possible. "Sound" means interview quotes on tape. So you will want to gather facts from the most important people involved.

Nancy's Accident Story

Let's have some fun here. Here is a simple example of an on-camera reporter's work and you are the reporter.

There's been a car accident and you and your crew are first on the scene. Whom do you want to interview? There are lots of targets, so how do you figure out what interview to do first?

Part of the answer is the urgency of the situation. In other words, if someone is about to leave the scene, by all means talk to him or her before they leave. That could be an eyewitness or an ambulance person. Once you've gotten the interviews that you would have lost if you had waited, then move to the next most important. You want to interview someone involved in the accident, the driver if possible. You want the policeman on the scene and the ambulance people and a good eyewitness.

Facts are the bones of a news report. Don't stop asking questions until you are sure you've got all of the facts . . . and have all of them right. Often you will hear conflicting pieces of information. Be alert to those and follow up on them — somewhere is the truth of what happened. Use information gleaned from one interview to lead you to questions for the next person you interview.

From these interviews, the "sound bites" or "sound" will be able to tell most of the story. In addition, what "sound" you don't use in the report, you may well use informationally in your narration.

It's Television, Get Video

"Sound bites" from your interviews will tell part of the story. Your narration and the pictures you shoot at the scene will tell the rest. As a reporter, you are gathering notes on the scene. As an on-camera reporter, that means gathering up pictures of the scene on tape.

To be a good reporter, you must be a good observer. That means, in our accident example, shoot video of the wrecked cars, of course. But look closer. Did the air bags inflate? Shoot those pictures. Are there tire tracks from one car that indicates it had to brake sharply? Take pictures of those tracks.

Later you ask the policeman a question prompted by your observation about the tire tracks. The policeman may say, "Yes, it appears from what you see that one car was moving too fast." It is good reporting (good observation) that got the answer. All of which was prompted by that observation you made. And, of course, you have the pictures to help you tell the story.

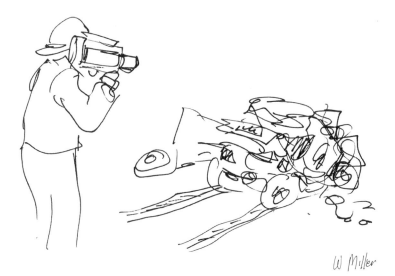

W Miller

Fig. 4-1 Get video.

See It, Shoot It

Always take those pictures as soon as you see them for two reasons: First, you may get sidetracked or pushed away from the scene, or get rushed at the end. Then you didn't get what may turn out to be an important picture.

And two, there is no harm. If your instinct tells you that it is suspicious, or important, then shoot it and shoot it right away. If it turns out not to be important, then don't use it.

Action is always a good way to start a taped report. Action accompanied by the sound of the action (in our case the siren) draws the viewer into your story immediately. If you are talking over a siren while taping, you will not be able to use that siren mixed with your chatter. You cannot erase your interview sound from the siren sound without erasing them both. What do you do when the ambulance arrives, siren blaring, during your interview? You ask the interviewee to hold that thought and get pictures AND SOUND of the ambulance. That may be the way to open your taped report. In addition, the sound of the siren didn't interfere with the sound of your interview.

Establish the Scene

Always shoot a wide shot of the scene — called an *establisher*. This is very useful, and may be the opening shot of the report. It can also be used as the closing shot or to cover a general line of narration such as: "There have been six accidents in this same spot in the past year."

Also shoot pictures of specific details at the scene. Say one of the people you interviewed, like the eyewitness, describes something specific — the overgrown bush that blocks the warning sign for drivers at the curve. You think this might be important for your report when you hear the eyewitness mention it. So be sure to shoot the picture of that overgrown bush and the covered sign.

Be sure to get pictures of those you interview doing something at the scene, not just talking to you. Have your cameraperson shoot the policeman as he is investigating, the eyewitness watching from the sidewalk or talking to the officer, the ambulance people helping the victims.

Those pictures of the scene, wide and specific, will help you when you come to writing your narration for the report.

Cut-Aways, Reverses and Jump Cuts

You must shoot cut-aways of yourself, also known as reverses, for all your interviews. This is a shot of you listening to the person you just interviewed. It's done AFTER the interview.

Here's how the reverse shot is done: The cameraperson has been shooting the interview from in back of your shoulder. When you finish the interview, he or she takes the camera from in back of you to in back of the person you just interviewed and shoots pictures of you listening.

It is important that the cameraperson goes less than 180 degrees from where the camera was first shooting. Simply put, if the

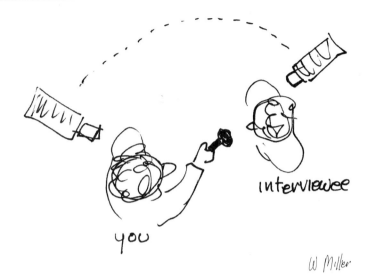

Fig. 4-2 Shooting a reverse.

cameraperson is shooting the interview over your left shoulder, the reverse of you should be shot from the interviewee's right shoulder.

This shot cannot be exactly opposite from the camera position used during the interview or it will look like a jump cut.

Jump Cuts

What is a jump cut and how to solve it?

Let me give you an example: Say you are interviewing someone who has a cold. During one very important statement, she sneezes, apologizes and finishes the statement. You might ask for the statement again, but if it was so well delivered (except for the sneeze), emotionally strong and otherwise perfect, you can use the reverse and cut out the sneeze. Like this:

"My son was such a good person. Why did he have to die? Why? Why did they do this to him?
ACHOO.

Sorry, sniffle, sniffle.
What I mean to say is, I...will...never...forgive...or forget."

The camera is located over your left shoulder taking pictures of her the whole time and you have recorded all of this statement. You need it for your piece; it is clearly the money sound bite. But you don't want to use the sneeze and sniffling. You are about to be saved by the cut-away.

After the interview, the cameraperson moves the camera to a spot behind her right shoulder. From there, he shoots a picture of you listening to her. That shot, the reverse shot, will go between her two sound bites. In effect, we will be listening to her, then briefly "cut away" to a picture of you, then return to her picture and sound to finish her comments. We have cut out the problem sneeze by covering her two sound bites that we put together. So the final piece would look like this:

"My son was such a good person. Why did he have to die? Why? Why did they do this to him?//
(Your picture from the cut away here)
I...will...never...forgive...or forget."

What we cut out was:

ACHOO.
Sorry, sniffle sniffle.
What I mean to say is...

If you had cut this part out and not covered it with your picture from the cut-away, the person's head would have jumped. No one has her head at the exact spot a few words later. If you butted the top of her sound bite to the bottom, her head would jump from looking at you to looking down. That's why it's called a "jump cut." Note that you are just using the video from the shot of you. All of the audio comes from her interview. There is no audio space between her two bites.

In addition, using a cut-away of you brings you visually into the interview, reminding the viewer that you are the one asking the questions and bringing them the news.

NANCY'S RULES

You must shoot cut-aways with the person still where they were for the interview. This is honest and for your own credibility.

Have your interview subject continue to talk about the topic. In fact, it's best to ask another question that is on the subject but not so important that you'd want it in the piece (don't forget, the camera is no longer on her, it's on you).

If you continue the conversation, then the reactions you have will be in the same feeling as the interview. In other words, if it has been a serious interview, don't lighten things up for the cut-aways. Laughs or smiles during the serious interview will look jarring and out of place. By the same token, don't get serious in the cut-away shooting after a laugh riot of an interview.

If you continue the conversation with questions, you might be able to use one or two of those on-camera questions in your piece. If the question during your cut-away shooting gets an answer that you'd like to use, by all means, you should use it.

Reverse Questions

Cut-aways are different from reverse questions. Reverse questions are done after the interview. They are like a cut-away, but the reporter re-asks the questions that might be used in the piece. The reporter then has his face on camera asking the question that was not shot during the interview.

I personally don't like them. They look staged and ring a false note. At some stations they are allowed, even encouraged. But if you do use a reverse question, make sure the interviewee is still there.

Otherwise, it looks really fake and you can get into some real ethical issues.

More Tricks of the Trade

Know what you are after and communicate this to the crew. This is an accident story. If someone comes running down the street with no clothes on and you are in the middle of the interview with the dazed driver before the ambulance arrives, what do you do? You stay with the interview. The streaker probably has nothing to do with your story. As my grandmother said: "Stick to your knitting — stick to the point." Don't over-shoot what you won't need.

The pictures of the scene, wide shots and specific shots, will help you when you come to writing your narration for the report.

How To Start Your Taped On-Scene Interviews

I like the simple approach. Introduce yourself: Your name, you are a reporter for the local station and: "Can I ask you a couple questions?" If you are polite and professional, most people will answer a few questions.

W Miller

Fig. 4-3 What do you do?

Listen to the person. Ask questions that follow the information you are getting, as you would in any conversation. If the driver asks you what time it is, you would answer that and follow it up.

"It's just after three. Why do you ask?"

Feel free to move the conversation back to the point of the story if it's getting off the subject. Do not interrupt, but after a good point is made, feel free to interject things like, "That's an interesting point..." and probe that. People love to hear they are interesting or observant or smart. Pay them a compliment and often you will be rewarded.

On the other hand, you have to know when to stop an interview. You must assess the quality of the material you're getting from this interview. If the interview is going nowhere, cut it short. You will find others who will be worth interviewing. Move on. Which brings up a big point you should always keep in mind.

NANCY'S RULES

Time is of the essence. Don't waste it.

Get to the most important questions first. This has the advantage of getting the most important answers on tape but also tells the person you are interviewing what you are after. When you have the material you need, or the person you are interviewing just doesn't know any more, its time to move on.

There is no need to be hasty to the point of being sloppy and careless. Just keep it moving. You will learn that you never have enough time in this business. Husband it. Don't forget: You still have to write the script, you still have to get it through the editing process and screened for final approval. You are going to want plenty of time for those parts too.

In addition, everyone has lots to do. This is not the only shoot of the day for some of the technicians. There are many shoots besides your piece to work on for the show that day.

W Miller

Fig. 4-4 *Time is of the essence.*

Know what you are doing. Unless it's a breaking story, you usually have some information to go on before you arrive at the scene. Do some fast homework. Get as much information as you can. Start to form some questions in your notebook. Don't improvise the interview. You should always be open to changing your questions if a new and better piece of information comes your way in the interview process. But don't come unprepared or without your questions.

Live Interviews for On-Camera Reporters

Nowhere is time more critical than in live interviews. Doing a taped interview gives you the luxury of wandering far afield, exploring aspects of the story that may be new or just interesting. You can always cut the stuff that doesn't work during the editing process. You can be selective but not when you are live. Every question has to be of value and every answer worth the viewer's time.

But the first thing you must do, if it hasn't been done in a studio lead-in, is introduce the viewers to your guest. Then get right to the point. If you are live you want to go for your best stuff first, and not mess around with nonessentials.

Have your questions written out. It helps speed the interview along and you will be sure you get to all of the important questions. BUT BEWARE: In a live situation, often a breaking news situation, be flexible. Things tend to change and if you are a slave to old questions the interview will be out of date too. You may miss the news. Or worse, you may be wrong. So listen carefully and stay with the story. It's still a good idea to write out the top questions.

For example: In our accident story, what are the top questions? What happened? What caused the crash? Was anybody killed? Anyone injured? Any arrests?

Make sure you get the answer to the question. Today, many people are trained to "stay on message." It's true of politicians of course, but also business people, medical people, lawyers and even police. So if you're very good and a very important question was dodged, ask it again. Ask it using other words. Be polite, but persistent. Your job is to get answers no matter how much their job is to duck the questions.

Another difference between the live interview and the taped one is the way you will present information. In a live interview, you don't have any way to give the audience some background, as you do in a taped report. So you may have to fill the viewer in through your questions.

For example: You are interviewing the police officer at the scene of an automobile accident. In a taped interview, you can ask, "Any news about the victims?" But maybe the audience doesn't know as much about the accident as you do. Live, you might put the question this way.

> "The accident here four hours ago sent two people to the hospital . . . can you tell us how they are doing?"

This way, you've given the viewer information in the question.

Be sure to set the tone of the interview to the subject. What might be appropriate for one subject will be wildly out of place in another. If the circus has just arrived, don't treat the interview with the clown in the parade as if someone died. By the same token, don't be light-hearted at an automobile accident. This may sound like common sense, but I've seen some very inappropriate behavior by young reporters.

When you hear the end, end the interview. In most cases, studio producers are willing to be flexible with time in a live interview (within reason — in a half-hour evening broadcast, it's likely you will get two to two and a half minutes for your live interview; in a one-hour news show, you might get four minutes; in a long form morning show, you could get five or even seven minutes for a major live interview).

But it's up to you to end it. Don't rush the interview, don't stop when it is going well and bringing up good stuff. On the other hand, don't drag it out either.

 Report from the Trenches

Jim Stewart in the CBS News Washington Bureau knew the end of an interview with uncanny ability. One example was so obvious, you may think, you would have known to end it too. But it takes confidence to do that and the awareness that you have covered the information. In Jim's interviews, there is no fat. You might just worry that you didn't get everything and revisit part of the story or explore some more. Jim knew he had it and when the end came, he'd turn and ask, "Did we miss anything?" The answer was always, "No, it's all there."

Once, in Montana, Jim was interviewing the parents of a son who had been shot to death, the result of an allegedly faulty trigger. Jim had asked what had occurred and what the fallout had been. Then he asked: "Some might say, this is all about gun control, you just don't like guns?"

The answer from the father: "This is not a gun control issue, this is a gun safety issue. ... Period."

That was the end and that is where Jim ended it.

NANCY'S RULES

1. It's the voice and face of the person you are interviewing you want on camera.
2. Keep your questions to the point.
3. Keep the individual you are interviewing on the subject.
4. Don't ask YES or NO questions. (See Interviewing chapter.)
5. Don't step on the answer.
6. If you're asking a question and getting the right answer, don't keep saying yes, mmmm, ahha. It will be very hard to cut tape when you get back to the studio. When you get back to the editing room, and you can't cut your piece, you will learn never to do this again.
7. The hardest thing is to keep your mouth shut. It used to be that there were very few live interviews for a reporter to do. But today many of them are live. Keep your mouth shut when your interviewee is talking. If a person says, "It was right then ..." and the reporter comes in with "that's when you jumped him?" You've violated one of Nancy's most important rules: **LET THE SUBJECT TELL THE STORY.**
8. **SILENCE IS GOLDEN** for reporters in other ways. Sometimes it's best to be silent when the person you are interviewing is not talking either. In this case, if you believe the person is holding out for whatever reason and simply stops talking, this tactic can work wonders. Just keep your mouth shut and watch the person. He or she will begin to get uncomfortable with the silence and many just blurt out anything to fill the gap. You might get your best stuff in the silent beats.

How long to hold for the response, how long to be silent? You have to sense this yourself. In a live interview, you certainly don't want too many seconds of silence because viewers will begin to think there is something wrong with their television sets. But in a taped interview it doesn't matter. You know you will cut that out during the editing of the report. The viewer will never see that silence.

9. As always, be polite, even friendly. People prefer talking to someone they like. People will respond with openness to someone they respect. You should use all your social skills in this part of the job. Don't get angry if someone refuses to talk to you, don't take it personally. There's always another way to de-fur the feline. In addition, you don't want to have a reputation as someone who has a short fuse.

10. And finally, get the facts right. You are allowed no mistakes. Your passing grade in reporting is 100%. Anything less than that is failure. You not only lose the trust of your boss, but more important, you lose the trust of the viewer and you may never recover it. In other words: Check, recheck and triple-check your facts, down to the littlest ones.

 ## Report from the Trenches

This really happened to a young reporter. Don't let it happen to you. This reporter was covering a board of education meeting that became contentious. The board had fired a very beloved teacher and the parents who knew this teacher were up in arms.

But at the beginning of the hearing, the board attorney made an announcement that the board would not take any questions about that issue and would not be addressing it at this meeting. He left open the question if the board would ever address the issue. This meeting was the first school board meeting the young reporter attended during which the board attorney spoke. The reporter did

Fig. 4-5 Beware of getting false information.

not know who he was because the attorney had never uttered a word in all the other meetings.

The reporter correctly focused his story on the issue of the teacher's firing and the board's reluctance to even answer a question from the public. Every question was met with the board attorney stating, "This board has no comment on personnel issues."

The community was furious and one member seated next to the reporter, was especially forceful in his attacks. The reporter used many sound bites from his neighbor in the report. Off camera, during the debate, he turned to the gentleman who seemed to be very familiar with the board and its members. The reporter asked him for the name of the board's attorney.

The man, who so clearly was against the board's attorney, gave the reporter a name. But, as you may have guessed, it was not the correct name. It was the name of a minor local thug. The report ran, with the board attorney incorrectly identified throughout.

While it was amusing to many in the community, there is a lot wrong with this mistake. It was embarrassing to the attorney personally and to the board. It made the station seem like it was taking sides in the debate, which it should not be doing. It embarrassed the station and cost credibility on other issues as well. It's a mistake that should never have been made. And it nearly cost the young reporter his job.

Checklist

- ❐ Gather the facts on camera.
- ❐ Get the facts right.
- ❐ Shoot an establishing shot.
- ❐ Shoot details that may be important.
- ❐ Shoot interviews and keep them tight.
- ❐ Shoot cut-aways of yourself after the interview.
- ❐ Shoot the sounds of the scene.

5

Writing the Script

So you've got the material for your report in the can. You've done your interviews in the field and you've observed the scene and shot the important video you will need to establish the situation and show the details. The next step is to put together a script, marshaling the facts you've gathered into an understandable report.

Your job now is really two-fold. You must accurately relate what happened. But you must also tell the story in such a way that the viewer will watch and remember. That is the mark of a good storyteller and there are tricks to doing this part well.

One thing I've noticed over the years in my classes is this: It's not just the best looking or the most polished students who have gone on to do well as on-camera people, it is the storytellers who have gone the furthest.

You should think of every report that you do as a story. Let's make one up. It will be a story with a simple set of facts. Let's call it our fire story.

Nancy's Class Fire Story

You are just packing up the gear from an interview you did for the morning news broadcast at a home on Main Street. You and the crew are just about to load everything into your truck and leave when you hear someone next door holler: "FIRE!"

You are the first on the scene. Your sharp camera operator immediately starts shooting. You are on top of your game, so this is what you get in the next hour.

Video of:

The house on fire.

The fire trucks (with natural sound of the siren) arriving.

Firefighters running to the back of the truck, pulling fire hose from the truck to the hydrant, hitching up and shooting water at the fire.

The resident of the house running out of the house (with natural sound of her yelling "Fire!").

A rescue of a resident from the second-story window by firefighters on a ladder.

The neighbors congregating at the sidewalk.

Police doing crowd control.

Ambulance arrival (with siren sound).

Rescued resident attended to by EMT personnel and taken away by ambulance.

A police sniffer dog held by an officer until the fire is controlled ... then they check the house for possible arson.

You stay long enough to see (and shoot) the fire trucks drive away down the street.

On-Camera Field Interviews

THE HOME OWNER — She is seen escaping on our video. The interview consists of nothing but her screaming, "Where's my cat Tabby? Have you seen Tabby?" and so on. She answers, "I don't know" to every question about how the fire started and what happened. She does say she didn't call the fire department and she does identify herself as Midge Connally.

THE FIRE CHIEF — He is a very good fireman but a really dull interview. But he is the best authority and the most important interview to get. He talks in fire department lingo: "The call came in at 0-eight hundred" (8 a.m.).

In a monotone, he recites the facts:

> The fire was "a two-alarm fire."
> There were "two pumpers on the scene and one fire/rescue vehicle."

Fig. 5-1 Fire chief.

"The men had to employ 800 feet of hose to get to the nearest hydrant."

The fire "did not fully involve the structure."

"An investigation will determine the cause."

In answer to your question, he acknowledges: "A witness did say she had seen flames shooting out of the electrical box on the side of the house."

Finally he adds, "All residents were evacuated safely."

THE EYEWITNESS — The next-door neighbor is your best interview — a zany character who is just down home. She is

Fig. 5-2 The eyewitness.

delighted to tell you what she saw. She is animated and exciting to listen to. You correctly spend more time with this interview than the others.

She is "Dang sure it started in that electric box ... and didn't she know about that cause she'd had a scare just like that on her house last summer." She had "Called Midge immediately when she saw that fire and hollered through the phone for Midge to get out." "There's a dang fire in your house, I told her." "Why I was scared half to death, I was." "Lordy I do hope Tabby made it out, I know how much that cat means to Midge."

She tells you the elderly person taken out of the second story is Midge's mother. They don't get along so well. "The two women and the cat are the only residents," she says.

THE AMBULANCE DRIVER — He only knows that everyone was safe after the fire chief told him. He did the preliminary check on the woman rescued from the second story.

"She is elderly and we are taking her to the emergency room as a precaution. She seems fine. She's a feisty one, she is."

In addition, you have taped a stand-up and a close for this piece (more on that later) which you will not use this time.

Let's Write the Script and Make a Package

You first screen the tape if you have the time back at the station. You take notes (usually with time code that shows up on the screen in the edit booth). You transcribe the interview "sound bites" you like and that are important.

If you have to turn this story around quickly, it's good to take notes during the interview of the sound bites as you hear them. You can write the script with these notes and your tape editor will find the pictures.

And you note the video that you will need for your narration and also the "Natural Sound." That is often referred to in scripts as "NATSOT" meaning "Natural Sound On Tape." It's a piece of audio that happened at the scene, like the sound of a bomb or a person hollering "Help me!"

Fig. 5-3 Take notes during the interview.

So whether you are back at your desk at the station ... or you are in the front seat of the truck because you will go live for the Noon broadcast, you are writing your script.

Where do you begin? How do you begin? Any number of ways. There is no single right way to tell a story ... though there are less than quality ways to do it. But you are going to focus on telling a story.

One very good way to capture the interest of the viewer is to start with some "Natural Sound" or NATSOT.

In our Fire Story, we have two good NATSOT choices. Can you figure out which ones I'm talking about? I favor starting with one over the other because of the logic of time. Can you guess which I like and why? The two NATSOTs I like as starters are the siren of the approaching fire truck and "Fire!" yelled by the owner.

Because the yelled "Fire" occurred before the fire truck arrived and because it is right on the point of the story, let's start with that. So we'll build a script:

FIRE SCRIPT/Nancy's class
NATSOT: "Fire!"

What's next? How about telling the viewer what happened. "Shortly after 8 this morning, a fire broke out at 1234 Main Street."

That's correct and it's serviceable. But BLAZE is more vivid than fire, isn't it? And here is a hint ... it is best not to start a sentence, especially the first sentence of your script, with a prepositional phrase (Shortly after 8 ...). How about a small tweak on this:

NARR: "A blaze hit the home of Midge Connally at 1234 Main Street shortly after 8 this morning."

(Note: NARR stands for Narration.)

Better, right? And we should identify the owner, the same person who yelled "Fire!," at the top of the piece.

What do we use for picture at this point? (Some TV lingo here: We call the picture or video you use "Cover" since it is covering your narrative script lines.) Let's use that wide establishing shot of the scene that you remembered to shoot. It helps the viewer to know where we are as the story unfolds.

So now we have:

FIRE SCRIPT/Nancy's Class
NATSOT: "Fire!"

(V/O wide shot of fire scene.)
NARR: "A blaze hit the home of Midge Connally at 1234 Main Street shortly after 8 this morning."

(Note: V/O is "Voice Over," which indicates video cover.)

This Is a Visual Medium

Don't forget it. You don't have to say everything. The picture can take care of a lot of the storytelling. For example, you don't have to say a fire broke out in a wood frame, two-story house, the viewers can see that. Similarly, you can let us know that Fifth Avenue, in New York City, is a place of wealth and power by the video that is shot. You don't say, "This street is one of wealth and power." But, if you shoot the tall elegant buildings, the store windows, we get the message. No need to waste time saying it when your camera-person can do it for you. Then you can use your time to tell the story.

Pace

For the purpose of a well-paced story, this report could use some "sound" from the scene here. It continues to bring the viewer into the story and pushes the information along. The one that sticks out to me is that NATSOT of the siren from the arriving fire engine. We'll "open the piece up" here and let the picture (the fire truck racing to the house) and its sound, the siren, play "in the clear" (no narration). This helps us in many ways. It puts the viewer there and tells the story without having to narrate every last thing.

So we have:

FIRE SCRIPT/Nancy's Class
NATSOT: "Fire!"
(V/O wide shot of fire scene.)

NARR: "A blaze hit the home at 1234 Main Street shortly after 8 this morning."
NATSOT: (Fire truck arriving) "Siren screaming."

Next, how about going to some of the good action footage you shot ... the firefighters getting their hoses attached to the hydrant and starting to put out the fire.

We could write it this way and be accurate: "800 feet of hose was brought by the firefighters to the nearby hydrant, to which they attached the hose."

Excuse me class, but this is DULL, is it not? Accurate but DULL. Why?

The first reason, and the main reason, is the verb. It's boring. Go for the right verb, the one that reflects action. Sure, the firefighters brought the hose ... but these are firefighters at a fire! They are hustling to get that fire out. Was the hose heavy? Probably.

How about they LUGGED the hose ... They hauled the hose ... They wrestled the hose ... SOMETHING other than brought.

Here's the other problem with this verb form. It is in the passive voice. That means something is being done to (Passive—bad) instead of something doing something (Active—good).

So instead of "the hose was brought" what about:

"The firefighters lugged 800 feet of hose to find water."

This is good because your pictures show it was the hydrant.

NANCY'S RULES

Active verbs are the writer's best friend.
Verbs bring the viewer into the story.
Go for the active verbs.
Never use the passive voice.

Language Is a Tool

Your language toolbox has more in it than just verbs. You should get to be familiar with other tools that will make your copy sparkle. Dan Rather has been a great reporter and anchor throughout his career. But what you may not realize is how artfully he uses language. He never misses a chance at using every tool available for broadcasters and that includes his writing. You can study it in any of the many books he has written. You will note his spare sentence structure, but at the same time note his flourishes. His use of metaphor and simile is legendary and many viewers looked forward to hearing them during election night. One particularly close vote brought this out: "The race is as tight as a Botox smile." This was only one of many that peppered his reporting. You will do well to take advantage of the language in your writing.

Back to our class fire script. So now with our active verb, we have:

FIRE SCRIPT/Nancy's Class
NATSOT: "Fire!"
(V/O wide shot of fire scene.)
NARR: "A blaze hit the home at 1234 Main Street shortly after 8 this morning."
NATSOT: (Fire truck arriving) "Siren screaming."
NARR: "The firefighters lugged 800 feet of hose to find water."

(NOTE: This is an editor's trick but I'll let you in on it here. Take the siren sound from the NATSOT and dip the level, trailing it under the next picture of the firefighters lugging hose, then fade it out. This is called an "L-cut" and helps weave the piece together. It is less jumpy, less jarring than cutting it out abruptly.)

Now we want to introduce our superstar interview, right?

Here we can use an old scripting trick that gives the piece pace and the opportunity to introduce who is talking. What we will do is use some sound from the eyewitness, then a line of narration introducing her, then another piece of sound from her. You can

Fig. 5-4 The eyewitness.

either break up one long sound bite into two parts (using them on either side of the narration) or use two sound bites with the narration between them. In both cases, it's best to use a shorter piece of sound before the narration followed by a meatier one — something like this:

SOT: "Why I was scared half to death, I was."
(V/O show neighbor then the electric box.)
NARR: "Neighbor Shelly Jones spotted the flame coming out of the electric box on her neighbor's house. She phoned her immediately."
SOT: "'There's a dang fire in your house,' I told her."

(SOT here means "Sound on Tape" and it's a part of your interview.)
So now we have:

FIRE SCRIPT/Nancy's Class
NATSOT: "Fire!"
(V/O wide shot of fire scene.)
NARR: "A blaze hit the home at 1234 Main Street shortly after 8 this morning."
NATSOT: (Fire truck arriving) "Siren screaming."
NARR: "The firefighters lugged 800 feet of hose to find water."
SOT: (Neighbor) "Why I was scared half to death, I was."
(V/O show neighbor then the electric box.)
NARR: "Neighbor Shelly Jones spotted the flame coming out of the electric box on her neighbor's house. She phoned her immediately."
SOT: (Neighbor) "'There's a dang fire in your house,' I told her."

As much fun as our interview with the neighbor is, we have to get to more facts and alas, leave her behind. It can be a trap to fall in love with a character who is not the key to the facts, so you have to be careful.

What's important now? Was anyone hurt? How much damage? Go there with your other interviews. The fire chief is the best authority but he is dull, so if you can, avoid too much of him.

You can use pictures of you and the chief as "cover" for narration about what he told you. You might use the best sound you have that is short or at least a tiny snip of his voice to lead into narration. This is also a good way to keep the viewer involved in the story. In this narration, you can say what the chief said. Like this:

NAT or NATSOT: (Again meaning natural sound ... even though it's the fire chief talking, it's not a sound bite ... just flavor of your interview.)
NAT: "... two pumpers on the scene ..."
NARR: "The chief told me that all the residents were evacuated safely."

Fig. 5-5 *Fire chief.*

Now that information came directly from what the chief did tell you. You could go from there to the daring rescue of the elderly woman from the second story.

This is not your only option. There would be nothing wrong with using the "sound" from the chief if you like. It might even set up the drama of the incident better.

SOT: (Chief) "All residents were evacuated safely."
(V/O rescue of woman.)
NARR: "The chief's men did a heroic job of rescuing one of the residents who was pulled from the second story."

Either one is fine. Then you'd go to the ambulance driver.

NARR: "The woman, identified as the mother of the other resident, was taken to the hospital as a precaution."
SOT: (Ambulance man) "She seems fine. She's a feisty one, she is."

So we've told the story and gotten everyone safely out. There are a couple of tidbits that should be included. How much damage? The chief told us not too much. And what about that investigation? How about one more line of narration:

NARR: "The damage to the home was minimal. An investigation is under way."

To cover this with picture, you could always use the shot of the damage you smartly got while on the scene. But I like book-ending the piece with the closing shot of the fire truck leaving. Remember we used the arrival at the top. Visually, it gives a nice symmetry, a nice balance to the report.

Now we have some dangling information. What do you do with that cat? Should it be up higher? Should it be in the piece at all? My belief is that it makes a nice tag to a piece as long as no one died or was severely hurt. So let's use it there.

LIVE (OR TAPED TAG)
"The only worry now is Tabby the cat who is missing. But here's hoping that Tabby hasn't used all of her nine lives."
Reporting (LIVE) etc. etc. (See next chapter for how to sign off.)

What about the ambulance attendant saying everyone is fine. He told you that the chief told him that. So that makes it third-hand information, doesn't it? Go to the source and ask the chief if it's important.

What about the neighbor saying they don't get along. That shouldn't be in this at all. It's not part of the story, it may not be correct and it could be actionable under law. Be careful of ever using gossip as fact.

How's our final script look?

FIRE SCRIPT/Nancy's Class
NATSOT: "Fire!"
(V/O wide shot of fire scene.)
NARR: "A blaze hit the home of Midge Connally at 1234 Main Street shortly after 8 this morning."
NATSOT: (Fire truck arriving) "Siren screaming."
NARR: "The firefighters lugged 800 feet of hose to find water."
SOT: (Neighbor) "Why I was scared half to death, I was."
(V/O show neighbor then the electric box.)
NARR: "Neighbor Shelly Jones spotted the flame coming out of the electric box on her neighbor's house. She phoned her immediately."
SOT: "'There's a dang fire in your house,' I told her."
SOT: (Chief) "All residents were evacuated safely."
(V/O rescue of woman.)
NARR: "The chief's men did a heroic job of rescuing one of the residents who was pulled from the second story."
(V/O How about using the fire truck leaving. You could use the damage of the house but that is a more literal show-and-tell.)
NARR: "The damage to the home was minimal. An investigation is under way."
LIVE (OR TAPED TAG)
"The only worry now is Tabby the cat who is missing. But here's hoping that Tabby hasn't used all of her nine lives."

On the CD-Rom, I've put in pictures for you to write your own script on the fire story. Go and write some. The more you practice, the better you will get.

Hard News/Light News

Let's touch on this for a moment here. What are hard news stories? They are serious stories. The fire story is an example of a hard news story. These are the stories that are usually placed at the top of the broadcast: war, a murder, a robbery, a new disease or cure are all examples of hard news stories. There are often tragic consequences. Consequences that the reporter must deal with. You become involved because you are shooting the story and you want to get the best interviews you can get.

In a hard news story the first thing you want to do is go to the highest available authority. In the case of our fire, it's the chief. In an accident it would be the policeman in charge of all the action there. That would be your first choice. The policeman might not want to speak with you on camera. You still want a strong interview. So you can search out a lesser authority, but a trustworthy source. Then you can go after the emotional interview. Sometimes the emotional interview ends up being the most important interview for your story because it is so powerful.

Your third choice would be a bystander — someone who viewed the accident. Eyewitness testimony, as lawyers know, are notoriously flawed. But you will get a sense of the scene and perhaps some facts that others did not provide to you.

Light news stories are fun and frivolous. They are not life-and-death stories and they usually don't affect your pocketbook. The local baseball team, a new movie, anything about healthy babies or animals and the rich and famous are all fodder for these light, chatty stories. The weather or an upcoming holiday is always a good story to tell if you can't find a good light one.

Use of "We" Versus "You" in Your Script

Although the Fire Script did not use this device, it is something that you should know about.

Let's say we wrote the tag differently:

"We all want to know what happened to Tabby, the cat who is missing."

Note the use of "We" here. To be frank, it sounds imperious, stand-offish and viewer unfriendly. Those who use "we" in their scripts think they are being inclusive. It comes off just the opposite. Substitute "You" for "We" and it does what you want. Here is an example where I've employed "You" and the use of a question that really draws the viewer in.

"You might have wondered what happened to Tabby, the cat who is missing? No news there at this time. But here's hoping that Tabby hasn't used all of her nine lives."

Much better, don't you think? This is a good device to use and is often a great way to lead a story. As always, don't overdo it, though.

Reporting from the War Front

Job One: Stay alive. You are no good to the station or the network if you cannot report — to say nothing about your family. Be the most alert you have ever been. Be wary of going places that might get you wounded, even killed. I know that may sound stupid since a war zone is a place where this could happen. But veteran war correspondents have the instincts and training to get in and out alive war after war. Others get hurt their first visit. Be smart about where you go in these dangerous places.

 ## Report from the Trenches
(*Real* Trenches)

Erin Moriarty from CBS News *48 Hours* was imbedded with a unit from Fort Wayne, Indiana, for the pursuit toward Baghdad during the Iraq War in 2003. She is a true professional, there to do her high-quality reporting. She was treated as a professional by the men in the all-male unit. She listened to their advice and took it. But at the same time, her job was different from theirs so there were times that Erin and the soldiers didn't agree. The soldiers were fighting an enemy; Erin was reporting on the war. If you are in a war zone with soldiers, there might well be conflicts. The lesson is: You must work with the soldiers and you must work out any issues.

They all returned to the United States safe and sound. The unit accomplished its mission; she accomplished hers. And the bonds they formed in that ancient desert are as deep as family. The soldiers probably have more respect for the press, and Erin has an enormous respect for the soldiers.

One thing that she would probably be embarrassed to have me mention here is the issue of peeing. In the full gear that was really required for being on the front lines of a shooting war, it's not so easy for women to go. But she did work that out too. If you are in this situation, there are questions you should ask during your training before getting to the battlefront. You might ask that one too.

Fat Head Advice

The great television reporters and anchors never forget they are journalists first. They keep reestablishing themselves by going on location to report important breaking stories, such as hurricanes and wars. What is most important to the network reporters and anchors I have known is not how they are treated, but did they get the story. The story is all-important to them. They are not arrogant. They are always interested in people. And this comes through in their work, especially in their interviews. They are humble in the sense that they do not make assumptions but keep seeking the truth by respectfully asking the questions until they can piece together what is really happening. When you get to be a top-level correspondent or anchor, always remember that you are a reporter first and by definition, you don't have all the answers.

Finding Your Stories and Developing Your Sources

Now you are ready to report your own stories. As a beginner, you will probably be assigned a story by the desk or your executive producer. But what boss doesn't love someone with initiative and enthusiasm? You should also try to find good stories on your own to suggest to your boss. This is a good way to separate yourself as a reporter from the pack. How will you find the great stories? Where do you dig for this gold?

Of course reporters have access to wire stories. They are a good place to search. But remember, if it's found on the wires, the story has already been reported.

A close reading of the Internet can help you dig for details on a story, but it can be overwhelming to really help you find your stories. So where do you find the unreported stories? Sources. If you have a beat, develop sources within your beat. This takes building trust and that comes from being an honest reporter.

For example, if you are on the education beat, you should know all sides and check in with them regularly. Check with the head of the board, of course. But don't forget to check with the members of the board who are against the majority as well as the superintendent of schools, the top principals, the head of the PTA, the teacher's union leader and even some teachers and students.

Local officials can be helpful and they should be cultivated. Also, folks in government agencies can be even more useful and usually more open to sharing information. Drop by, introduce yourself, start a conversation without camera or microphone. In other words, develop your relationships.

Lawyers who represent whistle blowers or others who are suing companies or agencies are often very cooperative with interviews and documentation. Union leaders will often point out failures of businesses and offer you interviews and documents. Unfortunately, too many companies and agencies have public affairs or public relations people who believe that the company should never talk about business and never comment on a failure or accusation. This puts you the reporter in the difficult position of saying the company or agency refuses to comment. The company may have a very good answer, but the public relations folks shut down any possible response.

Report from the Trenches

It is said at the CIA that no one ever got in trouble by not talking to reporters. But some companies built a trust with the public because they were open and honest. The classic case was that of Johnson & Johnson when someone tampered with Tylenol. The company came out immediately with all the facts, recalled all the bottles then on the market and was open and direct with the press and the public about what the company knew. It was and remains a textbook case of how to do it right.

Oddly, some years later, this same company declined to be interviewed when another of their products, Risperdal, came under fire. There were serious accusations that the depression medication for adults was being used on children with worrisome results.

The story came from a child advocate who had seen problems in a number of children under the control of a Florida state agency. Then a child psychiatrist backed up those charges with problems he had seen including the question: Why was the drug company encouraging doctors to recommend it for use on children when it had not been thoroughly researched on children? Johnson & Johnson refused an on-camera interview and in fact refused comment altogether. It was not its finest day.

It does not make sense for companies to pick and choose when they will comment. They should always comment. They should always be honest with you as a reporter. For your part, you should always be honest in your reporting and honest in your dealings with companies.

Conclusion to Writing the Script

Writing exciting copy is important for a correspondent. You are in the business of communicating. And this communication must be hard and fast. You do not have the luxury that a newspaper journalist has. No one is going to sit and study your text. Your story must be easily grasped and it must sound like a person talking with knowledge, authority and grace to another person. You must be a good communicator with your writing skills, as well as your speaking skills.

When you can trust your communication skills, you won't waste your time with constant rewrites and the insecurity of not knowing what you are doing. You must choose which are the important questions to ask. You must decide what it is that the viewer will want to know. In every broadcast time is limited. Above all else, with everything you do and say, you must never forget your viewers. They are your ultimate boss.

Checklist

- ☐ TV scripts have a unique syntax that you must learn.
- ☐ Know how to write into and out of SOTs.
- ☐ Understand the value of NATSOT.
- ☐ Pace your script.
- ☐ Don't be wedded to a minor character.
- ☐ Use verbs: active verbs, bright verbs.
- ☐ Write to your video pictures.
- ☐ Develop sources.
- ☐ In a war zone, stay alive.

Presenting the Report on Camera

There is the great divide between newspaper reporting and television journalism. It's a Mississippi River difference between the pencil press and TV. On the one shore is the newspaperman and on the other is you. Both of you have to know how to write, both have to know how to report. But only you have to know how to do it on camera.

The basic elements of the television reporter's news story:

THE OPEN
THE PACKAGE (OR INTERVIEW)
THE CLOSE
THE TAG
THE SIGN OFF

Studio Lead or Studio Throw

What is a studio lead? It is the words the anchor says that introduce the story to the viewer and introduce you as the reporter. The anchor will throw the story to you just before you go live on air. You will hear your show and your anchor through your Interrupt Feedback, known as an IFB. This is necessary when you are live so you'll know when to come in on cue.

The IFB is the piece in your ear. Through it you can hear the anchor and the producer, and anyone else who needs to talk to you. But you won't hear yourself. It's called "mixed minus," which means you hear the entire show (mixed audio from the anchors and the video that may be playing) minus your voice. If you hear your own words coming back in your earpiece, it is most difficult to concentrate. It has happened. You may have seen people pull the earpieces out during an interview or a live report. That was probably because they were being fed the broadcast audio, including their own voice.

The anchor will say, "And now we'll go to (your name) in midtown Manhattan." You'll respond with, "Thank you, Dana" or, "Yes, Dana." After the tag, you'll say, "Back to you, Dana." It is always preferable to send it back to a person in the studio. If you don't know whom it should go back to, it is OK to say "Back to you in the studio." But this comes across as impersonal and cold.

The Open

An open is what you tell your viewer as the camera starts to roll. You set up the story and give the facts. Do it brightly and tightly. Your open is what grabs the viewer to watch your piece. For taped packages, this might be live in the studio or live from the field.

Don't forget in your opens and closes you are talking to a real person through the camera, not just speaking to a camera lens. Keep your opens tight, and give the important details of the story.

Don't copy what is written in the wire copy or newspaper. You should do your own writing. A reporter in the newspaper is writing for readers. You are talking to the viewers.

Beware of the Same Copy

Something else to watch out for: Don't repeat the exact words that were just said in the studio lead to you. It is a waste of time and embarrassing to hear the following:

Anchor: "It might have been a lot worse, as our reporter Sam Smith reports."

Sam Smith: "It might have been a lot worse. Only two injuries from a wild accident . . ."

Poor Sam. He looks like an idiot for saying the same thing in the exact words that the anchor in the studio just said. The fact is, Sam probably wrote his before the anchor who stole the line. But if Sam is live, he should check on what the studio lead is going to say. In this case, since Sam is live, he could have made a second reference of it. Like this:

Anchor: "It might have been a lot worse, as our reporter Sam Smith reports."
Sam: "You are right. A whole lot worse, in fact. Only two injuries from a wild accident . . ."

You set up the story and give the facts. Do it brightly and tightly.

Sometimes there is no live open. Often the anchor will lead directly to the taped package. But even if you don't have a live open, you might have a live close to the package. Be prepared for anything.

The Package

You learned how to script a package in the previous chapter. But there are on-camera presentation items that we need to address here. Chief among them is the section of the reporting you do on camera.

Stand-Ups

What is a stand-up? It's you talking to the camera for a live report or for use in a taped piece. In the taped piece, stand-ups have two beneficial effects. It's always good to see the reporter in the package, to remind the viewers just who it is bringing them the story. It's a real live person and not just some disembodied voice.

It's good for you to be seen of course, but it is equally important for the viewer to know you as a storyteller. Without you, the storyteller, the story is not as relatable. Without you telling us, without you doing the interviews, the story seems distant and does not connect as well with the viewer. This leads to the chance that the viewer's mind might wander, or worse, the viewer might change the channel. That is something you cannot allow to happen.

So, what do I say in a stand-up? What kind of information do I put into a stand-up? It should be something important. If you are seen on camera, talking directly to the viewer, it will get the viewer's attention. It demands the viewer's attention. Therefore, don't let the viewer down. Give them something key to the story. It may be the whole reason for the story.

Report from the Trenches

During a presidential campaign, one of the candidates was visiting a small rural town in South Carolina. The candidate was set to make a major civil rights speech at the opening of a new church. The old church had burned down and the community, mostly black, had pitched together to build a new place of worship.

The correspondent and producer had done some digging and learned that a grand jury was about to indict the accused arsonists on charges. The prosecutors also had enough evidence to charge that the arsonists were members of the Ku Klux Klan. This was not only blockbuster news, but also the point of the presidential candidate's appearance — that civil rights was still a fight. And that became the stand-up, done at the site of the burned out church.

Be Creative but . . .

Creativity in your stand-up can make it memorable and make you stand out from the others. If you are trying to show how tall an ocean wave was and don't have pictures of it, then go stand in front of a ten story building and explain on camera that the wave was as high as this building. A visual helps those viewers who might not otherwise understand just how tall that wave was.

Be careful. Creativity can be overdone or too clever. For example:

Report from the Trenches

During a report on some severe flooding in her area, a young reporter got creative in a way you should not. She cleverly, it appeared, did her stand-up while in a rowboat as she floated down a flooded street. She was doing this live and as a result, she was found out. She was reporting from her little boat how deep the waters were when someone walked between her boat and the camera. The viewer saw the boots and knees of the person walking in front the reporter. It was obvious that the water was only a couple of inches deep. It was hardly the severe flooding that would require a boat.

W Miller

Fig. 6-1 Oops!

Wallpaper

Another good use of the stand-up is to present information for which there is no good cover (video picture). For example, say you have legal papers such as a deposition or a court proceeding where no cameras were allowed. Instead of using a picture of a pile of court documents — known in the business as wallpaper — use your stand-up to say what is important in the paperwork while holding the court documents. In the past, reporters would have to resort to that "wallpaper" — that generic picture: a shot of a bank if you were talking about a business story. It is generic and dull.

Bridges

And another useful stand-up is the bridge. The bridge takes you from one part of the story to another. It bridges two different things . . . it could be geography or time or people.

Let's say you are covering a hurricane along the Gulf Coast. The storm was aimed at New Orleans but veered to the west, spared Louisiana, but clobbered the Texas coast. You spent time in both states and your reporting addresses the effects on both states. In this example, your bridge is geographical, carrying the viewer from one place to another . . . from Texas to Louisiana. The top of the report told about Texas, the bottom reports on Louisiana and the bridge takes the viewer from one to the other. Something like:

> "While Texans here are returning to communities destroyed by the hurricane, residents of neighboring Louisiana are coming back to their homes — homes untouched by the storm."

Bridges could be temporal, carrying the viewer from one time to another.

> "James Joseph is a Nobel Prize winner today, but his teachers remember him as a brat."

Or a bridge can be communal, taking the story from one person or group to another. This is useful especially when you have two sides to a story: A bridge from Democrats to Republicans ... from strikers to management ... from young to old.

Graphics

Another valuable tool for you is graphics. They are getting more sophisticated and jazzier. The best thing about graphics is they help explain a complicated idea simply and, well, graphically. In addition, graphics help cover narration that otherwise might not have any great pictures.

Your pictures should speak to the viewers as much as your copy and your interviews. Never miss an opportunity to dazzle. Graphics will dazzle instead of bore your viewers.

 ## Report from the Trenches

A reporter got word that a doctor's phones were out and the doctor was beside himself. And well he might have been. He was a gynecologist with pregnant patients about to give birth. A phone was crucial. So he alerted the reporter of the problem.

He told the reporter that he had been trying for three days to get the phones back and was getting the run-around from every phone company involved. The doctor had signed up for bundled service that was supposed to save him money and consolidate all his long distance, local and DSL phone services into one. The problem developed when the phone went out. He called the company that sent him the bill — a long distance company. That company said they couldn't help because it contracted his local service to a different company and he would have to call that company. He called that company and a person there said he would have to call another company because the service had been subcontracted. He called that company and was sent back to the original long-distance company that had bundled all the services. He got the run-around and he got no phone service.

Since none of the phone companies would speak to the reporter on camera, the reporter was left to explain this complex dodge by using wallpaper cover of the company logos or headquarters. Not very exciting video, right?

The graphics department came up with a design that showed three phones each with the various company logos arranged in a circle. The narration said how the doctor was sent from company to company, and the graphic showed an arrow whooshing from one phone to the next and to the next and finally back to the first. It was a classic run-around.

It was a good example of how graphics can help a report.

File Tape

File tape, or tape that comes from some time in the past, can be very useful and illuminating.

Take our accident story from earlier. Say that street corner has been dangerous for some time. Remember we said there was a bush growing in front of an important street sign? Let's say there were a series of accidents at that same spot and that one of them had been the focus of an earlier report. It would be informative for the viewers and perhaps the folks in town who are responsible for the street signs if you used the old "file tape" in your piece.

The Close

This is an on-camera sentence or two used to sum up what you've learned from your reporting. It may also include advice and an update, if appropriate.

Generally you don't want more than a sentence or two at most. The close can be memorized or ad-libbed. It is given directly to the viewer. You definitely do not want to be looking down reading from your notes. You want to look through the camera.

A close can be a look ahead at what developments to expect, or a swift summing up of the interview or a clever snapper to the story if it isn't serious business.

The close is a terrific spot for useful information for the viewers. This is especially true for local news. The audience wants to know what's going on in their community. So if you can, be sure to give advice. Even if it is a large neighborhood, the weather, for example, will probably be the same throughout a large region, "Make sure the kids take their raincoats today."

For example: In an automobile accident story, you could say:

"The police have just closed off 5th Avenue from 55th Street to 60th Street. So stay away from this area. The traffic is horrendous."

Now practice. After you've written your opens and closes, say them out loud in a conversational tone and listen. If you have time try using a tape recorder to play them back. See how they sound. Listen to the words you have chosen to use. See if it sounds natural, if it holds your interest and leads you into the next part of your report.

There are certain words you don't use when you talk to another person (words such as interface). Be careful if you find yourself using them a lot. There might be the rare situation where they feel appropriate to you, then use them.

The Tag

The reporter's tag line is the final sentence or two in a taped package. Coming at the end, it should wrap up the story. It can be a clever line or a somber one. But it should be a satisfying end to your report.

The Sign Off

The final piece to add to this puzzle is your sign off or sig. It comes just after your close. Keep it short and direct.

A standard sig consists of YOUR NAME, WHERE YOU ARE AND YOUR CHANNEL. Save the channel for last.

An example of a live sign off is:

> This is (your name)
> Live from Greenwich Village
> For Channel Two News.

An example for a taped piece:

> This is (your name)
> In Greenwich Village
> For Channel Two News.

Several of my students forget to say their channel. Don't forget. After all they are paying your salary.

The sig must be in the same mood as your story and its close. If it was a light feature story, the sig should smile. If it's a serious report, the sig here should be stoic or modest. It too must match the mood.

Q and A

Don't think that a live close is the end of it for you. Not these days when technology gives the anchors in the studio a chance to quiz the reporter in the field. Sometimes the anchor wants to have a Q and A with the reporter after either the close or even the sign off. Sometimes your anchor won't tell you the questions beforehand because he likes the spontaneity. You must learn to handle this. If you don't know the answer to a question use my interviewee trick: "I'll find out and get back to you." Never try to make up facts when you don't know the answer.

Reporter's Notes and Notebooks

Let's talk about the notes you will be using during the LIVE remote. You must decide what size notebook you will be comfortable with in the field. I am personally not a fan of those cute reporter notebooks. They are about seven inches long but narrow, only about four inches across. To me, there is not enough space on these pages to write enough of your thoughts, but I will admit they work well if you are referring to your bullet points. You will also find that you will have to turn pages. Try doing this with the wind blowing, a mic in one hand and your notebook in the other hand.

These smaller reporters' notebooks are OK if you are wearing a lavaliere microphone allowing you both hands free. In addition, they can be stowed easily in a pocket or purse. Most network correspondents use them.

Do not use index cards. You don't want cards flying into the camera. The obstacles with these little cards are similar to turning the pages of your notebook.

Don't forget you are holding your mic in your other hand. So with both hands busy it becomes extremely clumsy to turn a page. It also is distracting to the viewer. You want to have enough room on the one page for the entire story. If you have to flip cards, and the wind is blowing, and it's snowing, you're really out of luck.

A legal pad is good as a stenographer's spiral notebook that you can quickly flip over to see the other side of the page. And you can do this with the same hand with which you are holding your notebook.

Bullet Points

❖ You want your notes to be as easy to read as possible.
❖ Don't write in paragraphs.
❖ Write notes in bullet points.
❖ Bullet points are the main words taken from the information gained from your research, your reporting and your questions.
❖ The names of places.
❖ The names of people.

Fig. 6-2 Don't use file cards.

❖ The numbers involved in the incident.
❖ Important quotes.
❖ Whatever is essential should be in your bullet points.
❖ This way you can quickly see what you need to with just a quick glance down at your notes, can't you?
❖ The purpose is to make sure you can see instantly what you need without having to study a whole paragraph. This way you can look at the camera most of the time, while presenting your live report.

When you are first starting out on the job, you may feel the need to begin by writing out your story in paragraphs. If this is you, you must also make a shortened version, and translate it into your bullet points. You may also want to number the bullet points. This way you won't lose your place as you might if you are trying to read paragraphs of notes, especially with all the myriad distractions. When you look down to bullet points, you can easily see where you are in your story. This will also help you look at your interviewee or at the camera and not face down in your notes.

Lots will be happening when you're covering a story, so you want to help yourself as much as you can to make everything you've written down as clear as possible. Bullet points are the strongest and clearest way I have found to read from your notes.

Magic Marker

Another trick is to bring a magic marker with you. Highlight the names of people and anything else of great importance. With one glance you can see everything easily.

So to make your reporting life easier: NUMBER your bullet points and HIGHLIGHT the most important words. This whole process takes practice.

Microphone Position

For the most part, you will either use a hand microphone (known as the hand mic) or a lavaliere mic, which is smaller and attached to your clothing.

For the hand mic, there is a right way and a wrong way to hold it. In one hand you will hold your mic, leaving your other hand free to hold your notes. So don't get into the habit of holding your mic with both hands. And even if you never use notes, you still don't want to hold it with both hands.

Don't place the mic too close to your mouth as the singers do on MTV, you will pop your Ps and hiss your Ss. Don't place your mic too far away from your mouth, you won't be heard.

So let's find out the best way for you, the reporter, to use the mic. You can determine the exact placement for your mic if you put the tip of your thumb against the bottom of your chin, make a fist and hold out your pinkie (see Fig. 6-3). Your mic should be at the level where your pinkie points to your chest. You don't want to cover your mouth with the mic. It should be approximately 6 or 7 inches from the bottom of your chin.

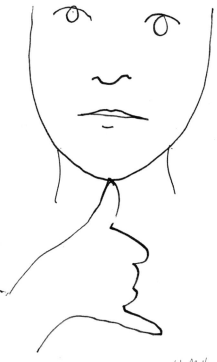

W Miller

Fig. 6-3 Microphone position.

Where Do I Look?

When you are at a live shoot, there will probably be only one camera. You will do your open directly into the camera, speaking directly to the viewer. If you need to look at your notes, do so but don't linger looking down any longer than you must. Then you return to your original position talking into the camera to the viewer.

If you have a live guest on a remote and you have to do an open before turning to DO your interview, a very good way to help get your subject's face on camera is to do your open facing the camera (see Fig. 6-4). Then pivot so your back is to the camera but the interviewee is facing you and the camera (see Fig. 6-5).

You are standing closer to the camera at an angle to your guest. This way your cameraperson can shoot your subject over your shoulder. Your questions can be directed to your subject. Whenever you need to send it back to the studio, you can easily pivot so you return to face the camera.

It's All in How You Ask the Question

The words you choose when you ask your question are crucial. The specific words will help determine the kind of responses you receive.

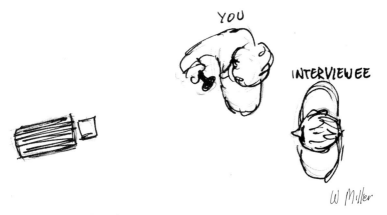

YOU

INTERVIEWEE

W Miller

Fig. 6-4 First address the viewers . . .

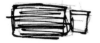
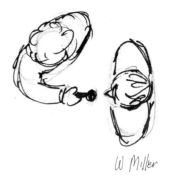

W Miller

Fig. 6-5 Then turn to DO the interview.

For example, in our accident story you might ask the driver:

> "How did it get started?"
> "How was it to drive in this weather?"

You can ask the eyewitness:

> "That car was about four inches from your skirt?"

That should certainly get a reaction out of them.

Do not ask a leading question. That implies you have a point of view, which of course you should not have. For example:

> "Don't you think the president's proposal is wonderful?"

That is a leading question, leading your interviewee to say:

> "Yes."

Better:

> "What do you think of the president's proposal?"

The words you choose should excite and nudge your interviewee into giving you answers that are vibrant, getting you good sound bites.

You can use the Vic Miles trick. Vic was a terrific reporter for the New York City market a while back. He would often confront the person he was interviewing — not rudely but cheerfully — and often get a strong response.

For example, he might say to the cab driver:

"A lot of people I talk to say cabbies these days are just plain reckless. You see cabbies all day long. Are they?"

The cabbie would explode with an answer. "No we aren't, it's the pedestrians. ..." Vic's style always got great responses and the viewer's attention.

Report from the Trenches

Vic did this once: It was at a particularly dangerous city intersection. Five Corners, it was called, and it was a block from an elementary school, so lots of kids crossed these streets both in the morning and in the afternoon.

A school crossing guard did her best but with traffic coming at all angles and kids of course crossing at all angles, it was an almost impossible task. Inevitably, a truck hit a kid in the crossing and fled. Fortunately, St. Vincent's Hospital is on one of the corners and the youngster was brought right into the emergency room.

Vic was assigned the story. He wanted to talk to a trucker or cabbie that traveled through that intersection. But no one would stop. Finally, he took his microphone and hopped onto the running board of one truck that was near the sidewalk. Vic smiled at the startled driver and asked:

"You didn't run down a kid here earlier today, did you?"

The trucker erupted in a loud denial that, NO he was not the hit-and-run driver.

Vic said he knew that and followed up immediately with:

"It's a pretty dangerous area, isn't it?"

The trucker, still hot, blamed the city for making a dangerous place and for not looking out for the kids. Great stuff.

Intention

It's not only the words you choose to ask the questions with. It is also the intention with which you ask them.

To get really good responses to your questions, become aware of the way you ask the questions. People want to feel that you are interested in their answers. They don't want to feel that you're just using them for your story. So remember you are talking to a person who maybe has just had an emotional shock, or who may be a bit nervous about being interviewed, especially with a camera rolling. So be warm or sympathetic, in a sad situation, or open or excited if it is something light and chatty.

In other words, be flexible. But above all remain curious, interested and respectful when you are asking the interviewee the questions. Delve deep and dig hard as you ask your questions, and always look right at your guests as if they are the most important people in the world, because at that moment they are.

Remember, don't just read your questions. If you do you'll get the equivalent of a nonresponse. You must really want to know the answer. Don't be perfunctory as you ask the questions. Keep your questions tight.

Should I Interview Several People at the Same Time?

The answer is Yes. Young people hanging together are always good for a sound bite. They give each other courage to talk. Sometimes you can use a crowd to good effect by turning the camera on them.

With many guests, it's tough on the camerapeople to get the shot of the one talking. If possible, warn the cameraperson ahead of time what you're planning to do. If you do this kind of group interview, indicate whom you are going to talk to so the camera can catch up with you. If someone jumps in before the camera is there to record it, ask the person to start again.

For example, if there is a town meeting going on with a group of people stuck outside who could not get in, you can ask them, "Are you happy with the job they're doing in there?"

Some Final Notes for On-Camera Reporter Interviews

Vary the length of your questions, as you might in a conversation. Remember, this too is a conversation.

When you have the time, and this would be with the main character in your story, you can take a person back to the beginning of a story, or to his or her youth. Often this can lead to a marvelous anecdote. "When did it begin?" rarely just gets an: "Oh last Saturday" kind of answer.

If your interview is off the mark, drop it. Move on. But be careful and be sure. The interviewee might be struggling and could well have something interesting to say. Again, you must make your best choice, and it will be based on your experience, your sensitivity, and your smarts.

When you are first approaching people to interview, you should learn whether they speak the language with enough fluency to be understood by the viewer. If not, be polite and thank them. You can certainly gather some facts from them, but don't use them for your on-camera interview. A slight accent is no problem. If the person has such a thick accent that they can't be understood, you have to move on for your on-camera sound bites.

The Five Ws and the Dreaded H

You all know journalism's five Ws: who, what, where, when and why.

There is nothing wrong with asking Why in the middle of the interview. In fact, there is a lot right with it. That question might probe deeper into the situation or the person's actions and help you develop a richer report.

Some other great questions are:

❖ When was that?
❖ Can you describe what it was like where you were?
❖ How did you do that?

But now there's another HOW question that's been creeping into the reporter's notebook. How ... as in: HOW DO YOU FEEL?

After a terrible accident the reporter may ask the victim or the victim's mother or wife, "How do you feel?" Here is my question for you: How do you feel about the "How do you feel" question?

Most of my students are shocked when I show them an example from a news broadcast. The mother is outside the burning home and one of her children is still inside, and the reporter asks, "How do you feel?" It's beyond insensitive. It's thoughtless. And worse yet, you will never get the answer you hoped for. It a naked play for cheap emotion.

Years ago a large local station insisted their reporters ask this whenever possible. It led to some pretty awful moments. It seems most vulgar when the situation is obvious, the subject weeping for example. Isn't it obvious to even the densest viewer or reporter how she feels at this moment?

Reporters who resort to this question have no imagination, are not trained or are not prepared. How painful it is to watch any interview with a coal miner's family as they await grim news of their loved-one's fate. It is horrible to hear the question, "How do you feel?" Horrible. If you can't find a better question to ask, don't ask anything. Have I made myself clear?

One Question At a Time

Ask one question at a time. Put another way: Don't ask several questions at a time. If you ask two or three questions at the same time, your subject can answer any one of them and ignore the others. Or they may innocently forget what all the questions were.

But beware. Many politicians and corporate officers you interview will have an agenda, an ax to grind. They are often trained to present their case well and, as a result, your television audience hears their platform without hearing your balanced report.

One trick they use is this: When you ask several questions they pull a word or two from your question and take the interview in that more favorable direction. You must be careful not to stay on their message for the entire interview.

When you start your interview, give your interview subjects a quick lesson on what to do. Generally, they won't know where to look. Tell them to look at you and ignore the camera. Do not let them address the camera. If they do, ask the question again with the reminder that the answer should be directed to you, not the camera.

Think of Your Priorities

You don't always have a choice, but you must begin to access what is most important for your story. Which person do you want to interview first? Which questions must be answered to help the viewer get the entire story? Don't ever forget your viewer, and why you are reporting. You are telling your viewers what they should know, about their politics, their safety or their teams.

You Are Going Live

Live location shoots so far sound simple to pull off. But there is a lot that can go wrong. This is not a controlled situation, as you would have in a studio. When you are live, people don't always do or say what you expect them to. Technology is a marvelous thing but only when it works. Murphy's law abounds in these live shoots. Anything that can go wrong probably will one time or another. So you and your crew will have to think on your feet. Veteran CBS News correspondent Phil Jones puts it this way: "Almost always something goes wrong, unexpected, in a live report."

Report from the Trenches

Phil was covering a major military trial, a court marshal, where no cameras are allowed inside. So the producer had planned to use signals when the verdict came in. Phil was live outside and here came the associate producer out the door with a signal ... but it was the wrong one. They had gotten their signals mixed up, leaving Phil with egg on his face.

It was the most confusing almost disastrous live shot that he could remember. "It was one garbled mess." He knew something was wrong. Instead of hiding the fact, he told the viewers that he wasn't sure he had it correct. He said to the viewers: "Just a moment, I don't think this is quite right here."

The lesson here is: Honesty, when things are going awry, will always be accepted by the audience.

I asked how Phil handled that foul-up.

"You handle it well because you have gone into this thing prepped on the subject. You know what the story is all about, you know what the issues are. And when you have to start vamping, have to start maneuvering, you have context. If you don't know the subject, if you don't know the story, you are dead. I don't care how glib you are, if you haven't covered it or researched it completely, it is going to show."

Stay Calm in a Crisis

Certainly in a LIVE report, time may not permit you to do more than one interview, so you need to make a choice. Stay calm. You may only have time to interview one person. Who will it be? And with time in such a tight constraint what will be your questions? Always ask your most important ones first.

You decide on your priorities. You must think on your feet. You must know who you want to interview the most. You may not always get to speak with the person you wish to interview. So you may have to use your second choice. You may have to rethink some questions quickly if you need to switch interviewees.

Beware of changed circumstances. Things are changing around you, especially in a developing situation. Don't get caught in the trap of preparing your report when all of a sudden the story changes.

 ## A Report from the Trenches

A reporter was supposed to report on the backup of trains during the morning rush hour. He went to the train station at 8 a.m. expecting to shoot mobs of people angrily waiting for their late train. When the reporter arrived, no one was on the platform. In his report he said, "So many people are angry that their trains are late." But the viewing audience could tell his reporting was false. No one was waiting on the platform and yet he stuck to the old script. He should have changed gears and found another story.

Don't Give Up

The desk sent one of my students to a newly opened restaurant. The assignment was to interview the famous owner, a big sports star. But the star didn't show up and the manager of the restaurant told the reporter, "Sorry." She didn't get mad but didn't give up either. She changed gears. She asked the manager if HE would show her around. When they were in the kitchen, she started asking questions. The workers there were all immigrants. Illegal immigrants it turned out. The restaurant manager wasn't happy but her boss was. She brought back a terrific story.

Substitutions

As a reporter, inevitably you are going to be sent on stories you either know nothing about or could care less about. But news is

Fig. 6-6 Substitution.

news and your job is to get just as involved in those stories as you would in your favorite topics.

So how do you do it? First, you do have to know something about the story you are about to report on. Ask the assignment desk or a researcher at the station to quickly get you as much copy on the story as possible. You can read it in the truck on the way.

But then, how do you deal with a report on a shooting when all you know about guns is that they shoot? I've found one way that works is to substitute. If you like shoes, and are scared of guns, think of the shoes. No one can see what is inside your head!

Try it. If it doesn't work for you, drop it. But it's a trick that some students say has been very helpful.

Crowd Control

In your work as a reporter, you will find that the television camera always draws a crowd. Sometimes it can be a noisy crowd. Often, simply asking for some quiet when you are on camera live is sufficient. If some people are shouting loudly you might say, "Everyone please move away. Allow me to finish this, then I'll talk to you."

Before you go on the air, if you have time, chat with the people who are there and ask questions. Often you can pick up a piece of useful information. In any case, you compliment the people by asking them questions. After, they will respect you and your wishes which means staying quiet for your shot.

For kids, I like suggesting you will tape them after you do your live shot, IF they are quiet. Then do it.

If there's a lot of waving or bunny ears behind the reporter, you can back yourself against a wall. This way no one can get behind you for the shot. Although this might not give you the best background, it will be safe and quiet in a difficult situation.

Most of the time, you will want a background that has something to do with the story. If it's a fire story, you will want the fire behind you. If the fire has already been put out, then you would want the charred remains behind you and would make reference to the fact that a fire had just taken place. For example, you might say: "A blaze 6 hours ago at this spot caused great hardships. . . ."

How Do You Handle Disagreements with Your Boss?

Carefully.

It's a very dangerous business. One reporter who has survived many battles with the boss put it this way: You disagree with the top person at great peril. But sometimes you must. Other times, you lose.

If you have a story and you think it ought to be on the air, you fight like crazy for it. You must learn to read your executive, however, and decide whether or not your arguments are going anywhere.

There are times that your boss decides something he heard would make a great story and you know it will be a complete waste of time. They come to you because it's a subject you know something about. What do you say? You've got to be careful. You have to pick your fights. You cannot fight for every story you think should be done or fight against every thin story the boss suggests. Test him with your arguments. If you see that he's convinced it's a story, you might try to offer a slightly different take on it that would be worth doing.

The most critical time has arrived: After you have shot the story, you've written the story, you've edited the story, now the trouble begins. It is then that a whole committee of executives takes a look at your report.

Many hands paw over your piece. Senior producers usually, but even the executive producer and the anchor will get involved in your piece. They want to make changes. They want you to make it shorter or they don't like a particular sound bite.

If they can't say anything else, you will hear: "It's kinda dull." Finally YOUR BOSS comes up with the most terrifying question of all: "Isn't there something better you've got?"

It is frustrating. But you have to fight for the integrity of your piece and for the reporting in it. All this happens with less than an hour to air. You are seconds away from making errors because of this nit-picking. You have to be knowledgeable enough about the story to stand up and say, "I'm not going to make that change." But you'd better be prepared to defend your argument. You try to go along with the senior producers and the executive producer, but there are times that you say, "Well I can't change that because I would not be representing the story truthfully." You always should stand up for accuracy, legality and principal.

Conclusion

There are many more reporters than anchors. This is true for every news show. So, if you are serious about getting into this business, you'd better hone your reporting skills. For your first job you may get reporting during the week and anchoring on weekends.

And one more note from Phil Jones: Local reporters are on the air live so much today that they've gotten very good at it.

Therefore, students: You must be good at live reporting — everyone else is.

Checklist

- ☐ Elements of a news report: The Open, The Package, The Close or Tag, The Sign Off and sometimes Anchor Q and A.
- ☐ On Cameras include Stand-Ups and Bridges.
- ☐ Graphics and file tape are useful.
- ☐ Learn microphone positioning.
- ☐ Intentions and substitutions.
- ☐ Wallpaper is dull.
- ☐ No "How do you feel?" questions.
- ☐ Use bullet points for live reporting.
- ☐ Stay calm in a crisis.
- ☐ Learn crowd control.
- ☐ Learn to deal with the boss.

Reporting Exercises

Some of these exercises can be reported as hard or light news, depending on your viewpoint. Write as a live report and tape report. Decide whom to interview.

Exercise 1:

- ❖ Fashion Week at Bryant Park.
- ❖ High winds.
- ❖ 4 × 8 plywood sheets fall through the roof of the tent onto the runway.
- ❖ All the celebrities are there (use whoever you prefer).
- ❖ Kate Moss is hurt.
- ❖ Chaos everywhere and people running all around.

Exercise 2:

- ❖ There is an antiwar rally going on in front of City Hall, when a bomb threat is phoned in.
- ❖ No one wants to leave (you're the first reporter on the scene).

Exercise 3:

- ❖ It's the Wednesday before Thanksgiving Day.
- ❖ At the Jefferson Market.
- ❖ People are lined up on the street to get fresh turkeys.
- ❖ There is a collision between two trucks. No one is hurt but traffic is tied in knots.
- ❖ Out of one truck, rolls and rolls of toilet paper spill out onto the streets.
- ❖ Out of the other truck, live turkeys come flying and running everywhere.
- ❖ Adults are running and trying to catch the escapees.
- ❖ Children are also laughing trying to catch the birds.

Exercise 4:

Here are two detailed stories. Do your stand-ups.

MIAMI, FL

In Miami, a man the FBI dubbed the "bumbling bank robber" was convicted after investigators matched his DNA to the gold teeth knocked out when a van hit the fleeing suspect, prosecutors said Wednesday. Charles Edward Jones was convicted of bank robbery Tuesday in U.S. District Court and faces up to life imprisonment, U.S. Attorney Marcos Jimenez said. On September 30, 2002, Jones walked into a Wachovia Bank in Miami, pulled a gun from his pocket and robbed a teller of about $16,000, according to trial evidence. As he ran out of the bank, he stuffed the gun into his waistband, accidentally firing it into his pants. The bullet missed him but when he stepped into the street he was hit by a van delivering school lunches in the area, investigators said. Jones managed to stumble to a waiting car, leaving two gold teeth, his gun and hat lying in the street, prosecutors said. The FBI later matched DNA from the teeth with Jones' DNA, proving he had been in the bank. Jones was arrested a few days after the robbery at a Miami hotel, where agents found a sock full of money from the robbery stuffed into his trousers. The serial numbers from the recovered money matched the bills taken from the bank, Jimenez said.

CONVINGTON, LA

Two dozen monkeys escaped from a research center and holed up in a forest, where animal-control workers used bananas and oranges to try to lure them out. The monkeys are classified as disease-free and pose no health risks to humans, but workers trying to capture the animals wore protective gowns and gloves as a standard precaution, said Fran Simon, a spokeswoman for the Tulane Regional Primate Center. By Wednesday, 8 of the 24 rhesus monkeys remained on the loose. "When they get hungry enough, they'll come back," Simon said. The Tulane Regional Primate Research Center, established in 1964, is the largest of the eight federally funded primate research centers, with 500 acres of land, eight buildings and about 5,000 monkeys. Its main study area is infectious diseases caused by viruses, bacteria and parasites. It was not clear how the monkeys escaped from a fenced area outside the research facility Tuesday, said James Hartman, a spokesman for the St. Tammany Parish sheriff. In the past, animal-rights activists have freed or attempted to free monkeys, but there were no signs that vandalism played any role in Tuesday's escape, Hartman said.

Beat Reporting

These chapters are about specific reporting areas, niche reporting or what are known as beats. We'll look at six different areas.

1. SPORTS
2. WEATHER
3. MEDICAL
4. LEGAL
5. ENTERTAINMENT
6. BUSINESS

You may be interested in one or two of these. But they are worth reading for any reporter because you never know: Most beat reporters started as general assignment reporters. You too might make that move one day. So read on.

7

Sports Reporting

Here's a question for you. Which is more important to become a top sports reporter: Knowing sports or knowing how to present sports on television?

The answer is: Knowing your craft is as important as knowing your specialty. Legendary NBC sports reporter Len Berman agrees with your teacher. You are not going to argue with him, are you?

"Both are important," says Len. "You can't have one without the other. And you can't have all of one without the other. For example: You can't be a sports expert knowing every bit of trivia and expect that alone to carry you on the air. It doesn't work without the proper television reporting skills."

You've just heard it from the best. Len believes you need a wide variety of skills to become a sportscaster. First and foremost, he says, is journalism.

"A sportscaster must be able to tell a fair story from all points of view. Writing skills are a must. So is computer usage. Those are the basics. After that, a working knowledge of TV production is most important. Use of video AND audio, which oftentimes gets overlooked in television. And then there are the on-air functions. A sense of ease about being on camera and an ability to deliver a story professionally. Being able to ad lib doesn't hurt either, not to mention mastering the teleprompter in a manner where viewers aren't aware that prompter is being used."

Fig. 7-1 Len Berman. COURTESY OF NBC

Of all the beats, sports reporting seems to allow, even encourage, a signature style. This has been true in sports dating back to radio days when the play-by-play baseball announcers had their "Going, going, gone" calls. ESPN anchors and reporters have taken the styling to all new levels. So do you have to have a signature?

Len Berman used to think so.

Report from the Trenches

Len knew a sportscaster in Dayton who would salute during his sign-off every night.

It sounds corny, but it was effective and viewers said they missed it when he stopped doing it.

W Miller

Fig. 7-2 Should you have a signature style?

Now Len thinks the signature business has gone too far. His feeling is there are so many sportscasters trying to make names for themselves that they're constantly trying to "re-invent the wheel" by coming up with new clever sayings.

"As a viewer," says Len, "just give me the scores, a couple of good sound bites, maybe something offbeat and get the hell off the air then."

But there is a unique style you are going to have simply because you are the only you. You will develop your style naturally. There is a story about the Albert family of sportscasters. They were brothers growing up on Long Island and the oldest one, Marv, used to practice from the time he was little by sitting in front of a televised sports event in his cellar, like a basketball game, and turn the audio down. He'd sit there and call the game as he watched. Great practice. Marv and his brothers went on to become great sportscasters with their own styles. Marv's basketball calls from the Knicks games were almost as important to the viewing as were the games.

"Gud," he'd say simply with a short and snapped "good" call when a basket was scored. Or "Two." As in two points. Simple and effective. His style. Nothing put on about it.

Before leaving the subject, one more note about personal style from Len. Be careful about going too far with your clothes too. "There was a time when sportscasters wore loud jackets," says Len. "Lindsey Nelson comes to mind. My philosophy is the viewer should be watching you, not your clothing." Great advice.

Len points out one mistake that many beginning sports reporters make: The assumption that everyone understands what you're talking about.

"A common mistake is for young sportscasters to use 'sports-speak,'" says Len, "instead of plain English. The great Marty Glickman once said a football player doesn't walk around the locker room saying 'look at me I'm toting my pigskin.' He isn't 'toting his pigskin' he's 'carrying the ball.'"

You're Still a Reporter

Len's point is that "reporter" is part of the job of "sports reporter." You cannot assume that the audience knows what you are talking about, knows the lingo. Like the "toting the pigskin" example, your job is to translate "jockese" into English just as a police beat reporter has to translate "contusions and abrasions" into "cuts and bruises."

There is another assumption trap you have to guard against says Len. "You can't assume people are sports knowledgeable. In fact, surveys show that the majority of people watching a television newscast are not sports fans."

Len gives this example. "Perhaps everyone knows that Joe Torre is the Yankee Manager," he says, "but if you say the name Tom Coughlin you'd be surprised how many people wouldn't know his job was the coach of the New York Giants football team."

Just as you have to watch out for someone feeding you false information in other news areas, you have to be on guard in sports too. For Len, it is easy to deal with the spinners. Simply have a healthy skepticism of everything anyone says. "Have your antennae up at all times," he says. "Always ask yourself 'where is he coming from?' After a while it becomes second nature."

But the fact is, that it's not just the public relations folks who are dodging questions or putting the best face on a situation. These days, athletes get media training. "Athletes nowadays are more guarded," says Len. "They are media savvy and know exactly where their quotes will wind up. I find the bigger the star (Tiger Woods, Michael Jordan, Derek Jeter) the more guarded they are." That does not mean you go into an interview assuming the athlete is going to cross swords with you. In fact, as always, try not to make assumptions. Len tells this story about that.

 ## Report from the Trenches

"I was at Yankee Old-timers Day one year and I timidly approached Roger Maris, the late Yankee home-run king, the man who broke Babe Ruth's single season home-run record. I had always read and heard that Roger was not a very friendly guy. He supposedly was downright surly during his chase of The Babe.

"Maris couldn't have been nicer to me. That day, or any of the other times I dealt with him. Moral of the story, don't always believe what you see or hear in the media. Enter with an open mind, and draw your own conclusions."

Breaking In

So you really want to be a sports reporter and you are thinking, "I don't stand a chance because it's so hard to break in." Len says you now stand a far better chance than he did. He thinks it's far easier today.

"When I graduated from Syracuse there was little cable or alternative media," he points out. "Nowadays there are a zillion choices. That doesn't count 'pod-casting' coming to a cell phone near you."

Weather Reporting

8

Marysol Castro is blunt about it: "I'm not a meteorologist," she says, "I don't claim to be a meteorologist — I have no desire to become a meteorologist."

But Marysol is the nation's weather reporter appearing on ABC Network's morning broadcast *Good Morning America*. When she was hired, she had never done weather before. What she knew was television. She'd studied it, worked at small stations and knew it inside and out. And she knows what people want. "Very few people at home know the difference between a low-pressure system and a high-pressure system," she says. "They want to know: Is it going to be cold? Do I have to put on a down jacket? Is it going to be hot? Do I get to wear this new dress I just bought?"

She says you need to be able to speak to viewers in a way that makes them feel comfortable. In other words, you need to be a good reporter telling a story. It just happens to be the story of today's weather forecast. What she does have is a well-trained scientist backing her up. "I have a meteorologist and he's the biggest science geek and I laugh at him all the time. I correct his spelling and he corrects my weather. 'No,' he says, 'not every low-pressure system is bad.' So I say, 'Is it going to rain or is it not going to rain?' "

But had Marysol decided she wanted to be the type of expert weather reporter you see on The Weather Channel, she says she

Fig. 8-1 Marysol Castro. COURTESY OF NBC

would have to know more of the science. "I'd probably go to meteorology school. I'd have to learn more about the science. You need to know physics."

Watch the Overhype

More than any other story, the weather tends to get hyped and overhyped. Too many reporters scream of the coming disaster and the viewer is left to think, "Ommygosh, this is the apocalypse."

Usually, it isn't.

Fig. 8-2 Marysol live on camera. COURTESY OF ABC

Report from the Trenches

A local weatherman on the East Coast came running into the news-room one evening as the producers were preparing the 11 P.M. broadcast. He was all lathered about a storm system sweeping up the coast. "This could be a doozy," he said. "Might be 20 inches of snow, maybe more, before morning if it hits right."

That got the producers' attention. They asked him to check back in an hour and they tentatively put the story in the lead of the broadcast. The next weather bulletin from the weather office was of even more snow.

The broadcast led with the weather story, the anchor tossing it to the weatherman at his map. He excitedly explained the track of the storm and concluded that the viewers were in for at least an inch or two of snow by morning. "An inch or two?" boomed the producer in the control room. The weatherman was brought in.

"You were saying 20 inches or more earlier?"

The weatherman said that was right, but he was just being cautious.

The snow story led the second section (after the first commercial break). This time the anchor led by saying that the weatherman had checked his maps and had more information.

It got to 8 to 12 inches in this forecast. The producer buried his head.

When the weather segment rolled around (in the last section of the show) the weatherman finally forecast that the storm could dump 20 inches of snow.

After the broadcast, the producer took the weatherman aside and told him that the forecast just presented to the viewers was snow is coming, somewhere between 1 and 20 inches.

It was a story that got hyped because the weatherman was so excited by the mere possibility of a big snow. In fact, the caution he showed in the first block was the right instinct. The storm barely hit that night. Less than an inch of snow fell. Incredibly, that forecast of 1 to 20 inches of snow was wrong.

Marysol sees her job as one of providing a calming voice in a storm. She says it is important to provide accurate information and at the same time to ease people's fears — not to hype them. Does this sound familiar? This is a fine definition of a reporter's job no matter what the story.

But weather stories, she says, are hyped too often. Too often they are presented as "The End of the World!!!"

"I can't tell you, being the smallest weather person in network news, I've had producers tell me: 'Get Castro out there, the wind will blow her around and it'll look great, it'll be a great picture.'

I have to say, I've done that. I've also known when enough is enough."

This is a constant struggle with the producers for her. "I get the assignment from my executive producer and when I get to the

W Miller

Fig. 8-3 Get Castro out there! It will look great.

location (more often than not the Gulf Coast or the state of Florida for hurricanes) I call him and say, this is what the story is. We might fight. He might say, I want you to find this person and I'll say, well, that's not the story," she says. "At times, your bosses have this idea of what they want. Then you get out in the field and it's a completely different story. And sometimes even a better story." (At one broadcast, even the senior producers were aware of it enough to have a name for it: The PCN — the preconceived notions.)

In fact, what Marysol experiences is pretty much the relationship most reporters in the field have with the show producers. Now comes the challenge to deal with that relationship. You will have to please the boss but also be an honest reporter. "But more often than not we come to a common ground. After they will say, 'You know, you were right.'"

After you prove that you are good at getting the right story in the field and doing it well, the battles will be fewer and even those won't go on for long. You will be able to say to the boss back at the station or headquarters, "Come on guys, don't I always come through?" They will have to acknowledge that you do.

Trust Yourself

You have to believe in what you are doing. Marysol says her sister, an actress, used to say, "If I don't believe in my character, no one else will." Marysol believes that is also true for reporters and their reports. If you don't believe in it, neither will the viewers.

"If I don't believe in what I am saying, the viewers can read right through me. They know. They can tell right away."

Be Fast on Your Feet

On her broadcast, *Good Morning America*, Marysol gets only about 45 seconds to deliver the nation's weather. "That is only a little bit of time to talk about a big country."

You may not get much time either. So you have to figure out — in advance — the most important weather story to tell. There has to be a headline that you give. Marysol gave me an example:

"It's June and it's cold so my headline says, 'It's summer but it sure does feel like late fall.' Something to get the viewer's attention."

Details

Following the headline, she then gives some details. And, she practices a lot. She doesn't use a prompter, relying instead on note cards and bullet points; though she does know weather people who

Fig. 8-4 Grab the viewer's attention.

do use a prompter. As soon as she sees the map come up full on the screen (so she is no longer in the shot) she looks down, checks her cards and follows down the bullet points as she checks the map.

One of her colleagues, Linda Church, has a camera in front of her and two cameras positioned — one to her left and one to her right. She stands in front of the green screen. That is where the weather map that you see at home is electronically projected. If you were in the studio, you wouldn't see it. It's just a green screen. The camera sees in green so the weather person cannot wear the color green. If she did wear a green dress, all you would see of her would be her arms, hands and face — the places where she wasn't wearing green. So those weather people have to look at a monitor stationed just off stage to see where the map that you at home can see.

Also, some weather people have a little clicker in their hands to change the maps. That's another place where technological trouble can brew. "Sometimes that clicker thing gets frozen," says Marysol, "and you're talking about the 5-day weather forecast and it's stuck on humidity. You have to be able to multitask when you are standing in front of a map generated on a green screen."

Luckily, Marysol doesn't have to. Otherwise, she says, she would lose her mind. Hers is a traditional monitor. So she appears on camera then the screen goes to a full screen picture of a map. Then she voices over the map.

She has a stage manager counting her down, telling her when she has 30 seconds, 15 seconds, 5 seconds. She has some thoughts about the stage manager. "I love my stage manager. If anyone gets into the television business, is on air, the people you want to make friends with is your cameraperson, because he can make or break you — can make you look wonderful or make you look horrible. And your stage managers are your eyes and ears to the control room. My stage managers will tell me when I screw up, 'Gosh, you missed the mark on that.'"

She appreciates hearing it from them because it is information given to help.

Airtime

Here is another example of the value of airtime. It is likely that you can think of some things you simply will not do on the air. But if it is a legit assignment, do it. Which leads me to this:

NANCY'S RULES

Don't turn up your nose at any legitimate broadcast assignment that gets you on air.

 Report from the Trenches

Marysol had just spent $80,000 on a Masters Degree from Columbia University School of Journalism. One of the first jobs at her first station was traffic.

She was the one in the helicopter telling viewers where the jams were and how to get around them. She wasn't all that happy about

Fig. 8-5 J-school to Chopper.

the assignment. "I thought, 'I just spent $80,000 to go to Columbia and I'm doing traffic? You've got to be kidding me.'"

But she learned there's something to be said for airtime. It's airtime that gets you noticed. That's what got the folks at ABC interested in her. "In the span of a three-hour show, I had 21 live hits."

Signature

Len Berman says he thinks the over-heated signatures in sports these days gets in the way of the reporting.

In weather, especially on the network level, a signature is required. The weather person throws to the local stations for a cut-in. That phrase must be the same every time so the local stations know when to jump in.

On the *Today Show* on NBC, Al Roker always says the same words: "That's what's happening around here, now let's see what's happening in your neck of the woods."

So, the folks at ABC told Marysol she needed a signature throw like Roker's. She didn't want to be like everyone else. But she did need a standard signature at that time so the local weather people knew when to start talking.

After hours of trying different catch phrases, she came up with, "Let's see what's happening outside your window."

It's not so much that it is overpowering. Having a phrase like that, even if you are on the local station and aren't throwing to a cut-away, helps identify you. You could use it as you introduce the five-day forecast or the graphic showing the current weather conditions. Such a catch phrase says something about you. I like it.

Geography

A mistake that comes up often in weather is mispronouncing the names of towns or cities. Geography is something Marysol did learn. Weather reporting is more than what's going to happen but it's also where. When she started, she was given a blank map of the

United States and her husband would quiz her and make her fill in all the states. You need to study the map.

This is something you might try if you are interested in weather as a career or even as an entry-level on-camera job. Don't forget, Diane Sawyer started as the weather girl on her local television station in Kentucky.

"The four corners I would mix up," says Marysol of her geography lessons.

You must get the pronunciations right. Marysol grew up in the Bronx. She has heard people drop the "the" and say: "In Bronx New York . . ." She lost all trust in that reporter. It's "The Bronx."

It's the same thing for people in all other parts of the country. Marysol remembers once when she said, "Yakima, Washington (pronouncing it Yah-KEE-ma — instead of YAH-ka-ma). I got the angriest e-mails. People are very proud of where they are from and when they see their town on a weather map, they want to know that name is going to be pronounced correctly."

A terrific point. Always get the pronunciation of the names of the towns right. That is true for all reporters and anchors and everyone on camera. If you aren't sure of how to say a name or a place, ask before you get on the air.

Weather-Speak

One more trap to avoid is what Marysol calls, "weather-speak." Just as police beat reporters should stay away from Cop-speak and medical reporters should stay away from Doc-speak, you are the translator. Stay away from the intricate science of the weather and stick to what it means to the viewer.

Getting It Wrong Is Not a Mistake

This is the only time I will say this. Weather forecasting is different from all other parts of the news. News is what happened. It already happened. Weather forecasting is doing your best to say what will happen. It hasn't happened yet. Marysol has a pretty sunny attitude about it.

"When I predict that it's going to pour and it turns out sunny and 70, I just grin and bear it and say, 'Just goes to show you there are forces beyond weather people.'"

"My husband puts it best, 'Marysol, you have a job where you can be wrong 50% of the time, and the next day you can still go back to work.' I don't think I'm wrong 50% of the time ... but certainly there have been times that I've been wrong."

Don't Hide Your Inner Ethnic

This isn't the last time you will hear this from me. The face of America has changed and so have the faces on camera. Almost any ethnicity is a plus for you. But one of the largest growing segments of the American public is the Latino audience.

Being Hispanic helped Marysol get to *Good Morning America*. She had an interview with anchor Diane Sawyer. She was nervous, she says, but "Diane was very lovely."

They were having a conversation when Marysol said, "You know, it wouldn't hurt you guys to cover more stories that affect the Latino community." Diane looked at her and said, "You are absolutely right."

She got the job on GMA, in some part, she believes, because she is Hispanic.

"Now is the time to be Hispanic or Latino," she says. "I went to cover the Indy 500 (automobile race) in Indianapolis, Indiana, in the middle of nowhere. I went for breakfast and heard as many people speaking Spanish as I heard speaking English."

Her heritage even helped her land her first job.

 **Report from the Trenches**

Marysol went to graduate school in journalism at Columbia University in New York. It was, she says, the hardest year of her life. "Sleepless nights," she says, but she learned everything about television and about newspapers and the news-media as well. She learned how to shoot a camera, how to edit a package; she learned how to produce, how to report.

"When I graduated, I wanted to be a producer. I had no desire to be on air. I graduated on a Tuesday and that Sunday was the Puerto Rican Day Parade in New York City. I was standing there with a couple of friends and I saw a local news truck pull up."

The reporter for a local station was a one-man band. That is, the reporter was also doing her own camera work and producing. Marysol murmured something about a "one-man band." The reporter heard it and turned to Marysol and said, "What did you say?"

"I just said it's too bad about being a one-man band."

"What do you know about it?" she asked.

Marysol knew a lot about it. They got to talking and the reporter asked if Marysol had a demo tape.

"Sure," she said. (By the way, that is always your answer to this question.)

She gave Marysol her card. Of course, Marysol had no demo tape. She had graduated four days before and was still drinking beer and champagne in celebration. She ran right back to Columbia, slapped together a demo tape from material she had. The next day she showed up at the station with her new tape.

They hired her.

It wasn't just her demo reel. She was fluent in Spanish. That helped. The boss told her the station was losing stories because not enough reporters knew Spanish.

This story actually gets better. Remember, Marysol had wanted to be a television producer.

She was sent out on a story the next day. She shot it, brought it back, wrote a script and handed it in. The news director asked, "Where's the stand-up?"

Marysol thought she would shoot the story, write it and hand it to a reporter. She was sent out to shoot a stand-up — herself — on camera. On that evening's 6 o'clock broadcast, Marysol

Castro was on TV, less than a week after graduating as a broadcast producer.

That should encourage every one of you. All it takes to get a job is a good education, being smart and being in the right place at the right time.

It does happen.

9 Medical Reporting

Marysol is comfortable having a meteorologist behind her who knows the science of weather. For her beat, knowing television is more important than knowing the science behind weather. Weather is perhaps the most technology-driven reporting — with graphics for maps, five-day forecasts as well as abundant use of video clips. Knowing television is crucial for the weather reporter.

But when it comes to the health and science reporter, it's just the opposite.

Do I Need To Be a Doctor?

One of the best on the medical and science beat is Max Gomez, health and medical editor at WNBC-TV in New York. To become a medical reporter, he believes you need some sort of scientific background.

"I don't know that you have to be an MD, or in my case a PhD, but I think you have to have scientific knowledge to understand the jargon, to be able to interpret data (and to understand those scientific journals). You just have to be conversant in the field."

So which is more important for a correspondent on the medical or science beat: knowledge of science or knowledge of television?

"In order to be effective, you have to know both," says Max. "I knew medicine and I learned television. I learned on the job."

Fig. 9-1 Max Gomez. COURTESY OF NBC.

Report from the Trenches

Max says his knowledge of science was what he was selling when he was looking for a job — that it makes more sense to take a scientist and teach him television than to do it the other way around. The fellow who hired him agreed. Max went to Channel 5 in New York where the medical reporter job was only part time. He was also full-time editor-in-chief of *Popular Science Magazine* and didn't want a full-time job because he was much too busy.

The station tried a general assignment reporter on the medical beat. That reporter knew television reporting well but did not know the science. After a while the station realized it needed someone who knew enough science to be able to get it right. The station figured the producers and editors could teach the television, so

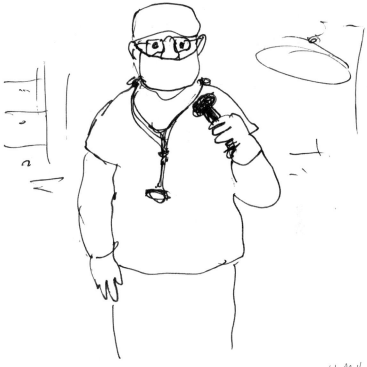

W Miller

Fig. 9-2 Medical reporter.

getting someone who knew the science was more important. The young eager scientist Max was the answer to the station's desire to expand the medical beat. "To their everlasting credit," says Max, "and to my everlasting gratitude, they taught me television."

You Need To Know Both TV and Science

The answer to the question then is: Eventually, you need both the knowledge of science and the knowledge of television reporting. If you don't know the television side of it, you are not going to be able to communicate the information clearly to the general public.

You also need to be able to translate complicated, arcane sorts of topics into plain language, so that viewers who are not scientifically sophisticated can understand it. The trick here is to translate it in a manner that simplifies but also accurately reflects the data. You must understand the medical or scientific information completely so you don't end up misleading the viewers because you didn't quite comprehend it yourself.

Another mistake is to use medicalese, in place of plain English. Your job is to take the information that is probably heavily scientific, filled with medical jargon, then translate it so the rest of the audience can understand it.

TMI

Beware of Too Much Information. It is the trap of trying to cram too much into one segment. "You want to cram information in there," says Max, "but if you put too much in there, people won't be able to follow it." He recalls one of his first efforts on television. It was his first lesson in cramming too much into one report.

 Report from the Trenches

"When I first got started, I was doing this piece on breast cancer — this was 25 years ago — in those days stories were longer ... two to two and a half minutes long. My tendency as an academic, coming from academia, was to cram every last bit of information into these two or two and a half minutes.

"A college class mate of mine was watching and he called me afterwards and said, 'You know, that was really interesting but I kind of had trouble following all the stuff in the story.'

"The light went off in my head. Here was somebody who was Ivy League educated, we were classmates at Princeton, so he's a very smart guy."

Max says because they were friends he was motivated to pay attention. That is not the way most people watch television. Most people watching television are cooking, or they are reading, or doing something else and they are usually not truly focused. But his old college pal was focused on the story. As focused as he was and as smart as he was, even he couldn't follow all of it. He called Max.

"The light that went off in my head was: You have to make it understandable and approachable in a way that everybody gets it — otherwise it doesn't make any difference how much important information you've got. Because if they don't absorb it in that first pass — which is the only time they have in television — it's not like newspapers where if you don't get it the first time you can go back and reread it until you do get it — you get one shot at it and if you miss that one shot, it's over."

Don't Worry

Max points out that if you are coming from a scientific background, you know so much about the topic you may swamp your audience with the complexities of the subject. Worse, you may get this terrible fear: I don't know if I will be able to distill all this down. As a result, you put too much in the report and people don't get it.

A word here about time, as in how long the reports run and how often. Max has a report on every weekday, always at 5:55. His garden-variety story runs about 1:45 ... with about 15 seconds of a live introduction and 15 seconds of a close. That means he has about two minutes to boil down complicated medical information and make it accurate and interesting to the viewer. That's the trick. A friend of his who is an arthritis researcher calls a two-minute report a medical haiku: the whole thing distilled down to a few lines.

Scientists who are new to the reporting side must watch out for writing in an overly formal manner to cover their insecurities. While technically correct, it can be a little off-putting.

"You don't need to sound like you are lecturing to medical students," says Max. "You don't even need to sound like the doctor we all know who talks to you in these very formal tones." The point is that you end up putting a distance between yourself and the person you are trying to reach — the viewer.

The beat journalist's job is to communicate, to establish a rapport and break down this distance between the authority figures and the viewers. Instead of holding the viewer at arm's length with formal syntax and language, you want to let them in. You want it understandable enough for your grandfather to get it. Most medical data is subtle and you need to understand it completely. It might be the difference of only a couple of words in a sentence. But if you misunderstood it, your report might not be accurate. Many of your viewers expect you to be as correct as their doctors. It's a huge responsibility. You just can't get it wrong on the air.

Says Max, "I'm glad that not everybody can pick it up otherwise I'd be out of a job."

NANCY's RULES

(From Max):

You've got to keep it clean and simple enough so people can absorb these chunks of information. If it's too information-dense, they won't be able to digest it. Make the report approachable — a cocktail party explanation in length and familiarity.

Legalities and Permissions

These rules and laws are ever-evolving but generally, if you are in a public place people have no reasonable expectation for privacy. Therefore, you can shoot television pictures.

Keep in mind that hospitals are private property. You cannot just walk in with a camera. You have to have permission and this you can usually get from the public affairs office.

Permission has gotten a little more difficult to gain in the medical world with the passage of federal privacy statutes. You have to be more careful about approaching patients. This is especially true from the hospital's point of view. It used to be that a hospital would identify a patient and his or her condition. Now they are more reluctant to release that information to a reporter.

Once you have permission to go into the hospital with your crew, you have only won half the battle. One of the toughest challenges is persuading a patient to talk to you, to reveal some of the most personal aspects of his or her life.

Max says this: "You have to be sensitive to people. They are revealing information that they would only talk about to their doctor or family or priest." These are people talking about personal medical situations. You may be asking a patient about a prostate problem, cancer or a cosmetic issue, or even the less serious but more private issues like hemorrhoids or PMS.

These are medical topics that were not discussed in polite company at all. To our detriment, says the scientist and the journalist in Max. No one talked about breast cancer. No one talked about colon cancer on television. They were considered too private; and information that could help people did not get reported.

"It was really around the time President Ronald Reagan developed colon cancer that colonoscopy stool samples, blood in the stool were discussed on television. Before that, there was very little awareness of these diseases and people died because of it."

Not everyone can give you permission — a child for example. Or if you are covering a story on a mental illness, there is an issue about whether that patient can give consent. There are people who legally can't give consent.

 ## Report from the Trenches

Max went to do a story on minimally invasive surgery on a hernia. He asked, "Can I interview the patient?" The hospital official said sure, and pointed Max toward the waiting room.

"I went over to the waiting room and there was this fellow handcuffed and chained to the gurney with three big burley armed guards standing around him." Max was told the guy getting the surgery was an inmate from a nearby county jail. "I asked, 'Do we have permission?' The hospital person said, 'Oh yea, he said it's ok.'"

But getting the prisoner's permission was not enough, as he soon learned. Max approached the prisoner and the guard said to him, "What are you doing?" Max was told he needed to get permission from the Department of Prisons and the warden and it had to be in triplicate and so on and so on. In practice, says Max, interviewing prisoners in hospitals never happens because it's too much trouble.

Getting Started

One of the beat reporting areas that seems to be expanding is health and science. Part of that is the result of the aging baby boomer generation. Nowadays, they want to know everything about health — THEIR health. And news directors want to give that large segment of their audience what they want.

In addition, young people today are far more aware and interested in health issues. Part of that may be the amount of information made available to the general public. Medical stories used to be reported in medical journals written for and read by physicians and scientists only. Now, newspapers have whole sections devoted to health and medical issues.

Now that everyone is interested in hearing about health issues, medical reporters are more in demand. The conventional wisdom has always been, you start out in a tiny market and work your way up. That's a little harder for medical reporting because small markets generally cannot support a specialist, whether it's a legal correspondent or a medical unit.

It's a tough road, says Max, because you have probably spent a lot of time and money to get your medical or scientific training. And now you are starting at the beginning of television, which means a big cut in salary.

Internships, suggests Max, are a good way to at least get a feel for the business and to get to know some of the people in the business.

A former intern of his is now a pediatrician who occasionally does a report for the station. She does it for free when she has the time. But it could lead to a full-time offer of a medical reporter's job at some point. And she's being taught on camera on the job. So for her, the tuition is free.

Max doesn't believe too many general assignment reporters are well enough schooled to be top medical reporters, but a good number have done it with the help of a well-schooled producer.

Max says this is an exciting time to be a health and science beat reporter. "When I first started out, it was sort of interesting. But the advances were incremental as opposed to revolutionary kinds of things. In the past five years or so the pace of discovery and development in science and medicine is just exploding."

Cancer researchers he has spoken with say that breakthroughs are coming quickly that will provide survival and perhaps even cures. He says science has just scratched the surface of human genome and genetics research.

"There are really fundamental shifts in the way we are looking at disease and the way we are approaching disease and pharmaceutical design — therapies for everything from cancer to heart disease to Parkinson's and Alzheimer's.

Where the Stories Are

Since Max has to have a report on every day, he needs to find lots of them. He says he finds them in all sorts of places. Here's his tip for you if you are looking for health or science stories.

Many story ideas come from the journals. Either he or his producer keeps in direct contact with the journals or with an outfit called Eureka Alert that monitors journals. Also, when he goes out to report a story, he'll return with two or three other ideas because he sat and talked to others at the hospital. The curious mind gets the story. Max will bump into a doctor or researcher and ask, "What's going on?" He says he gets a lot of ideas that way.

Also, he is generous with his time and makes appearances at many medical charity affairs. He gives and he gets in return.

He keeps his ears open at the charitable functions that tend to be run by disease-specific organizations: Heart Association, Alzheimer's, MS Society, Lung Association, Cancer Society. He says he often comes away with thoughts and ideas there. Sometimes viewers will call with a problem that turns into a story.

Sum Up

You have to get into health and science beat reporting for the right reasons, says Max. But he could be speaking to all my students when he says this. "I've seen people get into it for the wrong reasons, they get into it for fame and fortune. They want to be a star. Those people tend to flame out pretty quickly because there are not so many who do achieve fame and fortune . . . far far fewer than people imagine. It's not a particularly well-paid field outside of the top five or maybe ten markets . . . despite what people may believe. And the sacrifices in terms of stress and in time, time away from home, and time away from family to do it right — that's not insignificant. You have to do it because you really love it — you really enjoy it."

And for all reporters, Max has this final bit of advice: If you are in college, do not spend all your time studying television and radio. It's his opinion that that turns college into a glorified trade school. What makes an individual reporter valuable, whether you are on a beat or general assignment or anchor, is the breadth of your knowledge.

I feel as strongly as Max does that a solid liberal arts background is essential for a reporter — a medical reporter or anyone else.

Max suggests this: To learn television and radio, take a couple of television courses or learn it on the job if you can.

10

Legal Reporting

The legal beat is like the medical beat in one way, and this is not a malpractice lawsuit joke. Like the health-and-science beat, you do need some special knowledge or training in the law to get to the top. In the case of legal reporting, there seems to me to be no shortage of qualified candidates. I don't know what it is about the law business, but I get more students from that profession wanting to switch careers and go into television than from any business. And usually, they make terrific students in my class.

One well-known legal reporter and anchor never thought about switching careers. The television business came calling on her. But I'll let her tell you the story. This is probably not how it will happen to you, but it did to Catherine Crier.

 Report from the Trenches

"I've got a Schwab drugstore story," she says, recalling the Hollywood spot where starlets were discovered. "I'd just been reelected to my second term on the bench (she was the youngest judge ever elected in Texas) in 1988. I went to a Christmas party and I met a fellow who had been a former recruiter at CBS News — that was not the topic of our conversation, we were talking politics,

Fig. 10-1 Catherine Crier. COURTESY OF COURT TV

and he called me a couple of weeks later and asked me if I would ever be interested in doing a political show on television. I said, sure, sounds like fun.

"He brought over a camera on Valentine's Day in 1989 — two friends of mine who had written books came over to my house. We sat in the living room. I did an interview tape. A month later, I was doing a pilot for three different news organizations and six months later I was offered the Evening News with Bernie Shaw at CNN."

Catherine Crier went on to ABC and Fox as a news anchor and reported on almost everything but the legal beat. She finally got back to her legal roots as Executive Editor of Legal Specials and Anchor of Catherine Crier Live at Court TV.

She believes that training in law is essential for anyone tackling the legal beat. The reason: The law today is so intricate.

"It's dealt with too superficially as it is ... particularly on television ... and without legal training it would be even more so."

Fig. 10-2 You have to know the law.

But she credits her training for giving her some of the skills needed to be on air. "It was my many years as a trial lawyer, a criminal prosecutor and as a civil litigator that gave me the experience talking in front of audiences — albeit a judge or a jury instead of a television camera. And then as a judge you have not only to listen to the evidence and determine what the facts are and apply the law but you have to render social and public policy, which is very much what a journalist does. So all of that, in addition to the inherent training and analysis and sort of intellectual background that comes with a law degree, prepared me for many aspects of television."

Catherine says she knows now how that training prepared her. But in the beginning, she struggled when she took everybody's suggestions. She pleads guilty to trying too hard and not relaxing.

Report from the Trenches

She had done a pilot for CNN that got her that first job in television, the one as anchor at CNN. Before putting her on air, she was sent to a television coach (Not me!). She spent about two or three weeks being told things like, "This is a camera, this is what you do, sit up straight, pretend you have a rod down your back, talk like an anchor." Then she was sent along to anchor the news.

Six months into the job, the head of the network called her into his office. He said, "Could you emulate someone?" He played a tape for her. She was watching herself. It was that original pilot she had submitted to get the job. A time when, she says, "I had absolutely no training, no coaching whatsoever."

The boss said, "Would you be that person, please?"

"It was harder to let go of the rigidity that they had instilled in me than it was to fumble my way as a complete amateur. It took years. Now I'm laid back as all get out, for better or worse. If someone doesn't like it, they don't like it. I giggle, I make faces, I do my own thing, just going back to being myself."

Or as I tell my students, the best person to be on camera is YOU. That way, you don't have to try to pretend to be someone you are not. Catherine says she believes the audience reads that superficiality.

It may not be easy at first to relax and let yourself shine through. You may think you should project this image of an anchorperson and what they ought to be and sound like. But you shouldn't. Be yourself.

Skills for a Legal Reporter

A legal reporter should have the same journalistic skills as all reporters. Again, just as the reporter on the medical beat, you have to translate complex issues and language into plain English. None of that "party of the first part" legal mumbo-jumbo should ever make it on camera.

But more than that, Catherine says she would like to see more in-depth reporting on the legal beat. "I think a good legal reporter goes behind the obvious story and gives you the essence of the law and what's going on behind the scenes." Also, she says, "look a bit skeptically at the information that's being put out in the public. Say, wait a minute, who really stands to benefit here and what are the real issues at heart, as opposed to the horse race approach that we take to telling most stories, including legal issues. So instead of getting the inside story of what the law means to the public, for example, it's which side won in the vote? Or who seems to be ahead pressing some issue?

"So the in-depth reporting that I would want and would hope to see is oftentimes ignored in the rush or the pressure to tell stories as the horse race or left/right, good/bad, up/down issues."

Here is something else Catherine says you should watch out for: Trying too hard. She says she sees some reporters trying too hard to show how smart they are. They want to talk too much. They want to interrupt. They don't listen. Television, she believes, has gotten to the point where people don't listen to each other. She says she sees even professional interviewers committing this sin. "They ask a question then in the middle of the answer, they interrupt, look down at a page and ask the next set question. They don't have a conversation. I always find that real disconcerting," she says.

I find it disconcerting too. If you see an interview done this way on television, do not imitate it.

Catherine says she starts with prepared questions but usually doesn't need them. She just begins and they talk. Her very solid advice for you is this: "Go on to a conversation, know your material so that you can go anywhere with it."

One of the things Catherine has noticed these days is how hardened her guests are on the issues. Civil discourse seems to be a thing of the past. Now many of her interviews come in with their spin and try to stick to it.

W Miller

Fig. 10-3 Get them off-message.

"Politicians," she says, "have always been 'on-message.' Getting them off is almost impossible. Much more so now. Things are so hostile and so divided — culturally, socially, politically — that people come on, they've got a song and they are going to sing it."

She has some tricks to getting them off-message. When she gets the politician or spokesperson for a single-issue group who is relentless about staying on-message, she looks for the tiny concession. She might ask, "Can you at least concede for me X?" She takes a point that nobody could argue about. If her guest won't even concede that, the person comes out sounding completely irrational. If she gets that concession, she gets them off-message and then she says she will be able to go into a reasonable interview.

One other trick Catherine uses comes from hard work. She reads everything she can get her hands on about her upcoming guest. That homework pays big dividends.

 ## Report from the Trenches

"At Fox News, the back half of my show," she recalls, "I would usually do celebrities. I loved to research as much as possible to find some phrase, some quirky thing in their background that fell off the traditional format. Not one of the same eight questions they get from everybody. I remember Peter O'Toole. He had a quick interview with Hollywood people before I got on set with him for my program. I could see he was teed off. He was smoking like a fiend; he was mad at this guy who had done this interview. I knew his assistant, so first thing I asked, how is so-and-so. He kind of brightened up a bit and then I asked, 'Tell me about the knuckles on your right hand?'

"He just went white. 'You can see them?' He grabbed his hand. The story was they came from the time when the nuns were hitting him with a ruler in school. Then getting into boxing and all. But it was a little tiny thing that proves you have to read 20 interviews to find the little nuggets. I'd read a little squib about it."

Most people will ask the obvious questions. Catherine will dig to find the ones that are revealing. As a result, her guests chat about themselves in ways that few have heard before.

Advice for Students

Catherine says that for legal anchors especially, but for reporters too, you have to know how to read the teleprompter. And you have to read the teleprompter like you are NOT reading it. It's got to be conversational. It's got to sound like these questions just popped into your mind.

Fig. 10-4 TV as a screaming medium.

"The truth now is that I rarely read my scripts before. They can throw it up there and I can go along. It's a conversation."

Do not count on being able to do this for a while. She has some thoughts on how to break in on the legal beat. (That is assuming someone in television doesn't call you up when you've just been reelected as a judge in Texas and begs you to try being on camera.)

"I just had an intern here who has her law degree and wants to get into television. She wondered if she should go to a small market?" In traditional journalism the answer would probably be yes, go to the small market and work your way up. If you are talking about legal analysis, says Catherine, then the political world is a good place to start because politics and law have always dovetailed. Don't forget your politicians are the ones who write the laws in the first place. Clerking for judges, working in the legislature, are just some ways for the legal reporter to break into television.

Listen Up, You Idiot!

I asked Catherine if a legal reporter or anchor needs a special style or signature nowadays to stand out. "Oh, I hope not," she answered with feeling. She objects to the current fad of all that yelling.

"I'm one of those that thinks the argument culture, as Deborah Tanner puts it, has been very detrimental to television. I'm one that more and more turns off the set when I hear all the yelling and screaming.

"You see someone like Jeffery Toobin. He is Harvard-educated, articulate, smart as a whip — but soft-spoken. He's a gentleman. He will not engage in the yelling and the screaming. Take someone like that and you can still have really engaging intelligent sometimes feisty debate, but done appropriately.

"I'd say no to the screaming and yelling and yes to the personality."

In other words, class, all that yelling and screaming is interesting at first. It gets your attention the way a neighbor's fight does. But if that fighting keeps up day after day, you get tired of it, don't you?

This is not to say you shouldn't have your own personality and style. Catherine does, she is smart, gentle, tall, beautiful, elegant and unafraid to speak her mind. That's who she is. It works for her. It will work for you too.

Entertainment Reporting

Now here you can have style. Furthermore, according to one who knows, you should have lots of it. You should even flaunt your style. Push your style.

That advice comes from the guy who might be looking at you one day for a job. He is Vinnie Potestivo, Director of Talent Development and Series Casting at MTV Networks. Style or a signature, Vinnie believes, is absolutely essential for entertainment reporters.

"When you are dealing with entertainment reporting," he points out, "this is the person who is between the audience and the celebrity. What better way to make a celebrity comfortable than to come from the same world of glamour that they do. The celebrity comes prepared to be covered, the entertainment reporter should come styled too. The reporter should break down that wall immediately. And the first thing the reporter presents to the celebrity is the look. So visually the reporter is saying: I'm one of you, let's talk. I get where you are coming from. It makes sense from the viewer's perspective too because red carpets are about style and the reporter is on the red carpet too."

There is an MTV style to anchoring and reporting entertainment news. In most news operations, opinion is out. Not here. It is what the MTV-generation expects from its anchors and reporters.

Fig. 11-1 Vinnie Potestivo. COURTESY OF CHRISTINE COWAN

"They are more the voice of our demographic," is the way Vinnie puts it. "As they deliver the news, they are delivering opinion, they are delivering style ... they are the front line in what's happening in the celebrity world."

It's a tone that Vinnie is talking about here. Teaching that tone is part of his job. "Part of the responsibility of my job is overall talent development. So in addition to casting and developing vehicles for talent, part of what I do is making sure talent fits the tone of the network — that there's a unified tone to the network.

"We go over breathing technique, physical breathing technique. Connecting your body to your physical voice. Finding the core within your voice because that's what's going to carry. And there is the physical presence.

"My biggest obstacle is finding the talent. Now that the talent is there, the next step is taking your talent and fitting it into the tone of what's happening on our network."

That's what the MTV entertainment reporter or anchor sounds like. What does he or she look like? They are not very young — the youngest anchor is about 25 or 26 years old. They are sexier. "The main characteristic that differentiates our anchors from the main networks is style ... a younger looking, hipper style. It's a style that reflects what's going on in pop culture. A little bit of style, a little personality and a little bit of opinion." But note, even on MTV, you can go too far. It's one of the mistakes he sees.

"Over-styling is a big problem. Reporters who go too far, over-compensate based on what they see on the red carpet. We are fashion forward, we push the envelope and sometimes even we miss."

But not for lack of trying. If they miss, it's because they know style is important to the audience and they err on the side of effort, not on laziness.

Are You the One for MTV?

Who is Vinnie looking to tap as the next on-camera star at MTV? He shared the secret with me for your information. "Here at MTV, for entertainment reporters or news correspondents or news anchors, we look for someone with music or pop culture knowledge. Yet, at the same time, someone who can articulate what's going on within our demographic.

"The skills we look for are: Writing, producing and research. Our news correspondents don't really fall into the category of 'entertainment' because we treat them more as news correspondents. They were on the front lines of Hurricane Katrina in New Orleans — any place that is relevant in pop culture. It's not limited to just entertainment what we do here."

How different from traditional networks like CBS or NBC?

"We have a network here called MTV-U. The demographic is 18 to 22. It's a closed-circuit network, it reaches 750 college campuses ... about 5 million people. That's the only network we have that would be what we call 'Hard-hitting news.' We outsource the news from CBS News ... it is delivered to us. We do have our news anchors from MTV who appear twice an hour on there."

Where does he find entertainment reporters?

"It could be a producer who is camera-friendly, not necessarily great looking. Camera-friendly or telegenic. There has to be something about them, their physical presence that pops. It could be someone who works in the industry or a writer from a magazine that knows the ins and outs of the industry. Many of the best I've known come from the magazine world, they write for *Spin*, they write for *Rolling Stone*. They come with instant credibility and of course, a Rolodex of contacts within the entertainment world."

Like any reporter, the better your sources are, the better your chances are of getting a job with MTV. If you can, start filling up that Rolodex with contacts.

"The amount of experience you have will bring the expectation of the strength of your contacts. One of the things I work on when we have a new correspondent is setting them up with record labels and studio heads especially here at MTV."

Making a Reel for MTV

Here you are in luck. MTV has traditionally looked at every reel that comes in. The face of MTV2 came from a submission. If you want to know what the network is looking for, listen to my pal Vinnie.

"Style. It's big because we are working in the medium of television. Visually it is very important for us that it pops. We look for content. It's not necessary the production quality of the tape, it's the content that's important. It's what this person has to say and why they have to say it."

And beyond looks, he's looking for attitude.

"Something I look for is someone who's got an opinion. And the ability to support it with facts."

Your tape should include interviews in the field, man-on-the-street chats. Stay away from studio shooting with teleprompter. It tends to be stuffy, he says. "I prefer for them to be out in the field, free form, doing a man-on-the-street interview with somebody, interacting with somebody." When you are doing your interviews, don't try to show off. Your job, says Vinnie, is to bring out the best in your guest. Too many times, he says, the interviewer wants to be the star. That's a mistake. "They don't allow the interview to breathe. They don't give it room to actually become a conversation."

Thank you, Vinnie, for making that clear. It's a conversation you are having in this interview.

Also, he says, stay on the point of the interview. "Because of the hustle and bustle of Hollywood, it's easy to get off track. It's easy to take that tangent and go far away from the point."

The Question Everyone Asks

This has come up in my class often. Students want to know: When can the entertainment reporter or anchor expect to get their clothes paid for? So I asked Vinnie. He said, "Ha-ha-ha. I bet someone put you up to that question." In a way, yes. The answer is, you will get clothes to wear at no cost, but they probably go back.

"Wardrobe is something we handle in the deal, at the top of the game. It's safe to say when MTV puts the onus on you to represent our news department, we'll make sure that clothing is provided. There is a huge difference between providing clothing and paying for your clothes. Because we are a fashion-forward network, because we are a trend-setting network, we borrow a lot of clothing from venders, from showrooms in exchange for credit on air. They are borrowed and returned."

Fig. 11-2 Sorry, you don't get to keep them.

NANCY'S RULES

(From Vinnie):

Don't be stuffy.
Don't show off in an interview.
Stay on the point of the piece.
Don't overdress or underdress.

12

Business Reporting

There are so many outlets that feature business reporting now — not only on the networks but also overwhelmingly on cable. And for good reason: More and more people are interested in knowing how their money is moving, how secure their jobs are, how events will affect their personal economy and how to protect themselves financially.

One of the first to take business reporting away from Wall Street and into households on Main Street was CBS News correspondent Ray Brady.

His philosophy on business reporting should echo in the ears of all reporters. "Television is a populist medium. You could get real fancy about it but economics is really a science of how we live."

Skills

Ray says you need a special set of skills to be a top business reporter.

You need to know a little bit about economics and how the system works. "You can't go wrong if you follow the money," he says. That is particularly true if you follow business and Wall Street. As important as knowing about business, Ray learned that it is equally important to understand human nature.

You have two audiences when you do economic news, says Ray: You have CEOs of companies and the Wall Streeters, and then you

Fig. 12-1 Ray Brady. COURTESY OF CBS

have the man on Main Street. A business reporter has to satisfy both. The way you do it is to take the central point of your report and you humanize it. Always keep it in simple English so the man on the street understands what you are saying. But you must report the facts accurately and comprehensively enough so it satisfies the businessman at the top who thinks: This correspondent knows what he is talking about.

Ray cites this example: "You have to do a story on the rise in interest rates. How do you get across to the average Joe what this means to him? Well, you can say, 'Down the road, experts say, because of this rise today in interest rates, your credit card will charge you $200 more.'

"That way, you've satisfied the guy at the top who understands interest rates raised by the Federal Reserve and also how down the road they will impact people. And the people understand this too because you showed how it impacts them. And now they think, 'Hey, this is valuable information. I'll tune in tomorrow night and keep watching.'"

Voice

Ray insists that voice is one of the keys to a reporter's success, any reporter on any beat. How did he train his voice? He just listened to how other people used their voices, something you can easily do too.

 **Report from the Trenches**

One thing that Ray found out about television has remained a constant from the beginning. It will never change. "When I broke in," says Ray, "Walter Cronkite was the anchor — I kept studying Walter, what did he do on camera? How did he do it? Then all of a sudden it hit me: It was the way Walter used his voice. It was the main thing that made Walter Cronkite so popular. It wasn't that avuncular look or anything else about him, it was the voice."

This is something I try to make my students understand. The best-trained voices in television are on the air all the time. Listen to them the way Ray did. Break down what the reporter or anchor is doing with his or her voice.

Ray says he has noticed that a lot of correspondents on TV today really don't know how to use their voices well. They are losing out on an important tool. Remember: Whether you are reporting economics or a flower show, your viewers are receiving the report through their ears.

Looks

How important are looks for business? Ray doesn't believe they are that important especially compared to some other beats, like entertainment reporting. He says, "I really don't care how good looking a person is, I'm thinking about my wallet."

Is it harder for a woman than a man to become a business correspondent?

"Not when I look at the screen today," says Ray. "I have never seen a period in television where there were so many young women business reporters."

 Report from the Trenches

Ray recalled when opportunities for women really exploded on television. He noted that business channel CNBC started the trend

W Miller

Fig. 12-2 Women welcome.

with Maria Bartiromo. "You have all those male brokers down on Wall Street who looked and saw this good looking woman and they all went wild over her." Not only that, she got all the top interviews too. The Wall Street wags nicknamed her the "Money Honey." Viewers responded too. CNBC executives didn't miss the point of their success: "If they like one woman on the air," Ray said of the network, "we'll give them 150 women."

Airtime

One of the nice things about business and economics, Ray points out, is there is always some place where you can check the number. Another is that during the year, you are guaranteed several stories because of the release of government statistics. This helps you keep your face on the air and as I have said time and again, airtime is the gold ore for reporters.

A good example is unemployment statistics. The government releases them on the first Friday of the month so a business reporter has an automatic story 12 times a year. Why is it always a story? Because everyone is worried about his or her job.

Ray was always prepared to do a package on the day the numbers were released because not only did he know the schedule, he also shot material in advance. He didn't wait until the day the numbers came out to start. Ray says he would check with his sources and usually he'd have a pretty good idea of what the trend was. "But sometimes, we weren't so sure so we'd interview one guy who had a job and another who'd lost a job. Then we'd use which one represented the data."

It can take a while to dig up people, to find people to interview. But Ray developed a system and made notes along the way in what became his source book for himself.

This is valuable advice. If he had to do an unemployment story, he'd go to a union for a person out of work to profile and bring the story home to the viewers. If it's a story of a consumer being ripped off there are all kinds of organizations in Washington that protect people.

He dug around and brought his tattered notebook to me. "This is the book. THE book," he said as if he were carrying the Magna Charta or a first folio of Shakespeare.

His source book is filled with contacts, names and phone numbers or e-mail addresses. "Natural gas? The Natural Gas Supply Association. Oil prices? Sheikh Yamani, he was the most powerful man in the world at one point. Pensions? Pension Dynamics. Do you know how many people are being screwed out of pensions today? I'd go to these guys for a victim and an expert.

"Retail? Every year, there's a shoppers Friday, called Black Friday, the big shopping day after Thanksgiving that retailers hoped to get them out of the red for the year. It's always a story and that Friday is a dead news day. So this is how you get on the air too," says Brady.

"One year, I learned from sources in this book that the shopping was terrible but the sources wouldn't allow me to quote them. So I did a piece with stories of people saying, 'No, I'm cutting back this year.'"

Fig. 12-3 Learn sources' phone numbers.

He actually kept the book under lock and key. "It was my liveli-hood, that book." He didn't want to share it too much. "You give that all away and send out other reporters to do the report the executives begin to wonder, 'Why do we need Brady if any simpleton can do it.'" His sources made the difference. He knew his beat.

When Ray started out, he didn't have this source book. If you are a business reporter, or any other beat reporter, and haven't started a source book for yourself, start one now. Just grab a notebook and start writing in the names and contact information of any group that you think might be of value on a later report. If it crosses your mind, "Oh this guy's good, I better get his name down." Do it right then or you will forget or lose the information.

Light News Stories in Business?

You bet. Ray did many.

"At the time, it was an inflationary period ... and things like toy trains were going up in value. And we'd shoot it like it was a real train. Toot Toot ... and I'd write, 'Hear that lonesome whistle? Maybe you've got this train in the attic and it cost maybe $20 a few years ago. That train today is worth $3,000!!'"

These were very popular. "We did I think 20 of those ... all kinds of things were going up: Raggedy Ann Dolls, all kinds of stuff." (In fact, they came to be known in the shop as Ray Brady's dust-balls in the attic.)

When he was doing a story on the toy trains, he'd do a stand-up the way he was taught but with a twist. He'd talk directly to the camera but not all business.

"The same way though I'd have a smile and a glint in my eye."

Traps

Over the years, Ray has had people try to manipulate him into reporting a story for their benefit. So watch out, he says, when you are told a story that benefits the person who tells you the story.

It may not benefit anybody else. And, in fact, it could hurt your viewers who might invest only to lose money. You have to consider, when you are covering business and especially Wall Street, how the person giving you information could benefit. For example, in many cases, the person giving you the information might be helped because he owns stock in that company. Back in the boom days there was all kinds of lying. Today, you are supposed to find out. You must ask, "Do you own the stock?" Watch out for tips being given to you. Ray got them all the time. "But I didn't use them," he said. "As a reporter, you have to be very very careful."

It is against all standards for a reporter to accept inside information and benefit from it. Not only does this protect the reporter from being accused of biased reporting, but it may also reflect on the whole station's credibility. Furthermore, not acting on a tip may keep the reporter from being fired and even out of jail. Ray points out that someone will dig up your insider trading. Ray also says it's just practical to ignore these whispered tips. "I learned that for every tip you got that would work out, there might be 20 that didn't."

One important reason to keep your reputation in business reporting is a fact that Brady reveals that may be a surprise: You do stories that make you very unpopular. If somebody has an ax to grind, you might well be attacked. Your honest reputation can protect you from such attacks.

Get Them To Talk To You

Ray had a knack of getting people to talk when they didn't want to, often in investigative reports on companies.

"You get people who accuse them of wrong-doing," he explained. "Then you call up the CEO and you say, 'Mr. Smith, we have people saying you are a bad guy and we would like to give you time to answer this.' Invariably, you can get to them. I once asked someone at *60 Minutes* why anyone would go on camera with Mike Wallace. Because, they think: 'I'm the one that can beat that guy Wallace.'"

One story he recalls was about colleges selling the names and addresses of its students to credit card companies, and making a ton of money from these lists. "We interviewed a student who worked seven years to pay off her debt. A professor told me he was outraged. But the President would not appear on camera to say how the colleges were selling the names of their students. I stood in front of one of those red brick buildings at the U of Tennessee and said, 'The president won't talk to us.' That report went on the air without a comment from the university, which should have been embarrassing to the school."

Of course you want the university president to talk to you. But, if he refuses, say so in your report.

Getting Started

Ray started as a newspaperman at the Long Beach (New Jersey) *Daily Record.* He was assigned everything: Cops and Robbers, Domestic Court, City Council.

"There is no training like newspaper training. You learn how to write it fast and clearly, which is always important. It's money in the bank," which means something coming from a business correspondent.

But it is harder to make the transition since Brady started in television. There is such a technological divide between the newspapers and TV now, the learning curve is huge. And then there are more and more people who are good on camera and who know a specialty like business. But his training in reporting was for him and would be for you today, money in the bank.

Ray suggests that business reporting has some special aspects. Most journalists, he says, hate economics, hate numbers with a passion. After all, most of them were English majors. So that means you don't have that much competition. And, it gives you an independence from interference because the people you are working for probably don't know that much about it.

One last Ray Brady piece of advice for all on-camera reporters: "I would tell any correspondent: Get Fisherman's Friend. A lozenge to sooth a scratchy throat."

13

Anchoring I

The anchor is the creation of television journalism. In no other medium is a single person so involved in presenting the news. Nowhere else does one person have to be so informed.

The anchor is the single most important on-camera position in all of television. It is a huge responsibility, an enormous job and wildly rewarding professionally and personally. In many cases, the anchor has become the face of the station or the network.

In defining the anchor position, it is best to go back to the little known and often misunderstood root of the title. You may think of an ocean anchor, the device holding the ship steady in all kinds of weather. That fits. It's a logical definition. But that wasn't how it started.

Report from the Trenches

Don Hewitt, who started *60 Minutes* and invented most of the basic techniques used in television news, also coined the term "anchor."

It was an election night and he had on hand four reporters on whom he would rely for the broadcast. As he has told the story, he set them up as a track relay team. The final lap would be run by "the anchor." He was talking then of equals — reporters of equal stature — but only one would run the last lap. That anchor might have been the best among equals, but they were equals as reporters nonetheless.

It is worth noting that an anchor will do well to consider himself or herself an equal among reporters and stay humble. But the relay race has changed over the years. To continue with Don Hewitt's analogy, it is still a relay race for the anchor. Only now, the anchor runs the first lap too, hands off the story to a reporter, and runs the last lap as well.

Anchoring Is a Craft

Anchoring the news is a craft built on experience and hard work. Done well, it can be inspiring. In the hands of a top-notch anchor, a developing story is often presented so well that it couldn't have been better if a team of people had a week to prepare it. And that is a major point. Most of the anchor's work is done LIVE. Every broadcast is a live new show for the anchor, whether it is a two-hour morning show or a five-minute news segment. Each broadcast is a living thing unto itself.

The anchor has a conversation with the viewer, as if chatting over a backyard fence. You, the anchor, are on one side and the viewer is on the other side. You want to tell the stories as if you are talking with your neighbor who lives next door.

Credibility Is the Bedrock of the Anchor

Credibility is built on years of accurate reporting. The viewer begins to trust you because of your hard work. This trust can be lost in a minute of false reporting. The viewers know the difference. Value your credibility above all else. People will notice if you put on an act. Television is like a magnifying glass. It exposes your every flaw to the viewer and reveals a surprising amount about the person you are.

"So how do I act?" you ask. Act naturally. Be yourself. Be honest. People want to watch someone who is alive, connected to what they are talking about, vulnerable and confident. That probably describes you. The more natural you appear on camera, the better anchor you will be. This is not an easy task. The more at ease an anchor or reporter appears, the harder they have worked to achieve this. It takes practice and lots of it. But after a while, you will become centered and open to the ever-changing transitions in the stories. And I promise you, this won't take as long as learning brain surgery.

You may think that some anchors are just naturally gifted with an ease and grace in the anchor chair. If you saw the late Peter Jennings on ABC, or John Roberts on CBS or CNN, you might believe that this is some in-born talent they had. But all of them worked hard at their craft. Their ease in front of the camera comes as much from confidence as any ability. That confidence is built on hard work.

NANCY'S RULES

Anchoring is part reading and part performance.

As an anchor you may have millions of people watching you, but you shouldn't be thinking that way; you shouldn't be talking to a huge audience.

Television is an intimate medium. When I, as the viewer, am watching you in my living room or bedroom, or kitchen, as far as I am concerned you are talking to me alone. I am the only one present. So, as the anchor, always talk to one person, as if you are talking to a friend, a neighbor, who is just on the other side of that fence.

One of the most comfortable anchors ever is Bob Scheiffer. You must watch him to understand how to relate to others as an anchor. Study him during his chats with correspondents and note his conversational ease with the viewers. This comfortable relationship is the right tone to strive for.

Fig. 13-1 You are in my home.

Who Are You?

As an anchor you are reading from the teleprompter. You are at the same time talking to the viewer. You are performing, of course. But the viewer shouldn't see that. You have skills, you know how to speak clearly with a modulated voice, you present with more centered energy than you would use if the camera was not present. But the viewer is to know nothing of your skills. The viewer should only know the story you are telling.

Anchor Qualities and Skills

There are several techniques to learn to become an accomplished anchor. We will go through them in some detail. Probably the first thing you'll notice is the professional's READING PACE.

Pace

The pace for anchor reading is based on a 20-second copy story that is pretty much the standard reader story on television.

Generally, most anchors read about 60 words in that 20 seconds or about three words a second. Some are slightly slower and some slightly faster. Either is OK, just not too much slower or too much faster. I like to say 50 words in 20 seconds is the slowest you would want for pace and 70 would be the fastest read. Within that 20-second story you should get three to five sentences.

Here's a training trick: You can record your local anchors and the network anchors. Time the anchor stories with a stopwatch or use the timer that now comes on many tape recorders. Then transcribe their 20-second copy stories. See which of the anchor's pace you like best and use that pace for yourself, reading the copy you have transcribed.

Be aware that numbers take longer to say than they appear. If you are writing your own copy, don't think numbers save time. Take the number: "241." It may appear to be one word, and a short one at that. But if you read that number, it takes much longer. Write out the number and you will have a better idea of the time it takes to say the number. In this case: "Two hundred forty-one." It's really four words. That is a full second of reading at the proper pace.

Other Things To Know About an Anchor's Read

While you are watching the tape that you recorded of the anchor, you should also watch and listen to how he or she does certain things.

Watch and listen to how they make their points. They emphasize certain things so the viewer understands the point of the story. (This is not point of view but the point or the reason for the story.) It might be the word "up" in a stock market report or the words "New Orleans" in a report on the president's travel. Not every word can be hit for emphasis because then there would be no emphasis.

Listen to how the anchor uses pitch at the end of a sentence. Note that it usually does not dip.

Note how few pauses the anchor takes. The more time you give the viewer to break away, the more often you will lose the audience.

In many cases, the anchor will continue to read without taking a breath at every sentence. You'll be surprised at how long anchors go on a single breath.

Listen to how anchors vary the pace. This helps keep the viewer's interest by avoiding dull monotony. Also, the anchors will vary their reads, sometimes soften their voices for an intimate feel, say for a story about the death of a beloved community member. Other times the read goes rapid fire, as in a police chase story.

Watch the small physical moves the anchor makes. Notice the gestures. Also, watch for when the anchor leans slightly in toward the viewer. This is often at a transition point within the story or within the broadcast, such as a large shift in the mood going from a hard news report to sports or weather.

How Much Can I Move?

Keep your gestures to a minimum; television tends to make small moves larger and they can be distracting.

Here is a trick that will help you learn if you are moving too much or too little, though this is rare.

Get a friend or a trusted colleague to sit about a foot and a half from you. Tell the listener a story and check on how much (or little) you move your hands, your head or your eyebrows or any personal tic.

You are not on stage. You are in front of the camera. The camera exaggerates everything you do — every gesture, every movement. If you frown you will look terrible. Your constant frowning will distract from what you are saying. You do not want to appear like a mummy. But you don't want any exaggerated facial tics. This is something you must learn about yourself before you can take care of it. But do take care of it.

Connections

Another element of an anchor's presentation that sets the good ones apart from the rest is the ability to find a human connection to the

W Miller

Fig. 13-2 Check yourself. This is best done with a camera rolling so you can review your movements.

stories he or she is reading. Some of this is in the nature of the person. Students can learn a lot about connecting with a story from talk-show host Oprah Winfrey. Give Oprah any story and it will have that connection. But it is also something you can learn. You can find that place in you to care and it will come through. You don't want to be a sappy mess on the air, but a human connection is compelling.

Top anchors make it seem as if they care about every story, or at least know each story well. Watch how anchors appear to know what they are talking about. They are unusually well read about current affairs. They seem to know what they are talking about because they do.

Television anchors have been accused of being instant experts in everything. This is said as some kind of slap. I take it as a compliment. Anchors have to do lots of homework and have to care to know the background and the details of what they are talking about to do the job right. If you don't care, it will be apparent not only to the viewers but to the people who do the hiring.

Try Substitution

Just as reporters are given assignments to cover stories they know nothing about or care nothing about, anchors too are presented copy that they must read with understanding and enthusiasm even though they might not care much about either. But you will have to make all the stories interesting to the viewer.

As I suggested when discussing reporting (see Chapter 8), try substituting something you like in place of the item discussed in your story. This is a trick but not dishonest. If you like sports but couldn't care about dance, try substituting baseball for the dance and let your enthusiasm for that sport give your read a boost on the dance story. It doesn't work for everyone, but many of my students say it works for them.

Voice and Read

A warm authoritative voice is essential for a successful anchor. The viewer trusts and feels comfortable with a person who has a rich-sounding voice. Think of the people you have come to love to watch on television. Were they Oprah Winfrey, Dan Rather or Diane Sawyer?

One thing they all have in common is a strong and deep voice. I don't mean clownishly low. The voice should be resonant, not nasal or stuck back in the throat.

We will go into this more in the chapter on voice, but here are a few notes. An anchor's read is much more than the sound of his or her voice. It is also pitch, tone, modulation and articulation. An anchor uses the full extent — the full range — of the voice.

For example, if the voice softens, that is a form of communication. An anchor's toolbox includes EMPHASIS AND SUBORDI-NATION. When you are telling the stories, you must know what to emphasize and what to subordinate. That is done by using the voice.

Nowhere in your copy will you be called on to use emphasis and subordination more than when you have a story with numbers. Numbers simply fly over the viewer's heads. No one absorbs numbers well, so it is up to you to make sure they come through.

If 300 people die in some horrible catastrophe, that's a lot of death. If you feel that, the way you say that number will sound large to the viewers. Sometimes 8 can be a large number — earthquake measurements come to mind. It's up to you to make it big — or little.

You are telling someone the story, clearly with the appropriate attitude, which brings us to SUBTEXT.

Subtext and Intentions

Subtext is when you say it with feeling, not with words, that something is either wonderful or terrible. It is your attitude about the subject and it rides on what you are saying.

The key is not to read the story but to tell the story, to talk the story. For example, you have known adults who don't have children of their own. Did you notice sometimes they don't know how to talk to them or deal with them? They don't sound credible to the child. Again, it's how you tell the story to the child.

Intentions are slightly different. You already use them in life, when you chat over the back fence with a neighbor. You might ask: "Did you hear what happened to that Sarah?" The intention comes naturally. If you are scandalized and want to shock your neighbor, that's one intention: "... *that* (shocking) Sarah." If you are saddened and sympathize about something that happened to Sarah, it's another: "... that (poor) Sarah." You are thrilled, so you relish the news about Sarah, is yet another intention: "... that (wonderful) Sarah."

Same sentence, different intentions, different reads.

When you ask questions on camera, you should ask them with a purpose — an intention. For example if you were interviewing Mozart you'd ask, "Just how old were you when you wrote this quartet?" You might marvel as you ask the question. Or, if you think Mozart had someone else helping him, you might ridicule him as you ask the question. But whatever your intention behind your question or your story it must not be asked or told in a perfunctory way. When thinking about what intentions you are using it is most useful to use active verbs.

Let's return to numbers once more to examine subtext closely. When it comes to numbers in the copy, subtext is crucial. Business and sports reporters have it a bit easier since their audiences are prepared to hear numbers and already know the context of the stock market or a ball score. But that doesn't mean the sports and business people shouldn't give their numbers as much emphasis and subtext. No matter what you are reporting, you should report it with energy. Again, you do this naturally. Take the number 6. It means nothing just standing alone: 6. But if you were to say that the time you have to finish a task is 6 seconds, there would be an urgency to it. If you were reporting that 6 school children were killed in a bus crash, there would be a tragic aspect to it with lots of subtext.

We will examine this in depth in the voice chapter. As you become more experienced, and are more aware of technique, the different types of stories, the necessities of pace and contrast, and clarifying of content, you will be making thousands of speedy decisions. These will soon come naturally, just as you would at the back fence when you are chatting with your neighbor.

As you are learning the craft of on-camera presentation, be aware of subtext and intentions.

Segue

You will find segues important and very useful. When you need to make a transition to a different story, one way to help is with what I call segue words. These are words or phrases that take you from one subject to another. The words are used at the start of the next story. Useful segue words or phrases are:

Meanwhile
And
Well
Back home
Now to sports

Use of a segue word makes a graceful transition from one story to the next.

Hey! Relax!

An anchor must be relaxed. This comes with confidence. Confidence comes with experience. This may take some training, but it will come. I have a trick for my students: If you feel yourself tensing up, take a quick, deep yawn — one that fully opens the back of your throat — before you begin. If you can vocalize a deep "ahhhh" as you yawn, it will also keep tension out of your voice.

Also, this may sound like foolish advice, don't forget to keep breathing before you start. More on this too in our vocal technique segment.

Ad-libbing during live coverage is a skill you should acquire. You don't need to be brilliant. Just experienced. This takes practice and of course it takes being relaxed.

More and more technology is giving television stations the ability to go live to developing stories. So it should come as no surprise that news directors want to go to those live stories, those breaking news situations, as often as they can. It does give energy to a broadcast and it is what news is all about. So more and more anchors are being called upon to narrate live situations. That calls for ad-libbing. It's a tool all anchors must have. (I've put together some ad-libbing exercises for you at the end of this chapter.) Be careful about going overboard on ad-libs. You can get into a heap of trouble by ad-libbing after the hard news stories.

You can still ad-lib at the end of the light news or the kicker, if there is time. A kicker is that last light or frivolous piece to kick off the end of the show, just before your good-bye, so that you can leave 'em laughing, as they say in show biz.

An anchor must be sensitive, alert and in the moment. You will be doing live broadcasts where anything can go wrong or can change in a split second. For this reason alone, an anchor of a show must have focus and huge unwavering concentration.

Anchor Jack (and Jill for That Matter) Are Dull

As the old quip goes, "Early to bed and early to rise makes Jack a dull boy." Welcome to Dullsville, home of the anchors.

The anchor must get to the studio early enough to read and awake enough to understand the stories of the day, the stories of the broadcast.

Diane Sawyer (who is not a dull person at all) has anchored a morning show for many years. She arrives at the studio at 4 A.M., in time to look over all the copy and interviews for the morning's show. Yes, this wreaks havoc with your social life. (What social life?) One never gets used to those very early hours.

If you want to get ahead in this business you may have to sacrifice a few parties. But in order to get ahead, this business is so competitive, as I've mentioned before, you have to be hungry and passionate to succeed.

Fig. 13-3 Early to the studio.

Don't Forget Reporting and Interviewing Skills

To be an effective anchor, you should always remain a reporter first. To be a good anchor, the reporter in you must continually reestablish oneself as a working journalist. To hang on to the credentials is important. It is essential to keep your credibility.

That's why the top anchors all go to Baghdad or China, New Orleans or Jerusalem. They cover major natural disasters including tornadoes, earthquakes, tsunamis and Dan Rather's specialty: The hurricane. After all, it was when Dan Rather had his crew strap him to a tree during a hurricane that put him on the map. You must go wherever the story is happening, because it may turn out to be a big one.

Just as anchors have to remain sharp reporters, they must also be good interviewers. Keeping up on the news will help if you are thrown a late live breaking news interview to do in the middle of your broadcast.

In fact, the anchor has to be skilled at all on-camera television techniques. Interviews are hugely important. For the anchor, they are almost always live and they are almost always a surprise, based on breaking news. In fact, the later the news breaks, the more likely there will be an interview for an anchor since this may be the fastest way to get the information.

A package is unlikely if something breaks five minutes before air. But a live interview is very possible, especially with the technology available worldwide. So the anchor has to be well trained in late live interviews. That means absorbing the material quickly and being at ease with the situation.

Report from the Trenches

A young reporter at a local station got his dream break one weekend when the regular weekend anchor was on vacation. (You should know that weekend anchor slots are often used to try out young reporters to see if they have the skills to become an anchor, as was the case in this story.)

It was his hope that one day he would get the opportunity and here it was. He had been a terrific reporter on the streets and the management felt he was one to consider for an upcoming anchor post. He was a good-looking young man, a gifted writer and, though young, the top of the station's reporters.

It so happened that the weekend producer had worked up an interview with the publisher of one of the country's great business journals. The publisher had been in town for a conference and a major economic story broke that Saturday afternoon. When the newly minted anchor showed up in the news room, the producer told him about the great get ... that he would be doing a live interview with the publisher at the anchor desk during the 6 o'clock broadcast. The young man nearly had a nervous breakdown. He had never prepared for a live interview. Never trained or practiced or thought about it. And now he was being asked to do it live. He sweated, went to the bathroom several times and tried to study the questions prepared by the producer. But the interview was terrible. It was about the last time he was offered the job of anchoring.

Be Honest ... But Not Hard on Yourself

You should review your work every time. That means check the tape. Watch how you did. Don't beat yourself up, but study your work, as you would grade a student's paper. What did you do well? Remember that. Where did you falter? Work on that.

One thing that my students have a blind spot about is their idiosyncratic mannerisms — their tics. You must face the fact that if you have a tic, it can be a huge distraction. You must confront and control those distracting vocal or physical mannerisms.

In Indiana, It's Pronounced "Pee-Roo"

Here is something that sounds obvious but is often overlooked. The anchor must know all the proper pronunciations of names he or she will be speaking for the show: Asian names, Polish names, Arabic names. Each channel has its own way of pronouncing these names. Find out what it is.

Let's take an example: Saddam Hussein. Some say, Saaadaam or Sahdahm. Find out the preferred way at your station. There is never a penalty for asking. There is one when you get it wrong.

The folks who live in Peru, Indiana, had better hear the reporter call it "PEE-ROO" or they won't trust another thing he says.

Trust Me, They Love You

Trust your instincts and be yourself. You are trying your best to visit your viewer's living rooms. I am sure they wouldn't want a fathead or an overactor to join them for an evening. But YOU, the real you — you they would love. Television makes anchors bigger than life, but you must be just you to your viewers.

Television appears to be a series of contradictions. What you are learning is how to present the real you in the artificial world of the television studio. So you must learn your anchor craft with its "acting" techniques without being a drama queen.

This is an important distinction. Anchoring is not a soap opera. In fact, be wary of drama. If you tend in that direction — using long pauses and heightened emotions — pull back. Tighten up the pauses and tone down the reading. This is not the stage. The camera does the work for you. If you are a drama queen, save it for your friends. Drama won't work on camera and rarely works among your colleagues in the newsroom.

There are the rare instances when emotions take over the anchor: Walter Cronkite when he announced the death of President Kennedy or Dan Rather on the Letterman Show after September 11. It's rare when the human being comes through in extraordinary situations, but when it does, it is right.

The fact is, television exaggerates. To a degree, television depersonalizes. It is a one-dimensional medium and you must come across as a three-dimensional living, breathing human being.

Fig. 13-4 Television exaggerates.

Checklist

As an anchor, you must:

- ❐ Have a warm, authoritative voice.
- ❐ Be sensitive, alert and in the moment.
- ❐ Have focus and concentration.
- ❐ Find a human connection to the stories.
- ❐ Be thoroughly prepared and in command.
- ❐ Get to the studio early enough to read and understand the stories of the day.
- ❐ Know all the proper pronunciations.
- ❐ Be relaxed.
- ❐ Do your homework.
- ❐ Trust your instincts.
- ❐ Be yourself.

Ad-Libbing Exercise

Choose three light news stories from your newspaper or stories you taped off air. Pick an entertainment story, a weather story and something that tickles you. Read each story, then ad-lib a comment at the end.

Do this several times during the day, under different circumstances such as when you are having morning coffee, when you are taking a break from work, when you are exhausted before bed. Try this several days with different stories. Try it with a friend, telling the story and ad-libbing a comment to your friend at the end of the story.

14

Anchoring II

The TelePrompTer

You must learn how to use one. It is an inverted mirror placed in front of the camera that reflects the copy that the anchor is to read (see Fig. 14-1).

The TelePrompTer, known informally as "the prompter," shows the anchor about five lines of copy at a time. Each line consists of three to five words. The lines move upward. The camera sits directly behind the mirrored glass where the lines appear. So when you are reading those lines, you are looking directly into the lens. (You must practice this on the CD-Rom where there is a working simulation of a prompter for you to read.) At the networks, there is a person whose only job is to run the prompter. It used to roll a paper script at a preset timing. Today, it's all in the computer, there is no more paper prompter script.

In some situations, anchors may be asked to run the prompter for themselves. But if you have a prompter technician, that person should keep pace with the anchor and the anchor's idiosyncrasies, not the other way around. The anchor should not be trying to keep pace with the prompter. The anchor should be focusing primarily on telling the viewer the stories of the day with as much clarity as possible.

Fig. 14-1 The prompter.

The exact copy of the prompter script is on the anchor desk or in the anchor's hand, if standing. Why does the anchor need a hard copy script when they have the prompter? Is that just for show? No, anything mechanical can break down. The prompter can stop rolling. So be prepared with your hard-copy script. The script is an important backup that you as anchor should be ready to use in a graceful transition so the viewers don't know something went wrong.

 ## Report from the Trenches

It was a Friday night show with Bill Maher on HBO. He always does a 5- or 10-minute monologue as his close, well rehearsed and read from a prompter. He was about halfway through this night and he paused. He looked at us, the viewers, and said, "See that's the way it goes when technology fails." He brought his notes out of his pocket, a crumpled script and said, "It's like a Boy Scout, always be prepared." He finished the monologue without the prompter working, checking his notes and completing the section smoothly. The point: Always have the backup handy.

As Murphy's Law states, in a complex system, anything that can go wrong, will. Your script is your bible. You should always keep the hard copy, that exact paper copy, on the same page as the prompter. You must always keep track of your place as the broadcast moves along. That is why the prompter is written the way it is, one story to a page.

The Hard Copy

Most anchors go through the broadcast before air reading the hard copy of the script. It is the old-fashioned way, the words printed on paper that you can touch and hold. It's certainly a good idea to go through the copy before you go on live because the more familiar with the copy you are, the better you will do.

I suggest taking it one step further, at least until you have been anchoring for say ten years. Mark your copy as you read it in advance. Eventually, you will develop your own code. But underlining certain words is an obvious signal of emphasis. Some of my students like using a squiggly line for a different emphasis and others put a circle around words. For hesitations (taking a beat) you can use a slash or even a double slash for a full pause. And you can use arrows to indicate an inflection.

It's up to you how to devise your signals but it is a good way for young anchors to dig into the copy. What you will find as you become more comfortable in the anchor chair is that you don't need to look down at the copy to follow your marks. Just by having gone through the copy you will have made yourself aware of how to read the stories.

Some students like to note on the hard copy what kind of story it is, helping alert them to the transition. One way is to draw a face

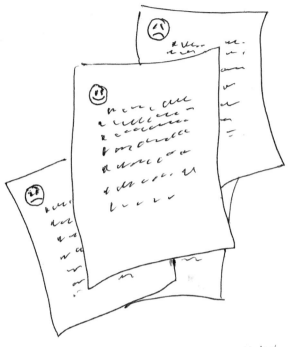

W Miller

Fig. 14-2 Mark up your hard copy.

at the top of the page. A smiley face denotes a light story, a frowny sad face signals a hard news story.

But all your best efforts won't stop things from going wrong. Most of what does go wrong is out of your control, but making things look smooth through the crisis is within your control. In fact, handling technical foul-ups or communication problems is part of the anchor job description.

Jim Jensen, an anchor who was on top of the New York market for years, had this to say about handling glitches: "They don't pay me for when things go right, they pay me for when things go wrong."

Maybe the sound is suddenly cut off, so that the people at home hear only silence. You must know how to handle this and other difficult situations that will arise. When the sound comes back on you might explain to the viewers, "There's been a gremlin in the works, we're sorry that you had no sound. . . ." You should let the viewer know what's going on so they won't think it is their television set or their fault.

Headlines and Opens

Headlines

Headlines are read at the top of the broadcast, usually only in the news broadcasts. These should be read with punch — really drive them home. It is, after all, the first impression you will make. Also, one more thing: This is one of the few times that using the present tense for verbs is a good idea.

> "The mayor is defeated."
> "School taxes are up, services are down. An investigative report."
> "The sun is headed your way. Complete weather and all the news next."

Many times, the headlines will be pretaped so they can be produced with video or graphics. But sometimes the headlines will be read live, when there is a breaking news story, for example.

Opens

After the headlines, the broadcast begins with you. You should be connecting with the viewer immediately, really looking through camera. In the old days, the headlines were referred to as the "Cold Open" and this part as the "Warm Open." That reflects your presentation of this copy well.

One of the tricks is where you place your head. For the open you don't want to slant your head to the side. You want your head to be straight on, and looking directly into the camera. To help it along a bit for opens, just slightly drop your chin. You then will be eyeballing the viewer. If you have a tendency to throw your chin and head upward, it looks snooty. You don't want that.

Everything you do in front of the camera counts. Everything is important. There are no throwaway gestures. You want to appear centered and in control, yet open and spontaneous. This is not a contradiction. This is how you are when you are at your best. You are freest, most confident, most relaxed and most focused.

You will get a countdown from the floor manager at the start of the show, coming out of each piece and at every commercial. You have probably seen it: The floor manager counting out loud and using his or her fingers ... counting backward from ten. The last vocal count is three, but the fingers go to two, one and then a ball. YOU ARE ON THE AIR. I suggest you take a breath at "two" so you are ready to go immediately when you are live.

After your open you want to move just a bit. Everything can be distracting, so you don't want any large or exaggerated movements. Yet you must always be truthful and connected to your material. When you say, "good evening," you must fill it with subtext leading to the next story that is the lead story in the broadcast. To put it another way, "good evening" is the opening line of your first and most important story.

Teases and Bumpers

The anchor is responsible for reading almost all of the bumpers and teases. It's a good idea to know how ... and what to watch out for.

What is a TEASE?

The tease is the copy the anchor reads after completing a news block before the commercial break. This is almost always live, not pretaped. As it says, it teases what is coming up next or later in the broadcast. Often the words, "Coming up ..." or "Next ..." is the beginning or sometimes the end of the tease. Teases usually end by saying something like, "So stay with us." And they generally run ten seconds or less. A tease can be accompanied by video — so the anchor is reading over picture; or the anchor may simply be on camera reading the copy without any video. It can be a straightforward line of copy, such as:

> "A big storm is headed this way. We'll tell you about it, NEXT."

or —

> "NEXT! Wall Street was hammered today. We'll tell you the numbers."

But a tease is best when it piques the interest of the viewer. A good way to do that is with a question that hooks them:

> "Why was a homeland security inspector so interested in Sister Bridget's bottle of holy water? We'll tell you, NEXT."

But beware of the overheated tease that a producer sends to you to read. I think most people are put off with a tease that is too coy — sometimes offensively coy:

> "How many people died in the crash on Route 95 this afternoon? We'll tell you, next."

If you see that when reading through the broadcast before air, say something. Get it rewritten.

If that copy comes your way and you have not seen it, you will have to be fast on your feet to change it. And you must change something that offensive. Anything would be better:

> "A report on an accident on Route 95 coming up next."

You are the last line of defense against this sort of thing. In fact, you are the last line of defense against mistakes of all kinds, including factual mistakes and mistakes of good taste. If that doesn't mean something, this should: It is your face there.

Let me digress while on this point.

Often there will be a mistake that no one caught before airing. Say a phone number for the local Red Cross was put up on the screen because of a blood shortage in your community, but the number you read from your copy did not match the number on the screen. Someone made a mistake, of course. And it wasn't you. It may have been the graphics department or the copy editor or the writer. It does not matter. When the show producer says in your ear through the IFB that there was a mistake in the last section with a phone number, you graciously take the blame on the air.

> "Just a few minutes ago, we asked you to help the Red Cross and gave you a phone number to call. Well, we didn't make it any easier for you to help. Many of you noticed that we said one number and wrote another on the screen. Here is the right number to call. (Read number.) And we do hope you can help. Thanks for letting us know we got it mixed up."

No viewer will think less of you. In fact, the viewers appreciate that kind of acknowledgment. It does you no good and does your station no good to blame someone while you are on the air.

> "Dumb graphics department. Bunch of dopes back there."

You look small, right? If you want to be the anchor, you have to take the credit and the blame. It goes with the job.

What Is a Bumper?

A bumper literally bumps up against a commercial. It's the spacer between the last story in the block of news and the commercials. It follows the tease.

During the Iraq war, the CBS Evening News did mini-productions about soldiers who had been killed in action. They were produced with video of the soldier and graphics. The copy was pretaped and edited together.

A bumper that was popular for a while was the "Factoid" bumper. It was a fact regarding a current story. If a hurricane was the big story of the day, the bumper might show the hurricane intensity scale from one to five and the corresponding range of miles per hour.

One morning news bumper had a lively graphic that showed the word "Triskadescaphobia" with Halloween colors and wavy lines. In this case, the announcer read the copy: "Beware! Today is Friday the 13th."

At three seconds before the hour, there is a network ID, usually showing the logo of the network. That too is a bumper, but there is no copy. But it does have an important meaning for the anchor. Usually, this means, your work on air is done for the day.

The Update

Just before you close the broadcast, be sure to update a major story that was covered extensively in your broadcast, especially if it is an ongoing story. This should not be overdone. But when there is a major developing story, an update is appropriate. First, give the viewers the latest you have. Then promise to keep them updated: "We will give you more information as we learn it."

The point of this is the same as the tease. It is to keep the viewers tuned to your channel. You don't want your viewer switching to another channel's reporter to find out if there is something new happening with your story.

Close

There is an art to closing the show as well. It should be as warm as your warm open. This is a good-bye. It is what you leave your viewer with, what the viewer will take away. You don't want it to be a dismissive: "Gotta go folks." Don't fling your papers down on the desk as if you've got a hot date lined up.

A good-bye should be spoken warmly, an invitation to your viewer to return, to meet again together tomorrow. One way to do this is to soften your voice. Speaking softly offers a quiet intimacy that can be effective for good-byes. Speaking more softly than usual will draw the viewer to you.

But this does not apply all of the time. You should stay in the moment. If the last story in the broadcast is a light news kicker that makes you laugh, then laugh. If it's a sad story, that emotion should carry over into your good-bye. In other words, there are many options but all of them are sincere. Not one is perfunctory or brusque.

Double Anchoring

You may have a DOUBLE ANCHORING situation at some point sharing the desk with another anchor. I hope you do have this opportunity because it can be more fun if you get on well with

Fig. 14-3 Double anchoring.

your co-anchor. Do your best to get along with your co-anchor. If you don't, one of you will have to leave eventually and that may be you.

In every profession politics comes into play. You might as well realize it and be smart. This TV news world is a very small world. It is very competitive and everyone knows the gossip. Try hard to make it work — usually you can. If not, then protect yourself by doing the best job you can. In heated office politics, use this advice: Keep your friends close and your enemies closer.

You must respect your co-anchors and never put them down or argue with them on camera. The two of you must really become a TEAM. Find a relationship that works. Then you can tease each other and have fun in the light segments.

Contrast Is the Name of the Game

Your rhythms should be different. Don't pick up your co-anchor's pace, rhythm or intonation. You must listen to the other anchor's story just before yours. For example: If your co-anchor is telling about a plane crash and you have an airline story or even another plane crash that follows, you should note that with your segue words into your next story. Note that these may not be written into the script but you should be comfortable enough to ad-lib them to smooth the transition from your co-anchor's story.

Also at the top of your story there should be contrasting rhythms, so that the broadcast keeps moving forward and doesn't become a boring monotone. If your co-anchor doesn't pick up where he or she should, it's your job to move the broadcast along smoothly. It's bad form and viewers do not like it when one anchor chides the other on a set.

This leads to the next point: YOU SHOULD KNOW EVERY-THING that's in the script, not just your stories or your questions. You need to be familiar with the entire script.

Another contrast comes within the broadcast stories — between the end of one story and the beginning of the next. Double anchoring provides contrast automatically. If you have two or more stories in a row or you are a single anchor, you have to provide the contrasting end/beginning between the stories. One way is to use those segue words we talked about. Another is to use your hard copy. After concluding one story, slide the page in front of you off the pile. This will naturally bring your eyes down for a moment. Then glance at the next story to note for yourself what it is and then start it, bringing your eyes up to the prompter, which is, as you know, the camera. It's a natural move and makes a very strong transition.

In addition, you will catch the words of the next story, preparing you for it. Since you have read through the script beforehand, you already know the story and how you will transition into it. You won't want to do this on every story, but it makes for a defined contrast between the stories when you do.

Light News

There aren't many times during a news show when the anchor can laugh and have fun. So take advantage of it when you can. Look for moments when you can switch gears from serious to fun and become playful. This is the way the viewer can get to know and love you and see the real you. You can share the light, fun stories with your friend across the fence. The viewer will relish this. Instead of appearing so authoritative, which you need to do with the hard news, you can let loose and show your silly side.

The light news, in most news shows, is toward the end of the show. Your show begins with the hardest news then moves to the lighter, with sports, weather, entertainment and often a kicker piece to complete the evening's news program.

My Court TV students yearn to find the rare moment when they can have fun and fool around with the viewer. There are not too many. In fact they are few and far between. If you want to joke — get out of the courtroom bloke! For the anchors on Court TV, sometimes it is only during the hellos and good-byes that it is appropriate for them to manage a small, warm smile.

Smile if the Story Is Light News

Don't smile AFTER you start to speak, smile just before you begin to tell the story. Remember, the action precedes the word.

The smile accompanies the start of the words, or comes just a second before you begin talking. In life, we think and *then* speak.

Smile When You Can

Usually the tag, your good-bye (ad-libbed), is given right after the kicker, your final story for the day. What kind of smile? It depends on how the story struck you. You have hundreds of different smiles and the right one, the appropriate one, will be there for you. All it takes is being connected with the story you are telling.

There are always exceptions to our rules, and if you are updating a tragedy you don't smile on your tag . . . you knew that, right?

The Morning Shows

The morning show is always much brighter than the evening news with a lot of chitchat, interviews and light entertainment interviews. Everyone is getting ready to go to work or to school, and you are joining the family at the breakfast table. So your open is warm and your good morning is to a friend. Keep it bright and cheery.

Even if you are going to talk about serious subjects you are still happy to see your early morning regular friends. Of course there always are exceptions when there is a huge tragedy.

Point of View or Proper Attitude?

There is a continuing debate about reporters and anchors carrying a bias. They do not, for the most part, in this country. And they shouldn't. But that doesn't mean you can't have an attitude about the story you are reporting. There is a difference.

Take a rape case. How would you report it if it had happened to someone you knew? Not with a joke, certainly. Your attitude would reflect the story. You must care about the story you are reporting. That's the human element the anchor can bring. That's what makes you, as an anchor, relatable to the viewer.

Television isn't like newspapers. In journalism classes you are told not to take any side, not to have an attitude, to remain impartial. But on television you can have an attitude because you are talking directly to someone who is looking at and listening to you in the same moment that you are relaying the story. Someone who is at home, in close proximity to you, reacting to you.

Physically and emotionally your attitude must be honest as well. Your attitude will change somewhat with each story that you read. Do you tell a light story with the same seriousness you just told the rape story? Of course not. You wouldn't across that fence with your neighbor, and you don't from the anchor chair.

NANCY'S RULES

Some Final Nancy's Rules for Anchors:

BE FAMILIAR WITH THE STORIES GOING ON THAT DAY.

You must be prepared if you are handed an update during the show.

DON'T LOOK DOWN WHEN SPEAKING.

Look into the camera in a forthright manner. Eyeball the viewer through the camera.

KNOW HOW LOUDLY TO SPEAK.

Your microphone is close by. It is probably on your tie, or on your jacket lapel. Now you know why anchors like jackets. There is an easy place on your clothing that won't fall down with the weight of the lavaliere mic that is clipped on to you. A sweater or a silk shirt is pulled down by the weight of the mic.

BE PREPARED.

On the rare occasion that you are suddenly called out of the studio to cover an important breaking story, keep a pair of sneakers handy, along with clothing you'll feel comfortable wearing in the field. This won't occur too often, but when it does you must be ready to move fast.

Room Service

Remember I told you about this rule in Chapter 1? Allow me to give you some advice when you do become an anchorman or anchorwoman. Whether you are a local anchor or a network anchor, you will be well known in your community. You must be careful about your personal relationships and personal life.

Report from the Trenches

An anchor was having dinner with a "friend" at a hotel where the anchor was staying. This wasn't the first time the anchor was seen with this "friend." Tongues were wagging. They had been seen departing in the elevator together often after dining in the hotel. It finally got into the local newspaper gossip column. A veteran colleague of the young anchor read the gossip item and sent off a note with the following advice:

I have two words of advice: Room service.

In other words, you are going to be something of a celebrity — certainly well known. You are vulnerable, so keep your private life private.

Nancy's Bedtime Story

You know the story of Cinderella and her ugly stepsisters. Those two stepsisters went to the ball to nab the Prince/News Director.

They all wanted to become the princess ... the anchor. They put on all sorts of acts to charm Prince/News Director Charming.

The Prince/News Director knew right away that these phonies were not the real thing. A little later in the evening Cinderella crashed the ball and wowed the prince and got the anchor job. She wasn't rich, she didn't wear a thousand dollar dress. What mattered to the Prince/News Director was that inside, Cinderella was the real thing. She was smart, likable, neat in her appearance and she was vulnerable and a risk taker. Did the shoe that Prince/News Director Charming had for her fit? Yes it did.

Checklist

❐ Practice the prompter (See CD-Rom).

Become comfortable with:

Headlines.
Opens.
Teases.
Bumpers.
Updates.
Closes.
Double anchoring.
Always be prepared.
Room service.

Exercise for Subtext and Intentions

When telling a news story, or asking questions, always use subtext or intention.

It is not only the words you use, but it's also the intentions you choose.

The intentions are HOW you ask the questions.

In real life you are always using intentions but you are not conscious of them.

Here's an exercise on intentions that my students enjoy.

You'll need that good friend to help you. Tell them to, "Open the window." Use those three words, no more no less.

Those are the only words you can use for this exercise.

Now tell them to sit still until they must move, because of the force and strength in the way you play your intention, when saying those words. They should not make it easy for you. They should not get up right away after you ask them the first time. "OPEN THE WINDOW."

Use just these three words, no more.

Order them to OPEN THE WINDOW.

Scold them to OPEN THE WINDOW.

Entice them to OPEN THE WINDOW.

Share a secret to OPEN THE WINDOW.

By imagining an *active verb*, you will find your intention becomes clearer and the result of your exercise becomes stronger. An active verb implies just what it says: You are taking action toward another person.

Tease, sympathize, lash out, needle, cajole, taunt, mock, invite, encourage, excite or sell them on the idea to OPEN THE WINDOW. The words remain the same, but the intention changes. And when you speak in order to affect another person (in this case, your viewer) you suddenly have instant subtext.

Once you become aware of this you will notice how you use intentions in your life. This is also a good technique to employ when you speak your opens and closes. You might be sharing a secret with your viewer, or teasing or exciting them about your open or close. Make your choice and try it on, "OPEN THE WINDOW."

15 Hosting

Hosting encompasses a parade of jobs including hosting parades. The skills needed as a television host are pretty much the same no matter what the hosting job; but the job can vary from announcing a hot air balloon named Kermit to announcing a hottie in a bathing suit.

Talk show hosts are usually in a studio, either seated in a living room–type set or standing in the audience. They can be Oprah on couches or serious news hosts at a desk. Or they can be afternoon syndicated shows where the host urges on some outrageous interview, often with audience participation.

They can be late-night comics or Sunday morning preachers.

And on cable, the music outlets like MTV and VH1 produce programs that require hosts for awards programs, pageants and major music productions.

Hosts for Lee Rolontz's programs at VH1 need the same basic skills that all hosts need. She shared her thoughts with me to help you learn what it takes.

What do you look for in a host?

"The first thing I look for — and it depends on the type of project — but certainly you want some kind of dynamic on-camera personality — meaning someone who is inviting and engaging."

Fig. 15-1 Lee Rolontz. COURTESY OF VH1

What are the skills a host should have? The skills of the VH1 host are the same skills of any good host, without the music. Listen to what Lee has to say:

> "A good host definitely has a relationship with the camera ... number one. If you don't have that, you can't be an on-camera host. A host has to have interviewing skills ... because interviewing always comes into play for a host eventually."

By interviewing, Lee means listening and responding. They are crucial for a sharp host doing a top-drawer job.

> "If you're not a good listener, even if you are hosting a pageant, you're not listening to what's going on — you are not going to be natural."

W Miller

Fig. 15-2 Inviting and engaging.

Listening forces you to stay natural and keeps you from self-consciousness. You have to be very in the moment. Another skill: You must be comfortable thinking fast on your feet. You must have the ability to grasp the subject, so you'll never be at a loss for words.

Lee gave me an example:

> "There is an amazing host over at MTV, he does it every day ... he is tremendously knowledgeable and can ad-lib at any point ... so especially if you are doing something LIVE, which is more difficult than taping where you can retape — to have someone who can ask questions or come up with commentary that is unique to him, that is fantastic."

What other skills should a host have?

"You have to know how to speak well and know how to speak at a pace that is proper ... some people speak too fast, some people speak too slow."

(NOTE TO STUDENTS: You want the Goldilocks' pace: just right.)

Other skills Lee required in a host:

You must have a well-trained voice. Not too high, not squeaky and well modulated.

You must have a clear definition of who you are in front of that camera.

You must have a speech with no impediments.

Be a Type

People are looking for types: The nerdy guy with superior knowledge, the smart and pretty girl, the smart guy, the fat girl, the old balding guy, the funny girl ... if you know you are a type, let it shine through.

"Sometimes you look at a tape," says Lee, "and you think, 'she's too pretty.' Maybe what you should do is be really pretty but also down to earth."

 ## Report from the Trenches

As luck would have it, when I was in Lee's office on Broadway in New York City, she was in the process of looking for somebody to host a music show. I asked her what she was going through.

"It's a music-based show, so the idea is to find someone who knows about music and maybe is a little bit of a celebrity so we could get something written about the show. We think about people who LOVE music because it is about older music.

So we are thinking about people like Jimmy Fallon, Jack Black ... celebrities who know music. But we would go with someone who really knew music, was an expert in music over a celebrity who didn't know music."

Sometimes Lee will choose personality over knowledge. In that case, she will get a strong writer and producer to work with that host. "Hopefully they have some sort of intelligence so you can coax them into knowing more."

Age Range

As to age range, this may surprise you: It's not so important.

"Here at VH1 we might go pretty old for a host —40s, mid-40s. At this channel our median age is 30 ... so we try to go around that age. But sometimes there is a younger person who is just great or an older person who is just great — it really depends on the subject."

VH1 has two regular hosts with whom Lee works. One is a woman, the other a man. The young woman had been with the cable broadcaster a long time. She came from "Much Music," which is a music channel in Canada. What makes her so good?
"She's adorable and pretty and smart."
VH1's other host is also from Canada. He honed his hosting skills on a daily Morning Show in Canada. (VH1 seems to like Canadians.) What makes him good?
"He is very knowledgeable about music ... and a smart guy."

What About Smart? What About Funny?

If you are bright, says Lee, don't hide it.

"You can have the broadcast news not-so-smart hosts and coax them, but the better hosts are the ones that are smarter."

Funny is good too.

"I like funny, but I'm in entertainment. If I was at a hard news channel, I don't know if funny is appropriate. For us, we like someone who is charming and engaging and also funny is great for us because we are light, we do entertainment."

Should I Get an Agent?

How does someone in Lee's position find the hosts she uses, I wondered. Are agents the answer? Yes, there are many agencies, she says. At her shop, there is a person on staff who does only on-air talent.

In Lee's entertainment world, the top dogs are the shows with the red carpets.

"When you get into award shows, that is a whole other level of hosting." Here Lee looks for someone with knowledge of the subject or a recognizable celebrity — or both.

But what about you — my students? Would Lee use someone who didn't have a track record or an agent yet? Would she even look at their reel? Yes, again.

"We do look at a lot of ingénues . . . and young people to train. You need to look at people all the time. We do look at people with no track record because we are trying to mold people. Some shows use people who are right out of college — most people go to college."

How To Get There

Here is what Lee is looking for.

"Hopefully they've done something in school — or there is a fake newscast . . . it's much better to have something on tape. They do have a terrific training system at MTV, which takes them through test runs, helping them — they have a whole department for that because they have a news division."

If you are presenting yourself to MTV or VH1, you don't want to be seen sitting at an anchor desk on your reel. Do a report on something that interests you and something you know about. Do a short documentary or commentary about your home town, she suggests. Promote your personality.

"What we look for is great personality in any setting that makes them feel comfortable. So they don't have to be sitting down and say here's the way I do the news — anything that excites them that shows them off the best way."

And Lee says your face is OK, no matter what you look like. Ethnic is in.

"In this time in America where it's no longer a white person's world the way it was 50 years ago ... any sort of combination of ethnicity is fantastic. Because it does represent who we are and what we are looking at."

But, she cautions, don't have too heavy an accent. You can look different, that's good. But you can't sound so different that you are hard to understand. "It's really hard if you can't understand what they say."

NANCY'S RULES

When something unexpected or newsworthy occurs during your event, DO NOT IGNORE IT.

OK, let's talk turkey. Or let's talk a hosting trap that occurred on turkey day. It was the Macy's Thanksgiving Day Parade marching

merrily along down Broadway on a windy November day in
New York in 2005. The featured hosts back then were the usually terrific crew from the *Today Show*: Katie Couric, Matt Lauer
and Al Roker.

Here's what happened.

Report from the Trenches

The M&M balloons were approaching Times Square when a rogue
gust of wind picked them up and pitched them over the heads of the
crowd stretching along Broadway. One of the ropes hooked around
a light pole and ripped the light head off. That heavy lamp came
crashing down onto the sidewalk, clobbering members of a family
from Albany, New York.

The accident, which injured but did not kill any of the parade
viewers, happened about 11:30 in the morning. The M&M balloons
were pulled out of the parade and did not arrive at Herald Square,
the end of the parade route. But instead of reporting what happened, NBC rolled file tape of the balloons from the parade a
year earlier and the hosts continued with the chatty (and ghastly)
prescripted copy.

"Will these classic candymen get out of this delicious dilemma?"
wondered Al Roker. MISTAKE!

How Should I Handle a Curve Ball?

If that had been said over the live pictures of the bleeding children,
you would have been rightly shocked. As it was, the words danced
sprightly over the file tape showing none of the real trouble. But
the children were bleeding. It was, I guess, a delicious dilemma, but
you, my student, would not say that, would you? I didn't think so.

These hosts worked for the *Today Show*, a news organization.
You cannot ignore news. The accident was all over the local news

radio stations and on the other local stations but not a word about it from these NBC hosts. Can you say credibility gap?

This occurred near the end of the parade and near the end of NBC's broadcast and that may have been why it went unreported. But it's no excuse. The NBC public relations people did not explain why it went unreported. But someone must have known of the incident. If the producer knew and didn't tell the hosts, then the hosts should be furious. They looked like idiots chatting goofy copy over file of balloons while people were lying in the streets injured from an accident caused by those balloons.

If the hosts did know, but decided to ignore the information, they made an even more glaring mistake. They looked bad in any case.

Host with Grace

To compare this situation to another hosting performance is instructive. Ignoring a news event as a host would have cost the viewing public one of the finest performances ever in the history of television broadcasting.

 ## Report from the Trenches

Jim McKay, a sports host working on the 1972 Summer Olympics in Munich, Germany, could have ignored the terrorist takeover of the Israeli team housing and continued chatting about the javelin throw or the U.S. swimmers. Instead, McKay moved gracefully from a sports host to the world's host of a breaking news event.

Host McKay detailed the killing of two Israeli athletes and the kidnapping of nine others. In the end, after a gun battle between the police and the terrorists, all the kidnapped Israeli athletes were killed and McKay said simply, "They're all gone."

If you get to the Museum of Broadcasting in New York, you can view this remarkable broadcasting moment. If you want to learn how to be a host when a curve ball is thrown at you, you should watch Jim McKay's fine work.

I repeat: When something unexpected or newsworthy occurs during your event, DO NOT IGNORE IT.

You cannot ignore the crash of the balloons on the parade or the crash of a light stand at a concert or a terrorist attack at a sporting event. This is not just for your own credibility but much more important, for your viewers.

Opens and Closes

One thing to keep in mind that will help: If you are an outgoing person, and I suspect you are or you wouldn't be getting into this business, then think of yourself as hosting a dinner party. You greet your guests, you entertain them and you say good-bye at the end. How you do this does matter.

You need a grabber of an open when you introduce your guest and your show to the viewer. (I have more about this in the anchoring chapter.) When you are the host for your own show, you must bring to your open more than just your personality. You must envelop the viewers so they become intrigued and want to continue in your company, even if they must sit through several commercials.

It is not enough to state that, "This is a very interesting woman." You should make the viewers think, "Gee, this sounds like an interesting woman." You might ask the viewer a question: "How would you like the opportunity to spend the weekend with Tom Hanks at his house or hang out with Julia Roberts at her place?" They would be thinking (if they are at all normal), "Yes I would." The question will immediately bring the audience where you want them to be: Involved with you in a conversation.

Then you introduce your guest who did spend time with those two stars. You are in fact telling the audience what's interesting about your guest by involving them immediately. You are telling them why they should stay and watch this show for the next thirty minutes.

The same is true of your good-byes. You want a strong close. Now that you have the viewers' interest, since they watched your fascinating show, you need to retain their loyalty. You don't want to let them leave, never to return again. Ideally you want to tease the upcoming show as specifically as possible. If you don't know what will be in your next show, be sure to close with your warmest adios so your viewers will want to visit you next time. You need to retain your base viewership and hopefully increase it. Your viewers are your guests. Treat them with generous hospitality and you will never lose them.

Checklist

A host should:

- ☐ Be dynamic on camera.
- ☐ Be a good listener.
- ☐ Have a well-trained voice.
- ☐ Promote your personality or type.
- ☐ Be prepared to handle a surprise while live.

Exercises for Opens and Closes for Hosting

Exercise for Opens

Choose a name for your own talk show. Make it snappy or have it say something about your show.

Choose a variety of fields. To practice, interview friends with different interests. This is an exercise, so use several different people to stretch your skills. Write three introductions for each guest: Make them different, keep them short, be imaginative.

Have fun with this. By doing this you will find the most exciting way to grab your viewer.

Find what will interest the viewers so they don't change channels before the interview starts.

Exercises for Closes

The close comes after you have thanked your guest for appearing on your show. Like the open, it is spoken to the viewer directly into the camera. It is a one-shot of you.

The close should be short. It is an invitation back even if it is a thanks for watching. It might tease the upcoming next show. But it is never a perfunctory, "Gotta go folks. I've got a hot date." It is a warm good-bye, and, as I said, an invitation to please return to this channel and watch the show next week, even if you don't use those words. These words are the subtext.

Try three different closes: One quite short, one a bit longer, one where you tease your next week's program.

Vocal and Physical Technique

Once you've learned how to recognize and put together a riveting story and interview, then you must ask yourself: How do I tell it in front of the camera? This is such a competitive business, in order to land the job and to move ahead to the next bigger job, you must sound and look your best on camera.

Not everything in this section will apply to everyone, but all of you will benefit from some of it. I have divided this section into three chapters: The Voice Itself, Techniques for a Good Reading, and Physical Techniques.

So let's begin.

16

The Voice Itself

I'll start with your voice. I'm going to teach you to become aware of what you can do to improve your voice: Its pitch, its tone and its resonance. I'll give you some narration-reading techniques so your viewer will stay with you.

But you must be realistic when dealing with your voice. You don't want to become self-conscious or embarrassed. As you try new ways of using your voice, that can happen. Many of my students are shy about it. So accept the fact that you will probably feel a little strange when you start to use these techniques as your voice becomes richer and more resonant. Be willing to try your best. Practice these techniques always out loud and loudly. When possible use a tape recorder so you can play it back and hear the new adjustments in your vocal technique.

One thing more: Just like any other skill, the more you exercise your voice, the more natural it will become. It's just like your physical workout at the gym. Your body and your brain become familiar with the weights, the exercises and the routines.

If you are an anchor, your voice is about 70% of what you'll be using on air. That means that your voice is most of your identity on air. So ask yourself: Does my voice express what I need it to, no matter what the subject or situation? Is it authoritative and credible? Is it one that people will listen to? Is it the one that people will WANT to listen to? The answers to these questions must be YES.

Your voice will help grab the viewers' attention and hold their interest. How you express yourself vocally is of the utmost importance.

A person's voice is like a thumbprint. It is unique to you, and only to you. You probably have retained some of your family and local idiosyncrasies, but still your voice is your own. You've added your own self to it. No one else sounds exactly the way you do.

Know Your Flaws

Now is a good time to ask yourself: What does my voice sound like? You should record something, it doesn't matter what, but a good plan would be to read some copy aloud. If you don't have a script, read a newspaper article. Listen to your voice carefully and critically. Note where it is weak. Be honest, not harsh.

Next, you should pay close attention to the speech patterns of the speakers you love to listen to — that includes both on television and in films. Ask yourself: What is it about their voices that I love? Is it a high voice or a low voice? Is it an unusual or husky voice? Note whether he or she speaks quickly, or slowly. Note the pace. Especially on television news, note how it changes inside a story, and from story to story.

There are professors and friends of yours who rivet you when they tell a story. Note what they do. They use words and rhythms in speech, in a way that is appropriate to the subject matter. They never drone on . . . and on . . . and on. They sound vibrant. They are interested and connected to what they are talking about. They are excited by it, and as you listen to them, so are you.

Can you remember the first time you heard yourself on an audio-tape? You may have cringed and said, "This doesn't sound at all like me." In a way this may have been true. Many tape recorders are of such poor quality that they make the voice sound quite strange; but it may not have been the tape's fault. You probably just never thought about your voice. You may have had no idea what you sounded like to others.

Consequently, it is more than the way you use the words and the rhythms. It is also the TONE and the RESONANCE of your voice. By resonance, I mean the timbre of your voice — it should not sound thin and weak, nor should it get lost in the back of your throat. No one wants to listen to a squeaky little girl's voice. (It is rare that a voice is too resonant but it can get so deep that it is difficult to understand.)

You do not want to sock your audience with a thick Southern or New York accent. If this sounds like you at all, then by all means get to work on that aspect of your voice and speech.

It's not as hard as you fear. It will take practice but it is something that can be done. Do not be discouraged. Once your voice and speech are as good as you can make them, you'll feel confident and be able to handle both the copy and your job better.

What about the quality of the tone of your voice? Your voice is one of your essential tools. The name "Television" could really be "Audio-vision." That is how much weight sound in general means in television and, in this case, the sound of your voice means. If you subtract the voice from your on-camera presentation, there wouldn't be much left.

I'm going to give you the exercises and techniques to improve your tone and your resonance. For those who want further and more detailed explanations there are many books on the voice. Our job together is to get that voice of yours in the best shape possible for your on-camera work.

Is This You?

Your voice should draw the viewer toward it. If you have a high, squeaky, immature voice, or a nasal one, or one that is stuck in the back of your throat, you need to fix it.

The most prevalent problem that many of my students face is either a voice that sounds too high or one that requires more resonance. The high, thin voice is usually initially caused by tension exacerbated by inadequate breathing.

Breathing

I hear you saying, "Nancy, I've breathed all my life. What's there to learn?"

Lots.

When you were a baby, you breathed correctly. You breathed with your diaphragm. Now you have to learn to breathe properly again. Again? Well, yes. You used to do it right, before all the problems of life started to tense you up. This bad breathing habit starts at a very young age. You need to have enough breath to speak for an extended time without taking lots of short breaths that will chop up your copy and make it difficult to be understood by your viewer.

Most adults breathe with their upper chest. Your lungs extend all the way down, almost to your diaphragm. Your diaphragm is

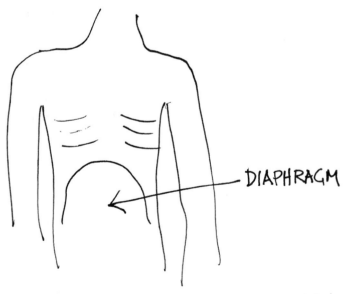

Fig. 16-1 Your diaphragm.

the muscle just above your waist and just below your bottom rib. You can feel your lowest rib, and you can feel your diaphragm muscle. It is not your stomach. You should breathe using your diaphragm.

When you breathe, air is drawn into your lungs. Your lungs are enclosed within your rib cage and as the air enters, the size of the rib cage is somewhat increased. That increase, which you feel, because your ribs move up and outward, is brought about by the expansion of your lungs, which press against the diaphragm forcing it to expand outward.

Tension

When you don't have enough breath, it's because you have taken the breath only into the upper part of your lungs. You have not completely filled your lungs with air, starting all the way from the bottom. You want to breathe in through your nose. As you speak, the air will be expelled through your mouth. In order to speak, if you do not take a full breath, you will end up relying too much on your throat and upper chest. When you have only the shallow breath, all the work is being done around your vocal cords. As a result, you lose that resonance you want.

Remember also, if one part of your body is tense, the rest will follow. You cannot produce a rich and relaxed sounding voice through a mountain of tension. So you must learn to relax and to have your breath support your voice in a manner that is as free of tension as possible. This is why you must learn to breathe using your diaphragm.

Usually people tense up when they are nervous. Your voice will never be rich as it can be until you breathe without raising your shoulders. This is particularly true when you take in a large breath before saying a long sentence.

If you doubt that you ever breathed using your diaphragm, try this: Go look in a mirror and take a deep breath. See if your shoulders move up toward your neck when you take the breath. If so, you know you are not breathing with your diaphragm.

Lie down on the floor and RELAX. Take a heavy book, your backpack or a heavy purse and place it on your waist. Take a few deep breaths. You will see the book moving up and down. Your diaphragm is doing the moving. Your shoulders will be completely relaxed; they will not have moved at all. This is how you breathe when you are totally relaxed. Now place one hand gently on your diaphragm and breathe easily. Place the fingers of your other hand on the side of your ribs. Become aware of your body and how your breath is moving. Breathe in through your nose and out through your mouth. There should be absolutely no shoulder tension or movement.

Now speak out loud. Say "Ahh." Say "Hello Nancy." How does your voice sound as you breathe properly? It won't be perfect yet, but there will be a definite change. It will sound lower than when you were standing up and taking shallow breaths using your upper chest.

In order to breathe properly and acquire a riveting speaking voice, you must have the ability to relax in a pressure filled situation. Psychological tension often brings about physical tension. Your focus and absorption in your work helps. So does relaxation, along with relaxed breathing. Many of my students and clients were never aware of how much tension they carried around with them until we started our work.

Exercises

In my classes, I have found that exercises are an integral part of learning about your voice. In these exercises, when using your voice or when asked to speak out loud, always do it BIG, LARGE AND LOUD. Do not be embarrassed or shy when doing the exercises. Do not do them for the microphone. These are exercises that you must FEEL AND HEAR.

One of your challenges will be to lose your long-entrenched bad habits and replace them with new, good habits. You must make some changes in your voice. I need to say that, for some people,

W Miller

Fig. 16-2 You can't work on camera with tension.

this is very scary. Good. That means you are aware that a change is coming. That change will be good for you.

If you are used to speaking with a small, high, breathy voice, it may feel uncomfortable to change to a lower, more authoritative voice. It may be threatening to you. It also may threaten some of those people who are close to you. They will suddenly feel you are someone to contend with. You will sound more like a take-charge person. It will, of course, sound sexier as well.

Anything new feels uncomfortable at first. But after a short time you will start to enjoy it. It will feel as much like you as the other voice that you lived with for so many years. So be brave. Make this change for the better. Your new rich voice will make your present life richer . . . I promise. It will also help your on-camera career.

So, commit yourself fully. I assure you this will not take too long. I have seen these exercises work on some of my students'

W Miller

Fig. 16-3 So relax.

voices in a few days, and for others in a few weeks. But you must work at it regularly and put in the necessary time each day for the exercises.

As I've said before and will again: To breathe correctly and to speak well, you must be relaxed. That is how we will begin.

Relaxation Exercises

Exercise 1

Standing with your feet comfortably apart, flop over from the waist (see Fig. 16.4). Be sure to bend your knees a bit. Keep your neck loose. Bounce the upper part of your body gently up and down — not fast, but easily. Be sure to let gravity pull your head and neck toward the floor.

While in this position, speak the deep vowel sound: AAAAH. Try to keep it in the lower range. Say it several times deeply and relaxed. AAAAH. Try even lower: AAAAH.

Simultaneously, while expelling this low, easy vowel sound, swing your body from side to side allowing your arms to swing

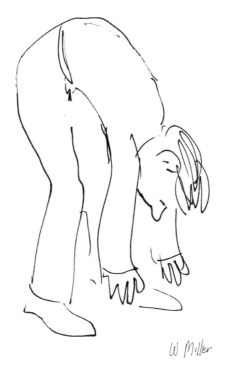

W Miller

Fig. 16-4 Relaxation exercise.

loosely. It will help if you can get a partner to work with you. Let the partner place a hand on either side of your back and move you from side to side while you are vocalizing your AAAAH.

Then have your partner tap your back with some strength, but not painfully, while you bark out HAH HAH HAH, like a dog. Do this with great energy, loudly and in a deep tone. You will be able to feel your diaphragm moving. These sounds may sound strange, perhaps a bit primitive, and they should come pouring out of you due to the movement of your torso. That's OK.

Now stand up slowly, uncurling your entire body, beginning from your hips, then your waist, next your shoulders, and finally raising your head. Do this smoothly, in very slow motion.

Exercise 2

Standing, drop your head from the neck and release the tension in your neck, letting gravity pull your head down. Now roll your head slowly in a circle, in one continuous motion. Your head is now dropping toward the floor, next you roll it to one side, then to the back, and then to the other side. Your head shouldn't go too far to the back, only as far as it is comfortable. (Remember this is about relaxation.)

Then reverse your direction. Roll your head to the other side slowly in a circle and return to the front again.

Do this exercise four times in each direction. And don't forget to KEEP BREATHING throughout all of the exercises.

Exercise 3

Separate your feet so that you are standing in a comfortable position. Stretch your arms and body to the ceiling while breathing in. Let your fingertips reach for the ceiling. Stand on tiptoes if you can to make the stretch taller.

Then come down off your toes, slowly letting your arms float down, as you breathe out. Your legs can bend a bit. You don't want to keep your knees locked.

All your relaxation exercises must be performed easily and slowly, without any swift, jerky movements.

Breathing Exercises

OK. You are now somewhat relaxed. We are ready to continue with your breathing exercises.

Exercise 4

This gets more difficult. You are going to replicate the same action you accomplished so easily lying down on the floor with a heavy object placed on your waist. If you are seated, stand up slowly.

Standing, you are going to press the tips of your fingers onto your diaphragm. This will be just beneath your lowest rib, with your hand facing your body. Take a deep breath and feel your diaphragm move outward, and slightly downward. There may be some movement in your stomach as well, but the diaphragm is what we are searching for here. You should also feel air entering the bottom part of your lungs. Feel your lungs fill up as this air fills your lungs from the bottom to the top.

NANCY'S RULES

DO NOT move your shoulders up toward your neck and ears. Keep your shoulders down and relaxed.

This is the hardest part. If you can, ask someone to help out. Have your partner place both hands on your shoulders in order to help you keep your shoulders down, in a relaxed position. You don't want the shoulders to work their way upward as you practice breathing.

If you listen to anchors or reporters using their voices well, you'll realize how their flow continues without taking a breath for what seems like quite a long time. For those of you who say I never have enough breath, try this.

Exercise 5

Blow out all your breath. I mean all of it, as much as you can. Then start talking. HelloNancyhowareyouIamfine etc. Continue talking without stopping as long as possible. You'll discover that you still have breath and when you really don't have any more left, the breath you require will simply enter your body. There will be no need for you to inhale a large breath of air.

You don't have to take a breath. The air will naturally enter into your lungs. Nature abhors a vacuum.

Exercise 6

Take a full quick breath. Use your diaphragmatic breathing. Count to 10 aloud, using up all your breath by the end of your 10 count.

W Miller

Fig. 16-5 Try to count to 50.

Now take another breath. Fill your lungs, bottom to top. Stay comfortable. Now count to 15 out loud, not in a whisper. Increase the numbers by five each time. My students in a day or two can reach 50.

Exercise 7

Here is your next controlled breathing exercise. This is a stanza from Gilbert and Sullivan's operetta *The Pirates of Penzance.*

I am the very model of a modern Major General.
I've information vegetable animal and mineral, I know the Kings of
    England, and
I quote the fights historical,
From Marathon to Waterloo, in order categorical;
I'm very well acquainted too with matters mathematical,
I understand equations, both the simple and quadratic

About binomial theorems I'm teeming with a lot of news
With many cheerful facts about the square of the hypotenuse.
I'm very good at integral and differential calculus,
I know the scientific names of beings animalcules;
In short, in matters vegetable, animal and mineral,
I am the very model of a modern Major General.
(by W.S. Gilbert)

The exercise is to see how much of this patter you can say in a normal speaking voice in one breath. Remember your relaxed new method of breathing.

Take a good swift breath. Say the words as quickly and clearly as possible. See how far you can go before you have to breathe again. If your breath runs out, finish on a second or third breath, then try again. Once you become comfortable with the words, you will be able to proceed much further into this speech on a single breath. You may join the roster of students who can speak this entire piece on a single intake of air. But don't worry if you can't. The main point of this exercise is to maximize the use of your breath and to practice breathing properly. You will never have to perform these exercises in public. And be assured, you will never have to read copy this long in one breath.

Breathy Voice

When some people speak, they exhale too much breath on their sound. This is true of both men and women. The term *breathy* is easy to identify. Think of Marilyn Monroe, or Marlon Brando in *The Godfather*. If you feel you are in this group, here are two exercises that will take care of the problem. You must use your ears and listen carefully to the changes in the sound of your voice as you perform these exercises.

Exercise 8

Stand in a doorway. Think of the strongman Samson. Place your hands on either side of the doorjamb at about your shoulder level or just below.

Fig. 16-6 Stand in a doorway.

Make sure you feel fairly comfortable. Now press outward against the jamb with as much strength as you can muster. Speak loudly, but don't shout. If you are doing this correctly your voice should sound clear and not breathy.

Exercise 9

Sit in a chair with a hard seat and sit up straight with good posture. Let your arms fall straight down from your shoulders. Grab beneath your chair seat on either side, with both hands, and pull your seat upward against your bottom with all your might. While you are pulling speak with energy, loudly but not shouting.

Each of these exercises fulfills the identical purpose. Each can rid your voice of that gentle breathy quality. Try them both. See which works best for you.

Fig. 16-7 Grab your seat.

Resonance and Tone Exercises

Now that you understand the importance of relaxation and breathing properly, let's move on to exercises to improve the quality and resonance of your voice. Your entire body is a resonator, but the main areas are your nose (nasal sound), the front of your face and cheeks, the front of your mouth and your upper chest.

Exercise 10

After a few minutes of breathing correctly, try this. You will need a mirror.

W Miller

Fig. 16-8 Yawn.

Still standing, open your mouth wide. Yawn. Don't pretend to yawn. This must be a real wide yawn.

On the exhale of the yawn, sigh a long, vocalized, loud AAAAH. Go from a high pitch to a low pitch. Listen to where the sound takes you. It will probably be a pretty deep sound if you are relaxed. Put one hand on your chest so you can feel the vibrations.

Now, with that mirror you have, hold it in front of your face when you yawn to make sure you are opening your mouth wide enough. You may not be able to see yourself as you actually yawn. Here is something interesting — most people can't prevent their eyes from closing at the instant the yawn occurs. Do this several times feeling the vibrations of it in your chest.

Exercise 11
Still standing, keeping your lips together but relaxed, take a proper breath. Use your diaphragm. Don't let your shoulders rise up. Hum

loudly on a low comfortable tone. MMMMMMM MMMMMMM MMMMMMMM. Do this a few times. Feel the vibrations begin to tickle your lips. If you wish, you can lightly place your forefinger against both your lips and you can feel the vibrations with your finger. To improve your voice, you are using two of your senses: Hearing and feeling.

As soon as you hear a smooth rich humming sound as you say your MMMMMMM and the tickle on your lips feels strong, drop your jaw, open your mouth. As your mouth opens wide you should switch smoothly from the MMMM sound in your closed-mouth position, to an open-mouthed AAAAH sound.

Use your mirror again to make sure that your mouth is really staying open and not just open a tiny bit. Often my students think they are opening their mouths and dropping their jaws but they are not. Their lips are barely parted. The teeth should be more than an inch apart. Your tongue should rest flat on the floor of your mouth. The back of your throat should be open and your soft palate should be raised. You should feel relaxed, with no tension. Hold on to the AAAAH sound — let it be fairly loud. Don't keep it a secret.

Let the AAAAH flow as long as you can support it. Support it with your breath. Listen to the rich deep tone. This exercise releases two of your main resonators from the tension. Those two where tension most often occurs are at the jaw and at the place where the mouth and throat connect.

Exercise 12

This is an exercise to make you aware of your HEAD TONES. Practice this very loudly and with great energy. Though you may not LIKE the sounds, you will begin to FEEL the sound and you will learn how to control it. Your voice won't be catch as catch can. This is known as negative training — when you exaggerate the things you want to stop doing, they will start to be under your control. Negative training moves you toward a very positive result.

Choose a few paragraphs from a newspaper or a magazine. Read the first paragraph in the highest, squeakiest and loudest voice that you can manage. Think of a bad opera singer. Think Minnie Mouse.

You may feel foolish. It doesn't matter, take the risk. Think that you are a daring child. There's nothing to lose but your ineffectual voice. This voice that you are squeaking out is called the head voice, or the head tones. Get to know this sound, because this voice is one you will never want to use on camera.

Exercise 13

Now I want you to examine another tone you do not want. NASAL TONES. Gently place a finger on one side of your nose. Scrunch up your nose. Read the next paragraph out loud. Make it sound as nasal as you can. Lean hard and loud on all the M, N and NG sounds to increase the nasality.

As you continue reading energetically in this second obnoxious voice, you should be able to feel with that finger the vibrations of the sound in your nose.

 Report from the Trenches

For years on New York radio, the owner of an investment firm did his own commercials. He spoke about how you could trust his firm over others. But his voice was one of those off-putting "Noo Yawk" accents with nasal and head tones that you are now familiar with.

I always wondered how he could do those commercials with that voice. How good could his judgment be? If he was so lacking in judgment about doing a voice commercial with that voice, how good could his investment choices be? Maybe his firm was terrific, I don't know. But it became a credibility question for me and, no doubt, for others.

If this is your tone, get to work to eliminate it. You don't want to sound like that.

Exercise 14

I want to get back to tones you *do* want. Like FORWARD TONES.

Do that humming we worked on earlier. Keep your lips loosely closed and relaxed. With energy hum the sound, MMMMMMM in a low tone. Put your finger gently against your lips as you are humming. You will feel the vibrations. This is the start of your rich resonant FORWARD TONE. A rich forward tone is the one you want for your work on camera.

Exercise 15

Other good tones are CHEST TONES.

Place your palm flat on your upper chest. Take a breath and say in a low pitch, but with a great amount of energy, HAAA HAAA several times. Hold on to the vowel and don't allow the ending of each HAAA to become soft and lose its energy and impetus. You need to feel the vibrations. These are your chest tones. You can hear them, and you can also feel them. It should be a lovely deep sound.

I hope you understand now why hearing as well as feeling are your guides as you work on improving and changing your voice and your bad speech patterns.

Exercise 16

When you feel comfortable with all of this, lets try to combine the forward tone with your chest tones.

Start humming. Feel the vibrations on your lips. Segue into speaking the AHHH sound. Place your hand flat on your chest. Start bringing some of those rich chest tones into your sound. Feel the vibrations on your hand from your chest. Say Hello several times. Draw out tones. Lean on the vowels. Now read a paragraph. Hold it up with your free hand. Listen to your sound. Get used to it. Listen intensely to what your voice sounds like. The point is to blend both sounds, your forward tone and your chest tone. Listen to yourself.

Try using different amounts of both forward and chest tones. You may decide you want a little less chest tone, or a little more. You'll hear your voice become higher and lighter, or deeper and sexier. Play around with this. Listen for clarity of tone and resonance. See which combination sounds best for you. When you've found the sound that pleases you, that is the sound you should practice for your on-camera work.

Even better, make sure your tape recorder is running. You should be encouraged by the large change in your voice in the relatively short time it has taken to perform these exercises. Of course you must keep practicing so this new voice becomes second nature, and you can use it under the pressure of performing.

Reading Exercises

Exercise 17

As you begin to feel solid with the low tonal sounds of the HAAAA HAAAA, and are comfortable using your chest tones, keep that identical tone placement, and read a paragraph with this new rich sound.

Be sure to continue to stand, to use your good posture, and continue to breathe correctly. Hold the paragraph up high enough so you are able to read it in your standing position without bending your neck and head downward. You don't want to create any unwanted tension by pressing the chin down against your vocal cords.

Don't be concerned with making sense out of your reading. Your voice will probably sound monotonously like chanting in the beginning. But soon, you will discover that deeper, richer speaking sound that you want. You can't expect to work on everything at one time. Now you are just working with tone and resonance. Ideally you will not want your voice too low, and you want to take care that it doesn't start to sound muffled or that it is not gurgling, or making a frying sound in your throat.

Optimum Pitch Exercises

There is still one more important exercise that will help you to uncover your special resonance and tone. Since everybody has a different voice, you want to find your own personal optimum pitch.

That means the pitch of your voice that is the most natural, and that has the clearest amount of resonance as you speak. This exercise combined with the ones above should be of great help improving the quality of your voice.

Listening is the most important aspect in discovering the ideal placement of your voice pitch. Be aware that your normal speaking voice, your habitual pitch, may well be your optimum pitch. So when practicing this exercise, don't push too hard. I don't want you to hurt your vocal cords. Having said that, let's begin carefully.

Exercise 18

Stand against a wall, with your feet comfortably apart, but not too far. During this exercise, try very hard to press the back of your neck against the wall, keeping your head straight. Of course your neck is not made to do this, but try to keep pushing to touch the wall with the back of your neck. This is very important for this exercise to work.

Now, stretch your arm out in front of your body, as if you want to touch the opposite wall, and raise it slightly above your eye level. Start to count loudly. Start with the number one. Number one will be your highest head tone. Lower your hand slightly on each succeeding number. Let your hand guide your sound. As you lower your hand, intone a lower note. Catch yourself if you hear that you are singing a scale. You must SPEAK in descending pitches. Beware that you are not SINGING the notes. For this exercise to work, you must talk the notes and not sing them.

Exaggerate the vowel sound in each number you speak, lowering your hand slightly as you say it. Your hand will help to guide you to control your pitch. The number two is the next pitch down. It is still high, but a pitch lower than you spoke at number one. Number three is lower than two and so on.

Don't forget; keep pressing the back of your neck toward the wall. Let your voice hold on to the vowel in each number. Let the numbers flow strongly. Listen to the sounds.

If you hear yourself saying two numbers with identical pitches, do not keep going. Start over again. For this exercise, if your pitch remains the same on the following number, you must always go back and start from the beginning. If you want this exercise to work, you cannot take any shortcuts by pushing on when you have made a mistake.

Listen to how those numbers sound. When most people reach the number four, five or six, they are usually at their optimum pitch. You will know when you have reached your optimum pitch because the sound you hear will sound the brightest and it will have maximum resonance. Your voice will sound better than it ever has before.

Now start the exercise again but this time have something to read in your hand and get your tape recorder rolling. You should still be standing. Find your optimum pitch. Do not skip any of the steps for the exercise. Hold up the piece of reading material and read it using your optimum pitch. Remember: Don't be concerned about making sense of the reading. You are developing your tone. Then play back your new and wonderful sound. You can now use this small piece of tape as a kind of touchstone to check if your voice is where it should be when you are reading your copy as you continue to practice. You should hear the difference clearly. You are on your way to trusting yourself with your new, strong and engaging voice.

How To Keep Up Your Practice

Put a note near your telephone. Write on it OPTIMUM PITCH, or SPEAK WITH FORWARD/CHEST TONES, or MY RICH VOICE. Anything that will help you practice. The telephone is a good practice tool because most people just say, "Oh, I didn't recognize your voice." And that's just what you want to hear.

It is essential that you get used to your new voice. Remember that when you begin to use these tones you might find it a bit frightening. With stronger, deeper, richer tones you will appear more authoritative and sexier.

Some of my students have said their new voice has the effect of being a bit threatening to people they know, especially in their family or in their relationships. So no more being the baby in the family or the good, sweet, perfect child. Stay with your improved voice for your career. Those around you will learn to love it if they love you.

Get Your Mouth Around the Words

In television, you are going to have to say a lot of words quickly and pronounce many difficult names. You will need to get your mouth around the words with little or no rehearsal. You won't have any second chance to say it right. You can't fumble around with excuses. After all, that's what they're paying you for — to talk, to be clear, and to make sense out of the script.

Exercise 19   Tongue Twisters

Say each tongue twister five times as quickly as you can. Using your hand to punctuate the rhythm makes it easier.

Bright blue blisters bleeding badly
The big baker bakes black bread
This crisp crust crackles crunchily
How many cuckoos could a good cook if a good cook could cook cuckoos?
Twenty tinkers took two hundred tin tacks to toy town. If twenty tinkers took two hundred tin tacks to toy town, how many tin tacks did each of the twenty tinkers going to toy town take?
Ten tame tadpoles tucked tightly together in a thin tall tin.
Tommy Tye tried to tie his tie but tugging too tight tore his toe. Tom turned to Ted and told Ted to try to tie the tie Tom tried to tie.
The sixth sick sheik's sixth sheep's sick.
Toy boat *or* troy boat
Am I and Annie aiming anemic anemones on my many enemies?
Billy's big blue badly bleeding blister
Good blood bad blood
Red leather yellow leather
I go by Blue Goose bus

He generally reads regularly in a government library, particularly rich in Coptic manuscripts, especially during the months of January and February.

What kind of a noise annoys an oyster? A noisy noise annoys an oyster.

Practice, Practice, Practice

Get your mouth around the words. As an anchor or a reporter, you will be speaking at a crisp pace and some of the words may not be too familiar. You'll always have difficult foreign names thrown at you. So start getting used to saying the words — as Hamlet advised, "trippingly on the tongue."

The purpose of all these exercises is to extend your capacities so that whatever you are called on to execute, you will perform with great ease and confidence. All these exercises will serve you well. You will extend the use of your breath and breathe properly. You will speak more clearly, and you will gain greater confidence. As in anything, confidence is the name of the game.

S, Z, Popping Ps, Glottal Ls

There are specific sounds that many of my students have difficulty saying correctly. The first is the S sound. Sometimes the Z sound presents difficulties as well. Z is the voiced sound of the nonvocal S.

The English language is filled with these consonants, so you want to sound them as correctly as you can when you are speaking before the camera. The incorrect position of your tongue, when it is placed too far forward will result in a Th, a lisp. The other type of lisp occurs when the breath flows over the sides of the tongue instead of over the tip. Then a sort of voiceless L takes the place of the S sound.

If this is you, you need to make an adjustment in the placement of the tongue. The tongue can be placed in the right position for the S by beginning with the placement for the T. Pronounce your T very slowly so that the tip of the tongue is only slightly removed from the gums behind your upper teeth. However, the sides of your tongue should remain touching your upper teeth.

As you practice the S, keep the T placement in your mind. Keeping the T sound and position in your mind is imperative because you don't want your tongue to return to its position of your defective-sounding S.

There are a great many problems with poor S tones even when the tongue is in the proper position. The cause of these problems come from the amount of breath that is exhaled on the sound, the pressure of the tongue press or the portion of the tongue that is used.

One of the methods that sometimes helps in these necessary finer adjustments is to whisper the S first on a high note, and then on a low note. You will hear the difference.

Exercise 20

When you think you have a good S sound, practice leaning on the S lightly and follow it with the vowels as follows:

S...EE, S...AY, S...AH, S...AW, S...OH, S...OO.

Then reverse the order for words ending in the S sound, like peace, place or case. Begin your sound leaning on the vowels and end with the S. Get off of the S fairly quickly.

EE...S, AY...S, AH...S, AW...S, OH...S, OO...S

Many of my students hang on to their Ss longer than is needed. My general rule is, leave your S behind as soon as possible. This can be accomplished by rushing into the next vowel sound or just finishing them speedily. Also, sometimes lowering your pitch seems to help.

Exercise 21

When words become plural, we know that S turns into the Z sound so be sure to voice it correctly. For this exercise follow the vowels with the Z sound:

EE...Z, AY...Z, AH...Z, AW...Z, OH...Z, OO...Z

You will find lists of S and Z words on our CD-Rom with which you should practice if you have even the slightest problem with these sounds. Be sure to use your tape recorder.

Exercise 22   Practice the Sound: Z

silver	zinc	zigzag	bliss	alias
sort	Zulu	zipper	face	blaze
sod	zany	music	kiss	Celsius
sink	zebra	lazy	dross	demise
scene	lesson	lizard	fizz	auspices
sigh	gossip	busy	has	chasm
cell	faster	dizzy	crazy	docile
across	aside	rosy	maze	censure

Exercise 23   Practice the Sound: S with Some Silly Sentences

A stewed sow's snout. A sow's snout stewed.

Sister Susie's sewing shirts for soldiers, some skill at sewing shirts our shy young Susie shows. Some soldiers sent epistles say they'd sooner sleep on thistles than the saucy soft short shirts for soldiers' sister Susie sews.

Six swift horses started in the historic race at seaside.

Simon Sweet fussed about the small squeaking mouse.

Selma insisted that clever verse must be terse but no assonant.

Stevenson was a scientist who liked to be certain of his evidence.

Simon's stout sturdy sons — Stephen, Samuel, Saul, Silas — sold sundries.

Stephen sold silks, satins, and shawls. Samuel sold saddles and stirrups. Saul sold silver spoons and specialties. Silas sold Sally Short's stuffed sofas.

"Puss' In Boots" is a story for small children who like to listen.

The L and the Other L

The English language has two L sounds. Both sounds can be heard in the word little. And they can be heard in the alternating words, leaf, feel, lean, kneel. They are not interchangeable. The L sound to be spoken is determined by its placement in a word and by the sounds that follow it.

The first and simpler L sound, as in LEAF and LEAN, can be spoken properly when the tip of the tongue is in contact with the upper gums and your breath flows over the sides of your tongue. The rest of the tongue assumes a position close to the EEEE sound, with most of it close to the roof of your mouth. This sound is at the beginning of a word.

The second L sound — feel and kneel — is more difficult and is often problematic for many students. This sound depends on more than just the position of the tip of the tongue. It is called a glottal L. When the L is at the end of a word or followed by consonants, the glottal L is usually sounded.

The two Ls can be distinguished also by referring to them by their sound. The first is a clear L, the second a dark L. For the dark L, the tongue tip is still heading to the upper gums but the rest of the tongue takes a position curling downwards toward the bottom of your mouth.

But, when the L is at the end of a word and the following word begins with a vowel, the dark L morphs into a clear L. Don't you just love the English language? So in the phrase, lemon peel, peel ends with a dark L. But in the phrase, peel a lemon, peel ends with an easy clear L sound because the L sound is immediately followed by a vowel. And, as I said before, both Ls can be heard in the word little.

Beware of placing clear Ls in all final positions. Your speech will sound a bit strange.

The network anchor Tom Brokaw was probably the last person who could get away with his glottal L speech defect.

You'll know if you have this problem if when you want to say the words milk, field, bell, they come out sounding like miook, fieuoold, and bioo. So do something about it. This is difficult and takes practice but it is absolutely achievable.

Exercise 24   Some Words to Practice for Your Ls

luck	cull	pal	lap
law	wall	loot	tool
loam	mole	lurk	curl
lop	poll	lurch	churl
lead	deal	lip	pill
look	cool	loop	pool

Popping Your Ps

This consonant is rightly called an explosive. It causes every correspondent I know problems when they are using hand mics or doing narrations in the studio or the record booth. It happens because air is imprisoned behind the lips. The sudden release of air when the lips are opened gives the letter P its explosive sound.

The degree of aspiration varies depending on the speaker. It should never be made with prominence, but should be dealt with in a subtle way. The lips should open rapidly. One must never hold on to the breath behind the lips for any amount of time.

When a final P is followed by another similar explosive sound the first P must be stopped. An example of this is: CAPE PIE. A full stop must be made after CAPE. However these words cannot be separated by a pause. So the first P cannot be fully articulated. The difference between the phrases: HOPE TO, and HOPED TO, is revealed in the length of time between the two T sounds.

Exercise 25   Some Sounds to Help with Your Explosive P

eep pee ayp pay ahp pah awp paw ohp poh oop poo

Peter Piper picked a peck of pickled peppers.
Where's the peck of pickled Peppers Peter Piper picked?

Accents

It's best not to have too thick an accent. If you are from the south you probably have a drawl. There is one sound you should be wary of: The short i sound often wrongly replaces the short e sound. You will sound ignorant if you don't get rid of it. It's easy to do.

Here are examples of some short e sounds that my southern students often switch to short i sounds.

PEN becomes PIN
SENATE becomes SINATE
TEN becomes TIN
MEN becomes MIN . . . and so on.

Very few people have gotten jobs with a thick New York or Brooklyn accent.

"THE POINT OF NO RETURN," should not be spoken as "THE PERNT OF NO RETOIN." "Girl" should not become "GOIL." And be careful of excessive nasality, often a trademark of the NOO YOUK accent.

Most stations prefer standard American speech, or something close to it. So mark your script to help you eliminate any thick or detracting accent. You should make your own list of words that have your problem sounds. Use a tape recorder. Get someone to speak the words correctly onto the tape. Leave a space for you to repeat the proper pronunciation. Play the tape back. Listen carefully for your improvement.

If you do have an accent, it may be charming. But be very sure every word can be easily understood. You can do something about it. Do it!

A Closing Thought

Most people in television call the audience "viewers." They are after all, "watching television." However, the audience is involved through two senses.

They LISTEN to television, but they are not always watching. In the morning, you are making breakfast or getting dressed or doing your morning chores, and if the television is on, then you are likely to be listening and not watching. Viewers rarely turn down the volume.

All of this is to point out that your voice is far more important to the "viewer" than anything else ... even your appearance.

Checklist

- ❑ Practice, practice, practice.
- ❑ Your voice is who you are as much as your looks.
- ❑ Learn your flaws and fix them.
- ❑ Breathe correctly.
- ❑ Relax! Lose tension.
- ❑ Build resonance and correct tones.
- ❑ Find your optimum pitch.
- ❑ Avoid popping Ps, sibilant Ss and glottal Ls.
- ❑ Practice, practice, practice.

17

Techniques for a Good Reading

This will be useful for all anchoring work as well as for your narration for packages.

As you begin this work, don't shy away from the language. After all, language is your nuts and bolts. You must begin to relish it. You will need to become sensitive to the sound of words as well as to their context. You must be able to express the subtle nuances of what the words mean.

As a beginner, it doesn't hurt to imitate the successful anchors or reporters. Many of the most established anchors and reporters did this when they began their professional journeys. So, if you're one of those people who proudly say, "I never watch television," well, you'd better start.

Television can be an excellent teacher. The professionals on camera got their jobs against fierce competition. Why have these particular anchors won out? It's got to be more than a good set of sparklers. Try to figure out what it is.

This is the beginning of your first dose of reality. You want to discover what they are doing with their words that you are not doing. Listen and learn what makes this person sound so good. By analyzing what they do, you will begin to realize what skills you need to do the job — skills you now possess and which skills you need to acquire.

Fig. 17-1 Time to become a viewer.

Punctuation for TV Scripts

When you are beginning in the news area or in any area on television where there's written material, you must learn how to see a script the same way a musician sees a score. The musician can look at his score and know when to be quiet and when to be louder or when to be slower or faster. Your television script is your score and you must follow its directions as well. Your script will tell you how to pace the story as well as how to find the correct pitch. Much of the direction is in the made-for-TV-script punctuation.

For you, it is a good plan to review your script and to mark it with what have become these accepted television punctuation marks. They are different from general writing punctuation marks, but are there to do the same thing. They are much more obvious, much more emphatic. Subtle is not a good thing in television scripting. One top TV producer used to say, "Subtle is a four-letter word in television."

The COMMA: You know what that looks like. It is used but not frequently because it borders on subtle. As to the SEMICOLON, I have never seen it used in a professional television script. That is way too subtle. Instead of Commas and Semicolons, use . . .
The DASH: Looks like this—
That is a slight pause; about what you would think of as a comma.
Or the DOUBLE DASH: Looks like this— —
That gives you the clear signal to take a beat, a pause, like an emphatic comma.
The ELIPSE: Looks like this . . .
It is very useful, telling the reader to take a beat, a rest, a pause that is often used as a joiner — joining two thoughts without using connecting words. For example: The athlete faced three choices: Winning . . . losing . . . or tying.
The COLON: Looks like this :
That indicates a full stop with something coming after, teeing up what comes next. It's also very useful. See the above example, which would be read: The athlete faced three choices: (STOP) Winning . . . (pause) losing . . . (pause) or tying.

You should try to write some scripts using these punctuation marks for yourself for practice. Clip a newspaper article and change the marks. One other thing you should notice is this: Most newspaper sentences are way too long. Use lots of PERIODS (which look like this).

As you gain more experience, you will be able to see the pacing and intonations in a well-written script automatically. In fact, the best in the business can do it having never seen the script. That takes practice — years of it.

Tape and Ape

Beyond watching your favorite anchor or reporter, you should tape and ape. Record the voice you like on your trusty tape recorder. (I say tape recorder and not a video recorder because it is better to just listen and not to watch and listen, since this work is for voice exclusively.)

Then transcribe (write out) what you have recorded — every word, even noting the pauses. Next, read it aloud into your tape recorder. Now listen to the way the professional has read it. Then play yourself back. Become aware of the pace and authority of the professional's voice and the way he or she makes a point with it.

A professional voice will tell a story with clarity. It never sounds artificial. I like to call this NEWSPEAK. It is a combination of part talking and part reading. It does not sound like a casual off-the-cuff read, but it's not forced or over-the-top either. You must be credible and knowledgeable and have a confident delivery. As you start your reading, imitate the pros. I suggest this to my students and they seem to learn a lot from doing so. After a relatively short time you will find your own voice.

After you have taped and aped the delivery of your favorite anchor or reporter, it is time to get away from mimicry. You shouldn't try to copy the voice, but find your own. Emulate but don't imitate the softening voice and the pauses. The reason for this is that there already is a Katie Couric. You want the future employer to want *you*. So, your goal in all of our work is to be the absolute best YOU that you can be.

What you need to do next is begin to develop your own delivery and make your own read sound as good as it can. At this beginning stage, it will be best for you to just work on the readings: For narration in packages, for the prompter and for anchors' copy stories.

Reading but Not Sounding That Way

You will be reading copy but it must not sound that way. I am going to go through the separate elements, so you can work on each area, and then put them together.

Your read must be authoritative enough to cut through, but chatty enough to connect with the viewers. If your voice has a catchy difference, such as a low register, so much the better. If it's offbeat, that's great too; but it can't sound too extreme. You know what I mean by that: Daffy Duck's voice is offbeat but wouldn't work except in a cartoon.

Some readings sound low key and limited in vocal pitch and variety but still the story punches through. How is that? Often it's done with rhythm and tone — timing and a small variety of pitches so that you might not be aware of the limited range of tone.

All readings of news stories must fit the subject matter. The style changes according to the story and the rhythm changes, but the voice remains the same. You do not change your voice for a light breezy story or a sad hard news story. Your voice is always the same. You don't ever assume a character the way an actor would for a role.

You must always be yourself.

News readings must have integrity and honesty and believability. You must be sensitive to the changes within each news story and be able to express these transitions clearly.

Mark Your Script

In addition to the TV script punctuation that we talked about, you should consider writing notes to yourself on your hard copy. You can make up your own markings to help you, but I have some that you can adopt (see Fig. 17-2). Even though these clues will not appear on the prompter as it rolls by in the studio, they will still remain in your mind and assist you throughout the broadcast.

In order to improve reading the copy, you must make conscious decisions. To make sure you don't forget what these decisions are, when you actually read on camera, mark your copy so that it is

EMPHASIS _____ Underline. Or circle the (word.)

COLOR WORDS   Wiggly line under the word.

UP AND DOWN READING Arrows

HESITATION /

PAUSE//

LONGER PAUSE///

TRANSITION ****

THE END OF THE STORY #### or 0000

Fig. 17-2 Mark your script.

simple and easily seen. You may use any marking that has meaning for you.

This is different from punctuation. These are marks for your read after the script is written. You can adapt them or create more of your own. Some of you may already have your own code for marking a script or you can use these if they help you.

By doing this in advance, you will remember and perform your choices for your read. You will feel confident that you have a handle on what you are doing. When you are through marking your script, it should be as clear as a musical score.

How To Sound Great and Natural

DON'T SHOUT! OK?

Your mic is close by. If you are in a studio the mic is either clipped on to your tie, jacket lapel or blouse. If it is a hand mic or a desk mic, it should be a few inches from your mouth and you should use a conversational tone, not a stage voice. If your training has been for the stage, be very careful about this. For you, half of your stage voice will do.

If you find that you keep reading your stories in exactly the same way, here's a trick that often works. It's the QUESTION and ANSWER method.

Question and Answer Exercise

Read the first line and then ask yourself a question. Answer with the next line. After each sentence, pose another question that leads you to the next sentence. Try to really answer the question that you pose with the next sentence as if someone was asking you something that you knew about and cared about.

This technique will help you to get conversational and more natural readings. If you're having problems sounding natural and interested, this is quite a helpful tool. Of course you want to use it only for practice.

Loosen Up

Like the sound of your voice, you may not realize how your read sounds, what your natural pace is or what rhythms you have. But one other thing that you may be surprised to learn is how tight you are. If you are not at ease or if you do not appear comfortable on camera, your audience is not gong to be comfortable either.

 Report from the Trenches

A new TV reporter, fresh from newspapers, was put in the hands of a veteran producer. The new reporter was terrific at everything in journalism except he was grim-faced on air. The producer told him, "Smile more." The correspondent did smile what he thought was more. "More!" urged the producer. More is what the correspondent thought he did.

This went on and on. The reporter thought his smile was so big he probably looked like a clown. Finally the producer told the correspondent to read the copy with the broadest, widest grin he could make. The producer videotaped this newspaper recruit.

The reporter watched the video played back and was stunned to see what his wild grinning produced. It was a thin and very forced smile. After that he got it. But until then, he thought he was grinning from ear to ear.

Try Paraphrasing

A trick to help you to loosen up is to paraphrase the story. This is particularly helpful if you are working on light news stories, or kickers. For this kind of story you want to be loose as a goose. Paraphrasing the story, using other words and even ad-libbing some of your own thoughts, will help you speak naturally, have more fun, and become looser.

Take a few risks. If you make a mistake, good! If you feel silly, good! Be silly! Laugh! Let loose with those ad-libs. If you're making a fool of yourself in this exercise, the only one who will know is you. And the chances are you aren't overdoing it. Like that grinning reporter, you can probably even go further with your looseness.

Don't forget to put all of this on tape, so you can play it back. You might be surprised at how natural and fun you sound. If you find this difficult, jump, hop or skip while you're saying light news. It's difficult to remain solemn when you're hopping.

Monotone Millie

Don't be a Monotone Millie. Don't read everything in the same tone. Differentiate your words (more about this coming up). Point up the words that are the most important. Let your voice ride up and down.

Use facial expression, body language, anything you can do to get meaning out of the script. Make sure that you don't end every sentence at exactly the same pitch.

You Are Not an Announcer

No one wants to hear announcer types anymore. Use your voice properly. You are not intoning the script like it's the voice of God.

Talk to One Person

Television is not like the stage. You are not addressing a large audience. It is intimate. A viewer watching television must believe you are talking to him or her. You must adopt a personal attitude, a proper volume, which is never too loud. Remember, you are a guest in someone's living room, bedroom, kitchen and even sometimes in their bathroom. So speak as you would to a friend who is about a foot away from you.

Five Keys To a Great Reading

Lets do a quick summary and then go into more detail.

1. LEANING ON A WORD
   Emphasizing the word that will give the sentence the correct meaning.
2. COLOR
   Making words sound like what they mean.
3. FLOW ... and ... PAUSE
   The pause is the natural hesitation in the voice. It can be used to place emphasis. The pause can often be effectively filled with natural noises: Natural sounds, chuckles or verbal stammers. Flow is the ease with which each word accompanies its following word.
4. UP AND DOWN READINGS
   In natural speech the voice rises and falls naturally. Words rise and fall in pitch and emphasis right through the end of a sentence.

5. TRANSITIONS

Another word for transition is CHANGE. To change moods, the voice must go down in pitch, just before the change, then rise in pitch. There are many variations you can find. Experiment.

Now Let's Go To the Specifics

Leaning on a Word

To emphasize a word, you may be told to punch the word to emphasize it. That has never been clear to me. I prefer to tell my students to LEAN on the word for emphasis.

When you lean on a vowel sound in a word it draws the word out a bit. It extends it. It makes the word stand away from the rest of the sentence. Most people, when they are told to punch or hit a word, will say the sentence in a conversational tone and when they come to that word they shout it. If you lean on the vowel sound in the word, the word in the sentence will come out emphasized but not shouted. Try this for example:

HE RAN DOWN THE STREET.

Lean on the vowel sound in RAN. Say it: "RAAN." The word RAN will come out even more specifically if you use your hand. Now say it, and brush your hand out in front of you, as if you want to illustrate the word RAN. Imagine you are talking to a foreigner. It will sound right — not overexaggerated, just appropriate. You don't want that word to be the only thing your viewer hears in the sentence. But you do want that emphasis.

Many people use their hands when they speak. You can use yours as we practice. For many of my students, it can help them connect with what they are telling the viewer. Don't worry about your hand getting in the way of the camera for now. Later, yes. But for learning purposes, you can use it now. You can always keep the gestures off camera, or when you feel more confident you can cut back and do less.

It's important here to explain that when you lean on one word it will affect the rest of the sentence. Speaking is a little bit like yoga;

if you stretch one muscle it will do something to the other muscles nearby. If you just punch one word, by itself, it will sound as if you hit that one specific word and that you don't understand what you are saying.

So be aware that if you emphasize, or lean on only one word in the sentence, it tends to sound amateurish. Don't forget the other words. When you emphasize a word, lean on the vowel in the word. That emphasized word will and should affect the other words in that sentence. And, remember, improper emphasis can completely change the meaning of the sentence. For example:

I didn't say she kicked the cat.

You think you know the meaning? It's simple enough. Now read these sentences aloud, with the emphasis I've shown.

I didn't say <u>SHE</u> kicked the cat.

or

I didn't say she <u>KICKED</u> the cat.

or

I didn't say she kicked the <u>CAT</u>.

Now underline another word in this sentence and read it aloud, leaning on the underlined word. Every different word you emphasize will change the meaning of the sentence with the possible exception of the word "the."

Can you see how different the meaning is of each sentence, depending on which word you are emphasizing?

Let's break down the different ways you can lean on or emphasize a word to hold the audience's interest.

You probably used a few of these methods for emphasis in our "kicked the cat" sentence. Of course speaking the word LOUDER is the most obvious and the least desirable method. You can LIFT the word to a higher key. You can DRAW OUT the vowel in the word you want to emphasize, leaning on the main vowel sound, which I've mentioned before. Now how about SOFTENING YOUR VOICE on the word. This technique will really point up the word or phrase. GAPPING, leaving a pause just before or just after the word, emphasizes it also. This is a very professional way of adding emphasis. It's a trick that is commonly used by the pros.

Coloring the Word

If you are asked to COLOR the word, you should know this is really just another way to emphasize a word. It's used for adjectives and adverbs. Those are the color words. Words should be expressed so they sound like what they mean. You can DISTORT THE WORD, as in "coooold" or "rrrough": "Last night was a rrrough night for our baseball team."

Long words should be stretched to sound long, as: "For those firemen, it has been a looong night," or "The smooth surface of the ocean before the perfect storm...."

Learning how to color words is just getting back to becoming word sensitive. When you perform these techniques, you are not acting or being dramatic.

Pause and Flow

Pause   An older anchor said to a younger anchor, "I get more of the story across to the viewer with my pauses than you do with your words."

It makes sense to me. Does it to you? Let's imagine the words and the pauses as a ham sandwich. The words are the bread and the pause is the ham. In other words, the pause is valuable and special. You should use it with care. It will help you sound smart and professional.

❖ The hesitation is very short.
❖ The pause is longer than a hesitation.

Imagine a swift intake of a short breath; this is a hesitation, not a pause. Pauses can be many different lengths. It takes a great deal of courage to employ a really long pause. A medium pause is only that length because that pause is in contrast to the length of the shorter (hesitations), or longer pauses. But a word of caution: You do not want to overuse the pause, or any reading device for that matter.

Remember earlier, we used the pause as an effective emphasizing device. We placed the pause before an important word. The pause made the word jump out, and the sentence's meaning became clearer.

The pause also helps with the rhythm. It can impart a feeling of naturalness. You change rhythms as you speak and as you make your transitions. It helps you to sound as if you are really talking to one person. If you use a pause before a transition, then use a strong change of pitch or pace. You will have made a double attack at the transition. This can be powerful.

Gate words can be used as a signal that a transition is coming. You may sometimes wish to pause AFTER gate words, but not always. Some of these gate words are: *Remember, well, you know, ladies, finally, hi there, meanwhile, you see.*

Two and three word units, called duads and triads, are usually adjectives describing a situation, person or thing. You can read the first word up, the second word at a medium level and the third word down, or vary it a bit in any direction. Just don't read them all in the same tone and rhythm. Once again use your common sense. The idea is CONTRAST that will be appropriate and fit the material in the story.

Just because two words are butted together doesn't mean you read them similarly.

For instance, starving, malnourished and emaciated, or gorgeous, sexy and simply divine. Each word should be colored differently. Be careful not to overdo.

Flow   Some correspondents ... insist on ... breaking ... their sentence in ... just ... the ... wrong places. And now you know what FLOW is. Be sure your pauses are in the right place. This means your pauses and hesitations should be in the places that maintain the sense and the natural flow of the thoughts. You must make the copy hang together, not be chopped apart. To help you sound less choppy, let one word flow into another.

If you were to write out a sentence with words flowing into each other this is what the sound of that sentence would look like:

Youareoneofthosepeoplewhocanholdaviewer'sinterest.

Watch out for embedded commas. For example: "My teacher, Nancy, came late to class." Those commas may be good for grammar, but they are not good for you. Be wary of pausing after a name. The name and title go together without a pause as do the noun and the verb when you are talking. So let your words flow together elegantly.

All of these reading/talking techniques, the choices that you now know you have, are determined by your sensitivity, by your taste and of course by your intelligence.

Up and Down Readings

Remember the game you played as a child: "What do you put in Grandma's basket? You put in apples, pears, cantaloupes and grapes." You knew when the list was finished by the clues in the speaker's voice. You may notice when people talk they don't drop the inflection in their voice until they reach the end of a complete thought. At least they do this when they speak naturally. But suddenly when they pick up the script to tell a news story, something different occurs. Suddenly, they drop their voices at the end of each phrase, each clause, and each sentence. By dropping the voice at these improper places, the speaker sounds bored. And this dreary way of speaking certainly bores the viewer.

You have had teachers in your life who spoke to you in a bored, dull way, right? You and the rest of your classmates started nodding your head and not too much later, off to dreamland you sailed. You didn't learn a thing in that class. But the difference between that class and television is: You had to sit in that class but your viewer does not have to watch you. This may be one of the most important keys to holding an audience's interest.

NANCY'S RULES

Do not drop your voice until you've reached the end of a complete thought.

The drop in pitch indicates to the listener that you have ended your thought. But if your voice continues to be on the rise, on the uplift, at the end of phrases, clauses and sentences, the viewer will assume from your tone that you intend to continue to expound on your subject.

When I say uplift at the end of your sentence, I don't mean a sliding inflection. I also don't mean a very high pitch. You must retain your energy and your loudness, and not lose the final word in your sentences until you have fully completed your entire thought. Do not speak in a low pitch for your last word of your sentences. If you drop your voice in the wrong place — at the end of your sentence — the audience will assume you are bored with the subject matter, or you are reading or that you are finished with your entire subject.

NANCY'S RULES

Never read down until you come to the end of a complete thought.

You must use common sense. You know when your thought is finished, when it has reached the end. Staying up in pitch at the end of your sentences indicates to the listener THERE IS MORE TO COME.

This is also a great technique to use when you're reading a list. You stay up on each item until you come to the last one, and then you can drop your pitch. For example, listing celebrities:

Madonna, Johnny Depp, Tom Cruise.

or cities:

Paris, London, Rome, New York.

Now, just for fun, say your list and just before the last item, pause as long as you wish — the listener will be eagerly waiting for you to conclude your thought. Then say the final word, finishing with a strong lower pitch. Try it. Of course in the real world of television you will probably never pause for this long, but in a practice session you should try everything to discover the limits.

Don't forget, every word needs to be understood. When you come to the last word of your thought, don't drop your energy and say it so softly that it gets lost, or is swallowed in the back of your throat or thrown away.

The last word is even more important than the first. It is what you leave with your viewer.

Pitch

There are times when you may choose to come down in pitch — even though you have not completed your thought — to make a strong point. There are times you may choose to keep your pitch on the uplift even though you are finished with your thought.

This technique is useful when you are throwing to someone else in the field or in the studio. By not coming down in pitch, the audience's attention is kept riveted and you help keep the broadcast moving forward.

Transitions

The strongest change in pitch usually comes just before transitions. When people are speaking they constantly change the mood of their voices whenever they change the subject. When you're trying to speak and sound real and natural, if you wish to reconstruct the sounds of REAL speech, you must also reconstruct the change of mood. Since you don't really feel what you are saying (we know this isn't real life but reading from the prompter or from a script), you need to do this mechanically, at first.

Know that when a person ends a thought, the tone of the voice usually lowers. They give a down reading, as in the phrase, "get lost." Most people who try this technique are willing to go DOWN, or SLOW DOWN, but they seldom do both at once. Hence their changes of mood or transitions are weak sounding.

But ending the old thought is not enough! You must start the new thought correctly. You must RAISE THE PITCH of your voice as you begin the new thought to contrast with the low tone you made as you ended the previous thought.

And since you SLOWED DOWN as you ended the previous thought, as you begin to speak the new thought, you must now speak more quickly.

Contrast

Contrast is the name of the game. Contrast in pitch or in speed or both sends the listener the message that the mood changed.

Other methods of contrast:

SPEED UP (pace)
GO DOWN (in pitch)
SLOW DOWN (pace)
GO UP (in pitch)

The idea is contrast!

If you wish to hold the audience's attention, you must make transitions. If you don't, you will seem to drone and on and on. And on. And on. . . .

Here is one of the tricks of the trade: If you have a complicated subject or lots of words alternating your pace — say one line as you speed up, then say the next line slowing down. Give this a whirl. If you are thinking and connecting with your words, it will sound even more professional. This technique may be used when you have lots of copy to read. Use your good sense. As with anything, don't overuse this.

Giving a Level

Before you record your narration, you are often asked to "give a level." This does not mean to say, "Hi there, I'm Nancy Reardon." The sound guys are not doing this to find out if their equipment is working. They know it is! You are asked to give a level in order to assist them in setting the gain, the volume. They fit this gain to your voice. For soft voices they turn it up and for loud voices they turn it down.

So when you are told to "give a level," you should begin speaking the copy, the anchoring, or the open, exactly as you plan to do it when you do the real thing. And you should continue reading until you hear, "OK! That's enough!"

Time and Timing Are Important

Start becoming aware of it. Every show has only a certain amount of time. When you are practicing in your home or in class with your exercises it doesn't matter if you run over five seconds. But for a show with commercials and a format that is live, you must be aware of TIME.

Say you are running out of time. What do you do? One technique is to increase the speed at which you are speaking, but still make your points. No one will notice if you do. In fact, it might help. It is an interesting point that by speeding up your read, people will tend to listen closer and hear you better. (Of course, not way too fast.) That may not make sense, but it is true. You can also tighten your pauses.

But don't forget, everything is relative. You still will need to slow down at times, but it will be slowing down at a speedier pace. If you speed up and tighten pauses, you still need contrast. You cannot just garble your way through a piece.

The faster you go, the stronger you must make your points. This is a professional way to speed up your reading. Shorten each pause a little bit. Keep the sense exactly as you do when you are speaking at your regular pace. This way it'll seem the same as the way you have been speaking.

Don't Make Paper Noises

If you have several pieces of paper, separate them beforehand and carefully slide them apart. When you're using a TelePrompTer, be sure to slide the pages off the script quietly. In the field, be well enough prepared that you don't have to shuffle notes. Live breaking news events may be the exception.

Also keep your papers low. They should not be flying about in front of the camera. Doing that will distract from your story. The viewer will end up watching the papers instead of listening to you. If you're doing an in-depth interview, be sure to use a clipboard or a quiet notebook.

Exercises for a Great Read

Here are some exercises to practice. Try using your new punctuation.

Commercials are easy and very clear, with many instant changes. They will work your skills. These first two are real commercials, courtesy of Procter and Gamble.

Sure

❖ CHOOSING AN ANTI-PERSPIRANT SPRAY ISN'T THE MOST IMPORTANT DECISION YOU'LL EVER MAKE. BUT, SINCE YOU DO HAVE TO MAKE THAT DECISION, YOU SHOULD KNOW ABOUT SURE. BECAUSE IT'S REALLY DIFFERENT. LOOK, LOTS OF ANTI-PERSPIRANT SPRAYS GO ON WITH A MESSY POWDER, COMPARED TO SURE, WHICH GOES ON DRY. I'M NOT SAYING THIS PROVES SURE KEEPS YOU DRIER. BUT YOU CAN PROVE THAT TO YOURSELF. IN THE ONLY PLACE THAT REALLY COUNTS. UNDER YOUR OWN ARMS. TRY SURE ON ONE SIDE. AND, ON THE OTHER SIDE, TRY THE SPRAY YOU LIKE BEST. IF YOU'RE LIKE MOST PEOPLE, THE SURE SIDE WILL BE THE DRIER SIDE. BUT DON'T TAKE MY WORD FOR IT. USE YOUR OWN ARMS AND FIND OUT FOR YOURSELF. TRY SURE ON ONE SIDE. IT'LL CONVINCE YOUR OTHER SIDE. I'M SURE.

Ivory

❖ IF SOMEONE CAME TO ME AND ASKED, WHAT DO I DO TO KEEP MY SKIN HEALTHY LOOKING, I WOULD

PROBABLY SAY THE FIRST THING…WELL…IT'S A COMBINATION OF ALL THE BASICS. BUT WHEN IT COMES TO SKIN, I THINK OF LOTS OF SOAP AND WATER…AND WHEN I THINK OF LOTS OF SOAP AND WATER I THINK OF IVORY. I LIKE IVORY I THINK BECAUSE IT IS JUST LIKE THE WAY I LIVE. IT'S VERY BASIC, IT'S VERY NATURAL, IT KIND OF GOES WITH MY WAY OF LIVING. IVORY CLEANS IN A VERY GENTLE WAY…BUT…IT ISN'T ALL YOU NEED TO HELP YOU KEEP YOUR SKIN HEALTHY LOOKING. BUT I REALLY BELIEVE IT HELPS. BUT WHEN I THINK ABOUT IT, HELPING SKIN STAY HEALTHY LOOKING IS WHAT IVORY IS ALL ABOUT. SHOULDN'T YOU RETURN TO BASICS? IVORY'S JUST ANOTHER BASIC. BUT IT'S A VERY IMPORTANT BASIC FOR MY SKIN.

Tesela Light & Power

❖ HI THERE. WANT TO BREATHE A LITTLE EAS-IER? WELL, HERE'S A START. IT'S TESELA LIGHT & POWER'S SAVE-A-WATT TEST, AND EVERY "YES" ANSWER HELPS TO PROTECT THE ENVIRONMENT… EASE POWER EMERGENCIES AND REDUCE YOUR ELECTRIC BILL, SO, HERE WE GO. ASK YOURSELF: DO I TURN OFF THE AIR CONDITIONER BEFORE I GO OUT (YOU KNOW, LIKE SHOPPING OR A MOVIE)? DO I RUN APPLIANCES (YOU KNOW, LIKE THE DISH-WASHER AND THE CLOTHES WASHER AND DRYER AND VACUUM) BEFORE 8AM AND AFTER 6PM (HEY, THAT MAKES SENSE!). DO I TURN LIGHTS OFF WHEN NOT NEEDED? (I'VE GOT TO WORK HARDER ON THAT ONE). DO I REMEMBER TO TURN OFF THE OVEN? (GOTTA WORK ON THAT, TOO.) DO I TURN OFF THE RADIO WHEN I'M WATCHING TV AND VICE VERSA? DO I BUY AN AIR CONDITIONER OF PROPER SIZE AND EFFICIENCY? REMEMBER, EVEN THOUGH ELECTRIC POWER PLANTS ARE BY NO

MEANS THE WORST POLLUTION OFFENDERS, SAV-
ING A WATT JUST HAS TO HELP SOME. HOW ABOUT
YOU? HAVE YOU ANSWERED "YES" TO TESELAS
LIGHT & POWER SAVE-A-WATT TEST? IF YOU DO,
WE'LL ALL BREATHE A LITTLE EASIER.

Worths

❖ IN DENVER THERE'S A LANDMARK COMMUNITY
FILLED WITH HISTORIC HOMES AND OLD-WORLD
CHARM: LODO. AND IN LODO, THERE'S ANOTHER
LANDMARK, ONE THAT'S KNOWN THROUGHOUT
THE WORLD: WORTH'S. BUT WHILE LODO HAS
REMAINED FAITHFUL TO THE PAST, WORTH'S
DEVOTION IS ENTIRELY TO THE PRESENT, WITH
SPECIALTY FOODS FROM HERE AND ABROAD THAT
MAKE A TRIP TO WORTH'S LIKE A TOUR OF THE
GOURMET CAPITALS OF THE WORLD. AND SINCE
IT MAY BE DIFFICULT FOR YOU TO SEE THESE SPE-
CIAL FOODS AND WINES DURING THE DAY, WE
MAKE IT EASY FOR YOU TO SEE THEM AT NIGHT,
WHEN THE CHARMS OF LODO AND THE CHARMS
OF WORTH'S ARE MOST INVITIING. WE'RE OPEN
EVERY NIGHT TIL 9, INCLUDING SATURDAY. AT
NIGHT, ALTHOUGH THE PACE IS VERY RELAXED,
OUR SERVICE HASN'T BEEN RELAXED AT ALL.
WE'RE STILL FULLY STAFFED. EVEN ON A SATUR-
DAY NIGHT. SO ONE DAY HAVE YOUR WIFE MEET
YOU AFTER WORK, ENJOY A FINE DINNER WITH US,
AND THEN TAKE HER ON A TOUR OF WORTH'S FOR
FINE FOODS FROM AROUND THE COUNTRY AND
AROUND THE WORLD.

Pane Longo

❖ THE NEXT TIME YOU'RE PLANNING TO HAVE ROLLS
FOR DINNER, TRY PANE LONGO BREADSTICKS

INSTEAD. CRISPIER—MORE FUN. CRUNCHIER—MORE SOPHISTICATED. TASTIER—MORE EXCITING. LIGHTER—MORE IMPRESSIVE WHEN THEY'RE MAKING A POINT AND JUST PLAIN MORE ENJOY-ABLE. WHAT'S MORE, PANE LONGO BREADSTICKS COME IN REGULAR, DIETETIC, SALTY AND ONION. ROLLS, WHEN YOU COME DOWN TO IT, ARE ROLLS. PANE LONGO BREADSTICKS INSTEAD OF ORDI-NARY ROLLS.

1. Mark your copy as much as you can. Using your audio tape recorder read each commercial out loud.

   Pacing and Pitch   Read it in your regular pace and pitch.

   Now alternate your pace.
   Read one line quickly.
   Read one line slowly.

2. Now try using the techniques you've learned with this hard news copy. Make your strongest changes where you find the largest transitions.

   BREAKING NEWS THIS MORNING. WILMA MET ALPHA IN A MEGA-STORM, SLAMMING THE NORTHEAST. IN FLORIDA, MORE THAN SIX MILLION WITHOUT POWER. AIRPORTS SHUT DOWN. CURFEWS IN FORCE.
   BREAKING NEWS. WHAT DID VICE PRESIDENT CHENEY KNOW? WHEN DID HE KNOW IT? IN THAT C.I.A. LEAK CASE, A NEW REPORT RAISES NEW QUESTIONS. THAT AHEAD.
   AND REMEMBERING ROSA PARKS. SHE REFUSED TO GIVE UP HER SEAT ON THE BUS TO A WHITE MAN AND STARTED A REVOLUTION. THE MOTHER OF THE CIVIL RIGHTS MOVEMENT DEAD AT 92. A TRIBUTE.
   THE BIG STORY OF THE MORNING. MULTIPLE STORMS CONVERGING HERE IN THE NORTHEAST FOR WHAT

THEY SAY IS ANOTHER PERFECT STORM. THAT'S RIGHT. YOU TALK ABOUT WILMA MEETING ALPHA. IT SOUNDS LIKE UMA MEETING OPRAH. THIS ONE FANS OUT FROM FLORIDA ALL THE WAY UP TO MASSACHUSETTS. WE WILL BE TELLING YOU WHEN ALL THE LIGHTS WILL BE GOING BACK ON IN FLORIDA. YESTERDAY MORNING WE WERE TALKING ABOUT THE POWER OF WILMA. IF ANY PICTURE I THINK DEPICTS WHAT WILMA DID TO THE STATE OF FLORIDA, YOU TALK ABOUT ALL THE PEOPLE WITHOUT POWER, LOOK AT THIS MAN IN MARCO ISLAND, FLORIDA BATTERED BY THE WINDS OF HURRICANE WILMA. THIS STORM CAME ASHORE AS A CATEGORY THREE HURRICANE AND DID A LOT OF DAMAGE IN THAT STATE YESTERDAY.

3. Now try this with the light copy:

A SENSE OF MAGIC AND EXCITEMENT WAS IN THE AIR IN LONDON'S LEICESTER SQUARE ON SUNDAY AS "HARRY POTTER" FANS WAITED IN THE RAIN TO GREET CAST MEMBERS ATTENDING THE PREMIERE OF THE LATEST POTTER FILM—"HARRY POTTER AND THE GOBLET OF FIRE."
PRODUCERS DESCRIBE THE FILM—THE FOURTH IN THE SERIES ABOUT THE BESPECTACLED YOUNG WIZARD—AS THE DARKEST PRODUCTION YET. IT IS THE FIRST OF THE FILMS SO FAR TO ACHIEVE A PG13 RATING, MEANING UNDER 13 YEAR OLDS SHOULD NOT VIEW WITHOUT ADULT SUPERVISION.
DANIEL RADCLIFFE, WHO PLAYS POTTER, ATTENDED THE PREMIERE SUNDAY EVENING ALONG WITH OTHER CAST MEMBERS INCLUDING ROBBIE COLTRANE, WHO PLAYS HARRY'S FRIEND HAGRID, MICHAEL GAMBON, WHO STARS AS THE KINDLY ALBUS DUMBLEDORE, AND MAGGIE SMITH WHO PLAYS PROFESSOR MCGONAGALL.

THE FILM TELLS HOW THE YOUNG WIZARD, NOW IN HIS FOURTH YEAR AT HOGWART'S SCHOOL OF WITCHCRAFT AND WIZARDRY, IS SELECTED TO COMPETE IN THE QUIDDITCH TRIWIZARD TOURNAMENT AGAINST OLDER AND MORE EXPERIENCED STUDENTS FROM RIVAL SCHOOLS. HE ALSO ENCOUNTERS HIS FIRST LOVE INTEREST, A NEW CHARACTER CHO CHANG, PLAYED BY KATIE LEUNG.

Be sure to play back everything on your recorder. Do you hear the difference? You should hear how professional you sound!

Hesitations and Pauses

4. Read the following sentences into your tape recorder.

   a. Only one person could have killed her, and that person was you.
   b. (A politician concluding a speech)... and unless we destroy corruption in our government, I assure you our party will go down in overwhelming defeat, disgrace and humiliation, let's not let this not happen.
   c. One out of every four people in this country is mentally unbalanced; think of your three closest friends, if they seem okay, then you're the one. (Ann Landers)
   d. I have only one thing to say to you, you're a cheat.
   e. Help, he can't breathe, run quickly, call a doctor.
   f. I find TV very educational, the minute somebody turns it on, I go into the library and read a good book. (Woody Allen)
   g. Heaven goes by favor, if it went by merit, you would stay out and your dog would go in.

5. Replace each comma with a different length pause, and mark your script.
   S = short pause, M = medium pause, and L = long pause

Now read the sentences aloud, and record again. Be sure your pauses are really different lengths, particularly the middle length pause. Perhaps exaggerate a bit so you can become aware of these choices, and you can easily hear the difference.

You should now hear how well you hold the viewer's attention. (There are many more exercises on the CD-Rom.)

Checklist

- ❒ Practice, practice, practice.
- ❒ Learn TV script punctuation.
- ❒ Mark your script.
- ❒ Tape and ape.
- ❒ Don't shout.
- ❒ Don't be Monotone Millie or THE ANNOUNCER.
- ❒ Lean on a word.
- ❒ Color a word.
- ❒ Pause and flow.
- ❒ Up and down readings.
- ❒ Transitions and contrast.

Physical Techniques

Television is a magnifying glass. Everything appears larger than it is. Take the appearance of the studio itself. If you have ever been to a news studio, you may have been surprised at how small the anchor desk area appears. On your television it looks spacious.

The television monitor presents a flat, one-dimensional image, which includes the image of you. On top of that, most of the anchor shots are shot fairly close. People on television tend to be shot from the fifth button up, or even closer. Of course there are wide shots and establishing shots of the studio, but mostly television news and hosting is confined to close-ups.

On-camera Movement

If you start moving your body or hand quickly toward the camera, it will look distorted, like a fun-house mirror. Whatever the reason for distortion, it makes sense then to be careful, not to play BIG. This will be a distraction to the viewer. And remember, any distraction allows the viewer to lose the relationship and lose interest. Distraction is a four-letter word.

So think small. Small gestures, small facial movements or head turns. Every move on television is magnified. What appears normal then is less than real-life normal.

This will take some getting used to. In life, you are comfortable with the space around you and your actions within it. On television, it's like a minimalist painting. You need to keep your gestures and actions to a minimum. For the most part, your movements with any part of your body should not be fast or large.

You don't want to block your face with your hand. You don't want to wrinkle your forehead. You don't want to frown a great deal. You can do all these things in a very small way, once in a while.

You don't want keep shaking your head when you talk or when you listen. You can use your hands, but don't overdo.

Distractions

Physical issues arise far less often than vocal ones. However, if you have one, it can be very jarring to the audience. In addition, when these problems do arise, such as a physical tic, they are sometimes very difficult to eliminate. The first step is to recognize you have one, and the next step is to constantly be aware that you have it. Keep checking, and with continued awareness, you will be able to eliminate it. It will not be easy but it can be done.

For example, I had a student who unconsciously scratched his nose. Never scratch your nose no matter how much you think it itches. Soldiers will tell you that they never have an itch on their nose until they are ordered to stand at attention and not move a muscle. You too can learn not to scratch, even without the threat of a gazillion push ups from the drill sergeant. But if it helps, consider Nancy your drill sergeant and you will do those push ups, soldier, if I catch you scratching your nose.

At ease.

Another thing I see often, especially among women, is bringing a hand in front of the eyes to brush back their hair. Many people do this without changing their hair at all. It's a physical tic that comes from nervousness.

Having said all this, I still want you to be natural, spontaneous, alive, in the moment, charming and full of surprises.

A lot of your work will be taped. But some news stories and some news interviews take you, the reporter, on location to tell the story live. That's one of the pleasures of watching the news. It's one of the remaining productions on television that is still LIVE. So you have to be very confident in these situations. You can't move too much because your cameraperson will probably have limited room to move. You must be centered and simple. Keep your head from moving too much at an angle, though a little movement can be effective. One example: Take a few steps toward your camera as you begin your stand up.

Smiling with Teeth and Eyes

The news directors are all looking for this; so make sure to keep your gaze through the lens and on the viewer. Be generous with your smile (and teeth) when it is appropriate. If it is a breakfast morning show, certainly at the top of your show you should smile when you welcome the viewer. But always do what is appropriate for the story, for the moment and for the viewer. Of course if there's been a terrible tragedy you don't want to be wildly smiling.

Talk-show hosts generally don't have too many hard news or depressing stories. Because they have lighter fare, they tend to have more opportunity to smile. One of the great charms of Oprah is her wonderful and genuine smile emanating from a special heart inside.

Generally you want to smile when you say hello and good-bye to your viewer, just as you would if you met a friend on the street. Don't forget, there are millions of different smiles, and different intensities of smiles (more on this in the chapter on anchoring). Of course I don't want you grinning like an empty-headed nitwit either.

Your smile is a tool, and an important one that communicates so much without words. But a smile comes from inside. As in real life, your smile is an automatic response. Don't try to shut it down, and don't try to fake it.

Frolicking Eyebrows and Frowning

You do not want these. If you look at yourself on video and you see yourself frowning or moving your eyebrows up and down a great deal, you are not going to like what you see.

One solution is botox, but if that is not the answer for you, try this: Get some scotch tape. Tape it on to your forehead perpendicular to your eyebrows, or wrinkles, or between your eyes, above the bridge of your nose. Have a friend video tape you, if possible, while you read the copy.

While you are reading, you will feel every movement you make with your forehead. You can stop it. Of course you won't read as perfectly because you are focusing on the physical. Don't worry about that for a moment — you want to stop those facial tics. When you watch the playback video of yourself, you should see that most of those frowns or eyebrow lifts do not help your storytelling. They are a distraction.

Spreading Your Mouth Too Wide When Reading

You don't need to use your lips or mouth a great deal when you are speaking. For example take the long EEE sound, as in feet. No need to spread your lips to either side. Let your tongue do the work, not your lips or mouth.

Try this: Look in the mirror. Rest the tip of your tongue against the inside of your bottom teeth. Keeping it there, say the vowel sound EE. Then write a list of lots of words with EE in them, such as fleet, greet, meet and sleet, and say them looking into the mirror.

Watch that you don't say those EE words as if you are smiling with your mouth. When you watch yourself on video, be critical and watch for this and other exaggerations with the mouth. If you are using your mouth in an exaggerated fashion, become aware of it. It is not necessary. Your tongue will do most of the work for you.

Study the professionals you admire and notice how simply they use their mouths and lips. They never use their mouths to overenunciate their words. Exaggerating your lip and mouth movements will not aid your reading or voice in any way.

Of course on sounds like O, OU or AW, the lips and mouth must form an expanded shape. However, you probably won't need to exaggerate them as much as you think.

Your head should be centered most of the time. Women tend to tip their heads to the side submissively. But what you want is to eyeball your viewer directly. Drop your chin slightly so your eyes are looking directly through the camera.

You also don't want to blink too much. On your hellos and good-byes you always look directly at a friend when you say this in real life. You never blink. Try it — say, "Hello, I'm so happy to see you," to a real person. You will not blink. The same is true of the good-bye. "See you tomorrow, I promise." No blinking, and that's how it should be.

If you have tension in your hands, and your fingers are spread apart and slightly curled, this will be distracting to the viewer. Keep it simple, not fussy.

Summing Up

You are not an overacting circus clown on the air. Less is more on television. But you do not want to be a mummy — frozen in time and space. What you want is enough life on the set, or in the field, to pop out to the viewer. Like the smile, this comes from being relaxed and physically free and centered within this small space called a television monitor.

Checklist

- ❐ Don't play it too big on TV.
- ❐ Easy with your movement.
- ❐ Eliminate tics and frowns.
- ❐ Smile with your teeth and eyes.
- ❐ Don't fake it.

19

Looking Good

You must look as attractive as possible. Pay attention to how you look. This is not vanity, it's part of the toolbox of an anchor. Your face is on television, after all. If you were on radio, it wouldn't be important.

MAKE-UP!

In television, the good news is that lights will make sure you are seen well. The bad news is that there are a lot of very hot lights. Both women and men's skin wash out, so almost everyone on camera will need something to get skin tone back to the way it should look. In other words, make-up for television is needed to make people look normal.

People pay good money for make-up advice. But I'll save you some right here. This is a lesson from one of the very best make-up artists in television. For years, Christina Brice has been making up anchors like Dan Rather, reporters and the people they interview from businessmen to politicians to presidents, including Bill Clinton and George Bush. Here are her tricks of the trade for you.

Fig. 19-1 *Make-up at CBS News with Dan Rather.*

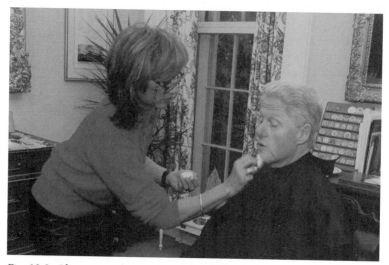

Fig. 19-2 *Christina making up President Clinton.*

Fig. 19-3 Christina with President Bush after make-up.

For Women

The days of journalist make-up, which is minimal, especially for women, are over, she says. Now, every woman on air has to be pretty and stunning.

Most female news anchors now are required to look at least a little glamorous. A soap opera actress playing the lead would have smokey eyes in her make-up. A news anchor would also have them now, just in a more subtle tone.

The morning news anchors especially are going with heavy make-up. Only Diane Sawyer keeps it to a minimun.

Oops! What To Watch Out For

What are the most common mistakes Christina sees among women on camera? She says sometimes the undereye concealer is too white so they look like raccoons. On color, many women tend to go a little bit too orange with their base coats.

For women and men too, get rid of the shine on your skin. It looks even worse on camera because it gets magnified.

What About Make-Up for Men?

Real men do wear make-up if they are in front of the camera. Men should wear a base make-up. The studio hot lights make you seem pale and flatten your features. If you have good features, you want them to be seen, of course. But even if you are less than a gorgeous male, your features are your personality and need to be visible. Make-up helps everyone under hot lights.

For men in the studio, use a foundation to help darken up. If you are outside, you should use a make-up to match your skin tone.

Many news people (and this is true for women too) have newsperson eyes. That comes with the territory — hours of work and hours of travel. So it's no surprise that one result is dark circles and bags under the eyes. Eyes are so important to your on-camera presence, you must do something about it. The fact is, it also comes with aging. So for the younger reporter, it's not going to be as much of a problem.

Fig. 19-4 Newsperson eyes ... fix 'em!

Lights can also help. They are one of the best friends of make-up artists. For example: Dan Rather sometimes uses lights oddly named pigeon lights. These are lights that are placed below his face and shoot upward. Many people use them. Their purpose is to get rid of dark shadows from under the eyes.

Men can get a little bit heavy and that can lead to jowls. Make-up to the rescue! Christina suggests that if this is you, you might want to shade under your neck with a darker color.

Some Tricks

It depends on what you're hiding. If you are hiding dark circles, you need to neutralize the blue. Think of an artist's color wheel. The opposite color of blue is red. So if you put something with a red tone only where the blue is, then go over it with a flesh tone color, you'll neutralize the blue. If you don't neutralize the blue and only put concealer on a dark circle, all it does is change the tone of the blue, and it becomes a lighter blue. The blue doesn't go away. You need to neutralize the blue color.

For students who don't have the luxury of a make-up person like Christina, there are things to remember. In the studio, she suggests you go darker a couple of shades in color. So if you are fair, darken down a couple of shades. "If I had a choice between too dark or too light," says Christina, "I'd always go a little on the darker side in skin tone. But not an orange intensity of darkness."

If you are fair, she suggests two steps darker because you will wash out under the lights. You can also do some subtle shadowing for the eyes and cheekbones.

If you don't know what you are doing, keep it simple with mascara and eye shadow. Brush a neutral color on your eyelid, use a little eyeliner and mascara. If you know what you are doing, you can play with the eye make-up.

For those out in the field, Christina suggests using very light make-up. It all depends on where you are. Obviously, if you are covering a catastrophe or something like September 11, you don't want to go out in full make-up. "In fact," said Christina, "I did people for 9-11 and did a 'No make-up look.'"

A little bit of mascara, a little bit of foundation, a neutral color … and out you go. (If you are in the field and there is heavy lighting, it's just like the studio. Where there is natural lighting, you won't be as washed out.)

What about blues and purples for eye shadow? She says she usually doesn't use them. But there are exceptions. Sometimes she might dot a blue color in with the eyeliner to pop the eye. You can use them, it's just the application.

The whole secret of make-up is application.

Lipstick

When it comes to lipstick, what about a color, like red?

Christina prefers more of a neutral lipstick and does not personally like reds. On the other hand some women look great in certain reds. Just make sure they don't bounce out too much. They can sometimes look harsh, so double check that the red you choose works for you on camera.

Try using a neutral lip color, Spice or Cedar — a light, rusty brown. The names may change, so look for a soft color that complements your skin, eyes and entire face.

Always check that you don't have lipstick on your teeth.

Make-Up for Young and Old

If you have a young, fresh face, keep it young and fresh. On the flip side, what if you have wrinkles? What can you do about wrinkles?

The secret to wrinkles, says Christina, is skin care. Pay attention to what you eat and how you sleep. Make-up cannot fix wrinkles. Make-up can only give you a product that will be a temporary mask. Make-up artists for the entertainment industry sometimes use little devices called lifts (a string with two tabs put behind the ear then through your hair). The make-up artist then pulls the strings tight and voila! Instant facelift. Today however, these lifts are rarely used since plastic surgery has become so popular.

Make-Up and Hair for Ethnic Skin Tones

If yours is a very dark skin color, man or woman — doesn't matter — without any make-up your skin tone reads blue or ashy. You will need to warm up your skin. Take a chocolate color and mix some reds in it. The red will counteract the blue and bring out the richness that you see in daylight.

In lipsticks, stay away from the reds with blue tones; go with the reds with warmth. The natural colors of the lips also vary. In the case of some African-American women, each lip can have a different shade naturally. It can vary widely, too, says Christina. She says she has worked with women who's lower lip is as much as ten shades darker than the upper lip. Her suggestion to even out the shades is match to the darker tone using lip concealer, then add lipstick.

Do Black Women Have to Straighten Their Hair?

This is a question Christina is often asked in the privacy of her make-up room. She believes that although the news business is changing, it remains a good-old-boy system, by and large.

"Every black woman I've worked with," says Christina, "has gone to work at one time or another with natural hair. And they all get negative remarks about it. Every single one of them.

"Rene Syler, on *CBS Early Morning*, is an exception," notes Christina. "She has very short hair and they do style it ... but it is natural. But pretty much as long as I've been working in news, when African-American women come in with natural hair (even behind the camera) it gets a negative response."

What about Make-Up for Asian Women?

The eyes, says Christina, tend to be the problem area for Asian women. "Some," she says, "wear a lot of eye make-up and it looks good but it is definitely high-end eye make-up."

For you as a beginner, Christina advises, "Less is best. It's always easier to add make-up than to take it off." If you do eyeliner, draw a thin line. Adding a little more mascara on the corner of the eye can give it a lift and open up your eyes.

Make-Up for Entertainment Reporters

If you are an entertainment reporter, you can go further with your make-up. Entertainment reporters wear make-up that rivals the make-up of the people they are interviewing: It is more glamorous, edgier. MTV would encourage a lot of glitter, maybe a trendy color like hot pink or bubblegum lipgloss.

"I have a concept about trends," Christina says. "When I first started make-up, I learned that if you wear clean make-up, it will be timeless. If you look at old Hollywood pictures, some of the make-up that was done then is still done now." If you choose classic colors, you will never be out of style.

Trends, like heavy eyeliner that comes to a point in the outer corners of the eye, false eyelashes on the top and the bottom, was hot in the 1960s but it's dated now.

Make sure that if you are working in the hot sun for any length of time (reporting from Iraq for example), wear a strong sun block. This is true for both men and women.

Tips for Men

Never wear heavy, or pancakey looking make-up. And don't wear blush. Men can dye their eyelashes and eyebrows, if they are too light or too dark. Men should keep their skin healthy, too. Don't laugh — eye creams are useful to you too. You will be wearing lots of make-up, day in and day out, so take care of your skin. Use a moisturizer.

If your hands are shown on camera a lot, it is good to use make-up on them as well. Dan Rather had to keep pointing to a board that showed the different states on one election night. His hands were made up. It would have looked strange to have his hands a different color than his face. This is an old Hollywood trick. Men don't like make-up even on the back of their hands because they are afraid it will get their shirt or jacket messy. The up side is, make-up base is a great concealer of veins and age spots. Even a light application does the trick.

Tips for Women

Use your concealer properly, says Christina. There is a tendency to have too much white under the eyes. If you shade cheeks, under your jaw or along your nose, blend the shading so it doesn't look too heavy or streaky and you don't see the lines.

There is no difference in make-up products for men or women. When applying a base coat on your face, always use a sponge for smoother blending.

Overall, for most reporters, beware of looking as if you've stepped out of a soap opera. Lean toward the conservative.

So Where Do You Get Your Make-Up?

Christina says she's used drug store make-up. These make-ups won't break the bank, and can be bought anywhere in the United States and work well. Some brand names are Max Factor, Revlon, and Iman's make-up. Remember, she's the model and wife of David Bowie. Even some very inexpensive products do the job well: Wet and Wild and Cover Girl. Christina says, "My theory of make-up is, it's all about application." When Christina says application, again, she means blending. Christina also uses high-end make-up. And they both work well.

What about going to one of those make-up artists that are in the department stores? She says she would definitely stay away from the department stores. They are using their own brand and they are there to sell. Beware of going to a make-up person who works for a specific company. They'll just use their commercial products and probably have no experience in how to use make-up for television.

Television Make-Up Products

There are a lot of professional products made for the television market today that work well, says Christina. "They are meant for television as opposed to make-up that's made for street wear."

The brand makers of television make-up are Visora, Bill Tuttle, Bob Kelly, Ben Nye and RCMA (Research Council of Make-up Artists). Several Make-up artists got together and created this make-up for the on-camera talent to wear.

Christina works with many different products, ones from Duane Reade and ones from Alcone, that are fabulous under lights, but quite expensive. (Alcone is a make-up store in New York.) If your budget is tight she will help you by finding less-expensive products. Lucky you if you live in New York or Los Angeles. But there are fine make-up people in all the big cities.

Hair Counts

Hairstyles for men and women anchors are important. A conservative hairdo for men and women is a must.

If you have long hair (hair that falls below your shoulders), put it behind your shoulders or cut it to shoulder length or shorter. There are a few women who look good with their hair pulled back.

If you are losing your hair, you can get a fairly respectable hairpiece. But please don't look as if you have a rug on your head, it's better to do without!

Color is also important — for men and women. Highlights around the face can brighten your eyes. Again, be strong and know what you want, at least to some degree, when you go to a hairdresser. If you are going to a new hairdresser, it's a good idea to bring a picture so that the stylist has a starting point. Communication is difficult when talking with someone new about color and style. Short can mean different things to different folks ... so can blond, so can wavy. So bring along the visual aids.

How you do your hair, and to some extent your make-up, becomes part of who you are to the viewer. So making a radical change in your appearance is something you should be very careful about.

For everyone with very dark hair, beware of the helmet look. You don't want sloppy, flyaway hair, but you don't want to look like a kewpie doll that's been sprayed to death either. The secret here is to get yourself a great cut. Then after that, put hairspray on your hands and run them through your hair to avoid those loose flyaway hairs. This way, instead of spraying the whole hairdo and making it look stiff and frozen, your hair will look natural but still have some movement.

If you like to wear bangs, check that they don't throw shadows onto your face. This may distract from the clean look you are striving to produce. And, if you have long hair be careful it doesn't brush against the lav mic you are wearing. If it does, it makes a swooshing sound that the viewer can hear while you are speaking.

If you are a man with a thinning hairline, try using a matching color eye shadow to fill in the hairless spaces using a clean brush. This works well.

Report from the Trenches

A young reporter was well regarded in the network. She was smart, perky and very pretty. She had this luxurious dark hair and stunning blue eyes. That wasn't why she was successful, but it did help. And it may have been at least part of the reason why the executives were considering her as the anchor of the morning show.

Of course she was excited and wanted the job. She evidently thought about how she might make an impression, but she didn't talk to anyone before taking action. She was scheduled to be the anchor for a two-week tryout. The weekend before, she went to her hairstylist and had her hair chopped very very short. No one had ever seen her look like that. It was a jaw-dropping difference. And the reaction from the executives shook her confidence.

Needless to say, the two-week tryout did not go well. She wasn't offered the job as anchor; and worse, she left network news shortly after that. The lesson here is: If you are an anchor, or are trying out for an anchor's job, and your looks are well known, be wary about making a big change.

Hair Spray

Hair spray in the field can be a lifesaver. The wind tossing your hair around in interviews and stand-ups can be so distracting to the viewers that they won't listen to what is being said.

But Christina makes a good point: Stay away from the camera ... spray in the opposite direction from the camera.

Eyes

Your eyes are vitally important. It is true that your eyes are the windows to your soul. People relate to you through your eyes. They can be a stunning attraction, the jewels of your face.

If you need glasses to help you read, try contacts, especially if you are beginning in the business. How many anchors do you see who wear glasses on camera?

If you wear glasses, they may bring you an identity that sets you apart. But be sure that you get your optometrist to put the nonglare coating on your glasses. This way the viewer will see your eyes, and you won't look like a 1950's game show contestant with the studio lights bouncing off your lenses.

For men, eyebrows should be trimmed and groomed so we can see your eyes. But for some men, it may part of your personality. Andy Rooney would not be the same without those bushy eyebrows.

Teeth

A word about teeth. Your smile can be a winning smile, which means winning viewers. This is about making you as approachable and attractive to your viewers as possible. Make sure your teeth look good. There are many ways to improve them. Straighten the front teeth if you have a major problem there.

Teeth should be white and sparkling. No make-up exists that you can buy to whiten teeth. The best thing to do: Go to your dentist. Some of the methods are not too expensive and what you spend making your smile better is well worth it.

Clothes Make the Anchor

As an anchor you don't want anything to distract from the story you are telling. You want your viewer to feel comfortable with you.

Wardrobe

You can help define who you are by what you wear. Check with your instincts and also check with someone you trust that what you are wearing is the best for you.

Most anchors prefer to wear a suit jacket. This gives them a comfortable and nice looking place to wear their lav mic. They can clip it onto their lapel.

A blouse can look sloppy if a lav mic is clipped onto the material. Most blouses are made from fairly lightweight material and when they are weighted down, even by a tiny mic, wrinkles will appear and look terrible. The kind of material will affect the way the lav mic sits on your shirt. Never use soft materials like silk. The lav mic will pull, making a mess of your blouse.

If the mic is attached to the collar of a high-necked dress, be careful that it is not placed too high up on the clothing. You want to be sure that it is the proper distance from your mouth.

Men can clip the lav mic onto their tie. Ties for men can be fun and individual; but men, be careful about the patterns in your ties. The general rule is don't wear plaids or dots or stripes. They moray, or appear to shimmer on camera, particularly the stripes in your ties.

Report from the Trenches

A very well-known network anchorman was preparing to tape an open for a package done for a news magazine show. The report had focused on fashion and the anchor had interviewed men's fashion designer Bill Blass for the report.

As a gesture, Blass sent over a selection of ties for the anchor. Knowing what was proper, the anchor sent a note back to Mr. Blass thanking him for the ties but explaining that he couldn't accept the gift without paying for them. So he sent along a check, too. Then he wore one of the ties for the taped open. The one he chose was a polka dot tie that he knew was an anchor no-no. He mentioned in passing he regretted that young men studying him on how to become an anchor might begin sporting polka dotted ties.

He sincerely hoped it wouldn't happen.

Also beware of the plaids in your jackets. They may look great in real life but not at the news desk for a broadcast.

Generally, for an anchor, it doesn't matter what shoes, skirts or pants you wear if you are seated at the desk. However, recently many shows have had their anchors standing with a full-body shot. This has been the case for weather reporters for years. If this is the case for you, everything you wear matters.

Bejeweled? Be Careful

Be careful of the jewelry trap. You may feel good about wearing that special piece of jewelry — a broach or ring that someone special gave you. But these may become distractions on the air.

I'd suggest staying away from wearing flashy jewelry. But also, whatever jewelry you do wear, be careful of jewelry sounds, such as a bracelet banging the anchor desk or a necklace that clinks against the microphone clipped near your neck. (The mic is threaded underneath your jacket or blouse and pinned to the lapel or tie.) The audio will pick up rustling or clanking if you are not careful.

For men, be careful of the banging sound of cufflinks.

One exception might be if you are covering a glamorous opening or charity ball. You should be well dressed, if you are live on

Fig. 19-5 Tooooo loud jewels.

location. If that means guests would be wearing diamonds or pearls, then you should, too. But be careful not to become so fancy that you lose your relationship with your viewers.

It's You, It's Your Responsibility

When you get to the NBC Network, you can relax about your own make-up. That network is moving toward a single "Look." The network is sending make-up artists to do a unified look for all on-camera people at all of its outlets, including cable. That is also true of its wardrobe look. One year, for example, all of the on-air talent wore clothes from Saks Fifth Avenue. That is the current trend at the networks with NBC leading the way.

Before you get there, your face is your responsibility. Even if your station has a make-up person, you know your own face better than anyone else. If you don't, become familiar with it. As they say in diplomacy, trust, but verify.

Remember Al Gore's debate with George W. Bush before the elections? He trusted his make-up people too much. His make-up made him look like the orange man from some badly shot cheap indie film. So know what looks good on you.

If you look at yourself in the mirror as if you are someone else, then you are in a position to assess what is needed for that face. Make-up is an important tool because your face, your hair — your look — is an important tool.

You should be able to learn how to make yourself up in a way that plays to your attributes on camera. As a young reporter, this will almost always be your responsibility. Later in your career, you will be better able to advise a make-up artist like Christine, tell her what has worked for you and what problems you have been able to overcome with make-up. The same is true for your wardrobe.

So look at that face and body, and bring out the best in them for your on-camera presentations.

Where To Go

I'm always asked by my students, "Where can I find a good make-up artist? Who can I go to get a good styling for on-camera work?" Well, there is a union for all the make-up artists and hairstylists who are professionals and work for film and television. The numbers of the union vary in each city. The three main ones that will assist you wherever you live are:

New York City, Local 798. Tel. (212) 627-0660. This is where you can find make-up references for the east coast, all the way to Florida.

Chicago, Local 476. Tel. (773) 775-5300. This local will help you out for the central states.

California, Local 706. Tel. (818) 295-3933. These folks can give you references for the west coast.

Give them a call for make-up consultants. They'll give you a few names. Try the artists out ahead of time to make sure you like what they do.

Getting the Job

20

Preparing Your Reel

Advice from the Trenches

Joe Duke is the point man for recruiting talent to CBS News. Before that, he assessed reporters and anchors from his post as news director in New Orleans.

He has seen presentation tapes that jumped out at him so much that once he hired a reporter in New Orleans when he didn't even have a job available. He's also seen reels filled with mistakes. So what Joe has to say about putting together your reel is the very best advice you may ever hear.

So How Do I Make a Good Reel?

A pretty good form for students to use in preparing a presentation tape is to open with a montage. Use stand-ups, a bit of anchoring, a snip of an interview situation, a live report from the field, and part of a package. It should present a series of different looks so the viewer, in this case the news director or the recruiter, can see what you look like — what you look like in the studio, what you look like when there's a big brush fire raging behind you.

These brief clips don't need to be total thoughts. It's purely the physical at this point — how you look and how you sound. You are giving the news director a fast first impression.

The montage is 20 seconds, with as many looks as you can give it. It's not about presenting concise, complete thoughts in the montage;

Fig. 20-1 Joe Duke. COURTESY OF MARIE WALLACE

it's entirely about impressions. In other words, style over substance at the top of the reel.

Joe says you should be aware that most recruiters and news directors will often look at the montage without looking at the rest of the reel.

NANCY'S RULES

Always put your best stuff on top.

Your reel is not a journalist's tape, it's a promotional tape.

At this point, the news director is not worried about the journalism. All that the news director wants to know is: Do you grab the viewers or do the viewers turn off when they look at you. Are the looks good? Is the voice good? To the people who screen tapes all the time, your qualities are obvious instantly — both your good qualities and your bad.

Joe will look at 30 or 40 tapes at a sitting, maybe more than that. While other recruiters don't get very much past the opening, Joe says he does.

"I watch more than people think I do and probably more than I should. But at the network level you are seeing people who are seasoned and you need to give them the benefit of the doubt, you need to go through and look at what they've sent. Maybe you spot something."

Don't count on the person watching your early reels getting that far.

What Goes on Your Reel?

This is a question many of my students ask: Should the reel have complete pieces or just parts of pieces and how many?

Joe says that after the montage, three pieces is fine. Three complete pieces. The reel shouldn't run more than eight or nine minutes max. He says most news directors get through the first two packages, maybe. If they get past that point, then they look for other skills. He says at that point he wants to see if you can write.

Remember, Joe and others who do this for a living want to be impressed. They are looking for people to hire.

What Does Not Go on Your Reel?

Joe has seen millions of bad tapes. He is astonished to see what so many young reporters put on their presentation tape.

"People continually put mistakes they made on the air on their resume tape," he says, "as examples of how they recovered. I always say, do yourself a favor, pull that segment out. You don't want a news director thinking you make mistakes. You know what's going through the news director's mind the first time you go on the air: I hope he or she doesn't screw up like the time I saw on that tape. Also, it shows something about your judgment that you would put a mistake on your tape. Why would you put that on a tape that you are showing a news director? What kind of person is this?"

Another mistake he sees is the weather disaster stand-up (you in the hurricane) in the montage. He believes you do yourself no favors using it.

"I don't think stand-ups in hurricanes, where you are being blown about, is very effective. People who are looking at tape want to see something that is more ordinary and they want to get an idea of what you actually look like. And you can't get that when you've got a hood over your face and you're holding on to a tree for dear life. Now if you want to put a hurricane piece on your tape somewhere, that's fine, but a stand-up in a hurricane in the montage is going to leave people cold."

Little things leave a big impression. It may not be fair, but when news directors watch the tape of a good young person and the hairstyle is all wrong, or the clothes are wrong, that often kills the reporter's chance of getting hired.

"All that can be fixed," agrees Joe, "but the problem is you are not going to get past the people who are going to make the decision who to hire because they say, 'Look at that dress,' well that's the end of that person's chance."

You have to be ruthless with your tapes.

NANCY'S RULES

Don't use any mistakes on your reel.
Make sure you look your very best.
Make sure you eliminate bad packages.

Story Lines for the Reel

Reporters have to be critical about the stories on their reels too.

Joe uses the example of the reporter who puts: "I jumped the fence to get this interview" into the script. Unfortunately, the interview that followed on the tape was terrible.

Joe is thinking, "He jumped the fence for *that*."

The news director doesn't care about the effort. All the news director cares about is the finished product. The means are of no importance. Oh, he jumped across the fence so he could show this crummy interview. No one cares about the effort except you. Do not assume news directors are going to think you are a great reporter simply because you jumped over a fence. Do not assume the interview you got that way will be good either.

Take it out. Be aggressive with your own material.

If you are doing a stand-up and the camera has a glitch, throw that out even if it was your best read and you looked great and there was a great bit of action behind you at that moment.

Remember what Joe says: Your reel is a sales tape; it's not a journalism tape. It's a process that starts with the montage ... saying hey, good to see you!

Joe says you see this every morning on the news shows. They open the door every morning, invite you in and you stay because you just like them. The viewers can also close the door real fast. They can turn the dial to another station, open another door, because the viewers have all these doors they can open. It's the same with your tape. Your montage gets the door open and then you have the opportunity to let the news director get to know you and hopefully get to like you.

Should I Use a Famous Person in the Package on My Reel?

You bet. The more famous the better. That would catch Joe's eye, especially if it's a young reporter.

"I think it can be very impressive," says Joe. Particularly if it's a young person. "What they've demonstrated is the ability to accomplish what I know can be a difficult thing and that is booking a well-known person for the interview. They actually got it and they actually sat across from say Kofi Annan and asked him questions. How valuable is that!"

What if My Story Isn't Mine But I Have To Have Something on a Reel?

Many of my students scrounge tape where they can find it. Tape from class, tape recorded from a news show and maybe tape from someone who has access to a tape library if they are lucky. From there you get interviews that you didn't do and video that you didn't shoot and put together a package that you didn't plan or research.

Is that OK to present on your reel? Yes, says Joe, if you are truthful. He knows this happens all the time and understands it.

"Lets take a college student or an intern at a local station," says Joe, who saw lots of them when he was a news director. "In many cases, how else are they going to get tape to use for a package to put on their reel? Many go out in a shadow way with a correspondent who is shooting a story."

Some of my students who do work as interns at television stations do this. They follow the reporter on the shoot so they know what was shot and what the story is. Many often use this trick: They will ask the crew to do them a favor and shoot a stand-up for them. They go back to the station, use some of the interview the reporter did, use the video the crew shot and write a story.

"I see a lot of tapes like that from young people who are really observers of the story being covered who then take the material and create their own story from it. I don't mind that at all honestly."

He doesn't mind it as long as it is your script.

"I'll know if a young reporter didn't write the story because it will be better than the rest of the reel." If you plagiarize, it will be apparent to professionals like Joe.

What about Production Houses That Provide Package Help?

There are places that do generic pieces for students. They provide the script and the video already shot and the student reads that script and does a stand-up, at a mall for example.

Joe sees them of course. And again, as long as you are honest about the origins of the piece, it's fine with him.

"I sort of don't care. Here's who really does that: It's people who are in schools where they don't have access to good production facilities, they have no tape or cannot shoot a stand-up. So if I'm a news director in Mobile and you come by and say I'm just graduating from South Alabama College and I'd like a job, I'm going to ask to look at your tape. You have a tape that might get you a job."

For Joe, it's all about that person he sees on the tape. And without a tape there is no chance. Plus, he believes the stations accept facts about newly hired reporters that might surprise you.

"If I'm a small market news director, here is what I am going to do: I'm going to teach them the journalism. If I'm market size 75 to 175, I just assume they can't write, I just assume they can't report. What I'm looking for is what comes across, what draws me to them. Part of that is the tape and part of that is the interview process."

Most young reporters start in small markets. The good news is you will probably meet a seasoned veteran who will continue your education. The bad news is you won't be making any money there. They just don't pay well. On the other hand, you won't be earning a tiny salary for very long, will you? You are going to get to a bigger market fast.

 Report from the Trenches

Joe tells a story about a young man who had just gotten his first job, starting work in a small market. He was all excited and told his parents about the job. His mother told Joe that the young man wasn't making any money. Joe told her that he wasn't going to be there very long, that it's part of the impetus to get him to a bigger market. In five years that young man was in one of the top markets in the country, working in San Francisco.

In small markets, says Joe, they're not going to pay you because they realize you're not going to stay. In most cases, they really don't want you to stay.

What Makes a Reel Jump Out?

For Joe it's more than the sum of the parts. It's always about the storyteller, he says.

"It's connecting with the person, it's always connecting with the person. You can take a double-decker bus around the city and you can get an animated, excited storyteller who makes you appreciate the Empire State Building ... or you can have somebody who drones on. In our business the really good storytellers cut through and make the material so pleasing that people get it. That's what a tape does too, the storytellers instantly come through or they don't."

 Report from the Trenches

When Joe was a news director in New Orleans, a top-50 market, he saw the tapes of many young reporters. This was one that jumped out.

"There was a woman who is now a correspondent at NBC who was a weekend anchor in Fort Myers, Florida, a small market. She had an agent who called me asking 'Are you hiring?' I said, 'No, I am not.'

"She said, 'I have somebody I'd like you to look at.'

"So she sends me this tape and I look at the tape and here is this woman who is young and wearing funny glasses and she's got on this flowered dress doing the news. You know, she's just big. She smiles and looks into the camera when they go to commercial and she says, 'Oh, I'll wait for you to come back.' Joe says he just bought into the whole thing.

"So I took the tape up to my boss and I said, 'I've got this person you ought to look at, and he says, 'We don't have any openings.' I said, 'I know, but you've got to look at this tape.' He looked at the tape and he turned to me and said, 'We just have to meet her.'

"I called her up and she flew in. I took her to lunch and I was smitten. I took her to my boss and he loved her too. So we hired her. We created a job. It came as a big surprise to the weekend anchor when I told him he was no longer going to anchor by himself, that she was going to anchor with him. We weren't even looking for someone and she just knocked me over."

For her, the tape opened Joe's door. Her interview and the stories she had done got her through the door and into a job.

"We met her, we spent some time with her. I saw more stories that she had done and I had a better picture of her than just the tape. Before you hire them, you've got to have more than just the impressions from the tape."

How Important Is an Agent?

This is a question I get from every class I have ever taught. Joe thinks it is essential to have an agent, but not right away.

"Maybe not when you are starting out fresh from school and no one wants to represent you then anyway. And likely not your first job and probably not your second job either. By the time you are moving to a market size 50 and above, you probably should have some representation. And when you deal with the big markets and the networks, it's important."

The table in Joe's office is stacked two and three high with tapes from prospective reporters. He sweeps his arm across them. "Most of these tapes come from agents."

What about Looks?

Looks are important, says Joe. So are clothing and neatness. Never ever assume that you are so good that it shouldn't matter what you look like.

"I don't care how good you are and how much you know what you are talking about, how well you have researched and written your report, your looks count. If the viewers are distracted or turned off by your looks on television, they are not going to listen to a thing you say. In newspapers you can be a troll and write well and you are great. In television, maybe there was a time you could be a troll and write well and be accepted but those days are long gone."

Report from the Trenches

There is a story that is still told about a fine radio reporter. She had a great voice and was a great reporter. She dropped hints that she wanted to make the move from radio to television news, which happens quite often because both are written for the ear and need to be tightly written.

So three of the top women in television, friends and colleagues of hers, invited her out to lunch to give her some helpful hints on how to go about it. One of their main objectives was to discuss her appearance. She was no beauty but she did have good presence. She was not a troll by any means.

But looks didn't count in radio and no one had ever thought to suggest to her about working on her appearance. So the women, all blonds by the way, delicately brought up the issue.

Did she ever wear make-up, they asked. They had never seen her wearing make-up. No, she said, and wasn't about to start. They moved gingerly to the big topic, her hair. It was a dull longish thatch of uncombed brown. After a few moments she caught the drift of the conversation and put a stop to it.

"Forget it if you think I'm going to be one of those bleach blonds you see on television all the time," she told them. Told the three blonds whom you still see on TV. Of course it's about her overall appearance. And she never did make a career in television.

To School or Not To School? What about Education?

My students are already in school studying television so this question doesn't come up much. But they do often wonder if it's a waste of time. Of course my answer is, "No way is studying with me a waste of time!" Joe thinks studying the craft is essential.

"If you are in high school and you want to become a television journalist there is a process that you will have to go through. Some short-circuit it, though not as many as you might think. You are going to have to go to a school and study communications and other things as well. Most everyone now is taking a communications course in some form. It may be called journalism, communications, mass communications or media studies.

"Then there's the other thing that's coming into play: I'm seeing more and more resumes with master's degrees in communication. It does nothing for me. Though why not have it."

Does It Matter Which School?

Within the TV journalism industry there are some schools that will stand out on a resume. "Northwestern is one of them," says Joe, "University of Missouri is one, Columbia, the Newhouse School at Syracuse and others."

Would it make a difference if a student didn't go to one of those but Joe liked the tape? "If I like the tape it won't make any difference at all."

What about Writing Skills?

If they are honest, most beginning reporters will admit that writing is not one of their best skills. For many, it ranks way down on the skill set. Yet writing is important for reporters. It's at least half the job. And being a good writer helps in other ways, says Joe.

"People who can write well and who are smart are also attractive. They don't have to be beautiful but they can't be distracting."

Many of my students think they are better at writing for television than they really are. News directors hear the same thing.

"They all think they are really good writers," says Joe. "Who's going to come out of school saying, 'Well I really can't write but I want to be a reporter.'"

My suggestion is to take a good writing course.

What Experience Does Joe Look For?

Weekend anchor is a good job to have because you can get experience both anchoring and reporting. Sometimes the reporter covering major stories is more like a field anchor, the point person for the developing story. That's valuable experience.

This happens more at local stations than at the network, but it happens often enough on the networks during major news stories. It happened during the death of the Pope, it happens during elections, it happened at the verdict of the Michael Jackson trial and of course during September 11.

What's the Key Thing I Should Worry about on My Reel?

Not worrying is the key. Use your best judgment, use your best stuff and be harsh. Joe and the other professionals will see everything about you. There is just no hiding yourself from them.

"The tapes reveal who you are," says Joe, "what you see is what you get. The style is in the way they write, the way they put words together, the way they conduct their interviews, the way they ask questions — I think all of that is going to show that personality.

"I look at a tape, I will see the potential, see down the road. And I'll see it right away, see it in the way they hold the microphone, the way they look into the camera, in the way they take five steps instead of three in the stand-up. The way they reach up and grab a leaf or the way they grab somebody for an interview."

More Stuff from Joe

In his position as a recruiter of reporters, Joe visits two major talent banks to screen tapes. Obviously this is a good place for your tape too. Here is some background on them.

Talent Dynamics in Dallas will put a tape up that will have 80 reels on it. "I'll just have the fast forward in my hand and I'll just fast forward through many of them."

Talent Dynamics is a talent bank, which was formerly part of Artists Research and Development — AR&D. Sandra Connell runs it. Joe would call Sandra and say he's looking for weekend anchors who might be great correspondents.

Talent Dynamics says it will review your video for possible inclusion in its National Talent Library. If it is accepted, it charges a one-time processing fee of $35.

Send a thorough resume with references and resume tape to:

Talent Dynamics
National Talent Library
600 Las Colinas Blvd., Suite 100
Irving, TX 75039
The phone number is (214) 630-9590
The website is Talentdynamics.com

There are video guidelines from Talent Dynamics for your resume tape:

VHS format
15–20 minutes long
Name and telephone on label of tape
Make sure it fairly represents your talents
Include a resume

At the Frank Magid Consultants in Marion, Iowa, it's a woman named Barbara Fry. You can reach out to these people yourself.

The Frank Magid website is Magid.com. There is no fee to be listed on that database.

Send your resume and reel to:

Frank N. Magid Associates
Talent Placement Service
One Research Center
Marion, IA 52302

A Few Words to Grow By. . .

I've given you plenty of rules but I have one more to add, and one more Report from the Trenches.

You are going to join a very influential business with a voice heard around your community, or in some cases, around the world. But you should know that it is still a very small business in spite of its outsized influence. For all its power, it is still a small community of people, most of whom you will work with at some point over a long career.

NANCY'S RULES

Make a good first impression.

The first impression you make will be the one that stays with you forever. If it is a good one, such as Melinda Murphy's who will give you advice soon, you will walk an easier road than others who have stumbled during their early steps. I mean this both professionally and personally.

Professionally, if you are known as a dedicated worker, that will stay with you. If you are not, that will follow also. If you are a terrific writer, a fast worker or a self-starter, that reputation will help you and will stay with you, too. So will the opposite. Make the right steps early and you will be rewarded.

I also mean this personally. No one likes to work with jerks. So if you have negative qualities in your personality, lose them. Bury them. Get rid of them. If you are self-centered, have a bad temper or are some kind of humorless, nasty individual, you will pay for it during your career.

 ## Report from the Trenches

You may not know this from his notoriety, but Bill O'Reilly really wanted to become a big time network correspondent, even a network anchor one day. But he spent his career in the cable world that has about a quarter of the viewers as network news broadcasts. Why? In part, at least, because of his reputation. He might argue his bad reputation is unfair and perhaps wrong. But network executives knew his reputation as self-centered and trouble. Say what he might, but I suspect it did hurt his chances of becoming a successful network correspondent or anchor.

Some of that reputation can be seen from a story that makes its rounds to this day. O'Reilly was a young reporter working for WCBS in New York City. He had the on-camera presence that news directors look for. He was a handsome young man, bright and well spoken. He was given a chance to be an anchor on weekend news broadcasts. This is often the place where the young reporters get their shots at anchoring. It's a great place for the news directors to try out their young reporters, and it's a great opportunity for the young reporters to show their stuff.

Unfortunately for O'Reilly, he showed some of the stuff that hurts you. On camera, he was fine. But off camera he was full of himself and let it show.

The anchorman at the station at the time was the legendary Jim Jensen, one of the top local anchors in the country. His office just off the newsroom was the most prominent, reflecting his importance. It was the biggest and the plushest.

Jim didn't work weekends. But often, he'd show up late on Sunday morning, carrying a cup of coffee and a stack of newspapers. He'd stop by the producer's desk and ask if anything of interest was happening. Then he'd get comfortable in his office and read the papers.

As the weekend anchor, O'Reilly usually showed up mid-morning read in. On one Sunday, not long after he'd gotten the weekend anchoring job, he asked the producer if Jensen was in. No, said the producer, he hadn't seen him. The producer didn't think much about it. O'Reilly left the newsroom.

What the producer didn't know was that O'Reilly went to Jensen's office instead of his own cubicle. The door was left open by the cleaning people as it always was on Sundays. O'Reilly had gotten comfortable with his feet on Jensen's desk, his newspapers strewn around.

A while later Jim Jensen stopped by the producer's desk with a morning greeting and a question about what was in the news. They chatted a bit and Jensen left in the direction of his office.

Then came the eruption. Screaming, yelling and all sorts of commotion blew into the newsroom. Then O'Reilly came scooting around the corner.

"Who the heck is that?" thundered Jensen to the producer. "And what's he doing at my desk?"

It was clear what he was doing. O'Reilly featured himself as the next Jim Jensen ... or at least good enough to be deserving of Jensen's desk.

His reputation was made. Many of the people who became network executives worked in that newsroom. And they all knew this story and what it said about Bill O'Reilly.

You can learn a lot from the cautionary tale of a Bill O'Reilly. But I hope you can learn more from the story of Melinda Murphy. Some years ago, this young and enthusiastic Texan showed up in one of my classes. She was tall, very pretty and as hard a worker as I have had in class. So it is no surprise to me that Melinda went on to a very successful on-camera career first in local stations and then in network television.

When I told her I was writing a book and would like her to give my students a few words of advice, she said she would. Here are Melinda's few words of advice. A whole chapter of them. Enjoy and learn.

How To Land a Job in Television

By Melinda Murphy

Passion.

Remember that word. Passion is THE key to getting a job in television.

And trust me, nobody in the world will be as passionate about your career as you will be. Your agent won't. Your best friend won't. Heck, even your mother won't. So if you don't have a burning fire in your gut pushing you to look for a job in front of the camera, you're not going to get one. It's that simple.

Why? Because your career is not as important to anybody else as it is to you. Sure, your agent (when you finally get one) will root for you. She'll send your tape to potential employers. She'll make the follow-up calls. But remember, you are not her only client. She may have ten or fifteen clients vying for exactly the same position.

So landing that job is really up to you. And this chapter has some suggestions to help you do it. But just know that looking for an on-camera job is tough. There are dozens of people who want that exact same job you do. So if you don't believe in yourself and if you don't market yourself properly, then you're never going to make it in television.

So passion is the key. Well, that and a great resume tape — and a marketing plan.

The passion part I can't teach you. Nobody can. Either you have it or you don't. And if you don't, you can stop reading now.

Fig. 21-1 Melinda Murphy. COURTESY OF CBS

"I Want To Be On TV" Is Not Enough.

When you approach somebody about an on-camera job you'd better have more to say than "I want to be on TV just because I want to be" or "I am curious about the world." Yeah, right. Tell me something I don't know. LOTS of people want to be on TV. But why would somebody hire you versus somebody else? If you're a beginner, that's a tough question. The best answer is because you know a lot about something else.

A great way to go about landing an on-camera gig is to become an expert in something first. Many of the on-air personalities you see these days started out as a vet or a lawyer or a chef or whatever and they were able to take that knowledge and use it to make an on-camera career for themselves. I met one woman at a conference who strongly discourages people from getting a journalism degree. She thinks you need to be an expert in another field first.

I don't necessarily agree, but I do think she has the right idea when she steers people starting out into learning a lot about another topic. Even if you don't get a degree in something else, it doesn't hurt to bone up on some important topics. If you want to be a political reporter, you'd better darn well be an expert in politics — even if that only means you've read every single article about this year's political race.

Read the papers. Follow your curiosity. Work hard. Network, network, network. That, my friend, will take you further than a piece of paper on your wall.

If you're still with me, then it's time to talk about your resume tape.

Your First Tape

There's simply no downplaying the importance of a resume tape. In a nutshell, your tape is you. It's your calling card, your one chance to make a good impression. So it has to be great — plain and simple.

If you're just starting out, you probably don't have a lot to put on a tape. And that's exactly why you'll find your first tape is probably the hardest to assemble. It's the true test of passion and tenacity. "What in the world can I put on it?" you think.

Well, for starters, you can include things you did in school or in a class like Nancy's. Additionally, I suggest renting a broadcast-quality camera, grabbing a friend and putting yourself on tape. Do as many stand-ups in one day as you can muster. Travel to a different location each time. Change your clothes between each scenario. Fix your make-up. And do each stand-up over and over until you get one in the can you like. And be sure to use every single thing you've learned. When you get tired, stop doing them. If you lose your energy, the effort is wasted.

It's important that you find a true friend to help you with this. You need somebody who has a sense of television and who will be honest enough to tell you what you're doing right and what you're doing wrong. That's what I mean by a true friend — somebody who can dole out gentle criticism. Be prepared to take it, use it and make your stand-ups better. This person must also have the patience of a saint because taping a zillion stand-ups isn't too much fun.

You'll want to emulate as many different situations as you can. Talk about water main breaks. Talk about the traffic. Talk about crime scenes. Try taping things in different kinds of weather situations. Do all the things Nancy has talked about in this book. If you're really smart, you'll actually grab a camera and show up at some real news scenes and tape a stand-up there, too. Just don't get in the way of the working press or police. Remember, you're not a member of the press ... yet.

If you're lucky enough to work in the television industry, ask a reporter if you can tag along on a real story. When the time comes, see if you can tape your own stand-up while you're on location. I had an intern who tagged along every morning one summer. And every single day, I let her tape a stand-up. Needless to say, her reel at the end of the summer was pretty strong.

But what would be even better is if you could tag along, tape a stand-up and then take the raw tapes and craft your own piece. That would be outstanding! Of course, you have to then sweet talk an editor into cutting it with you, but you can usually do that. Offering to pay him or take him to dinner is a good way to do it. And if he doesn't take any payment, be sure to bring a nice bottle of wine to say thank you. Never, ever forget to thank the people who help you along the way. Television is a team effort and there's no one player of the team who is more important than the others. That's a lesson you should carry with you throughout your career. I'll talk about this more at the end of this chapter.

If you are making a tape like this with "fake" stand-ups, you MUST disclose the nature of this tape in your cover letter. Tell the truth. This is not a tape of real news stories, but rather a tape of you showing off what you could do given the chance. If you position it correctly in the cover letter, they'll think you're a heck of a go-getter and a self-starter. Very few folks take the time to make a demo like this and it shows a great sense of dedication and passion.

What To Include on Your Second Tape and Beyond

Everybody always wants to know what to put on a tape. It's actually simpler than you think. Include stuff that makes you look good. That's it. Put nothing on that tape that is questionable. My personal theory is that a good resume tape is kind of like a good first date. The idea is to leave them wanting more.

I can't say this strongly enough. You must look good in each image they see. You must speak well. You must make sense. If there's even a slight doubt in your mind, don't include it.

To this end, it's really important that you make yourself look as good as possible before each and every time you tape a stand-up. That's true even if you've been in the business for ten years. Like it or not, television is a visual medium.

Now more so than ever, looks play a role. Heck, CNN fired a bunch of seasoned on-air folks and replaced them with younger, hipper versions. So just remember that while you don't have to be a stunning model or a handsome devil to get a job, you do have to always put your best foot forward — especially on your tape.

I know. I know. What does it matter if you can tell a good story? Looking good isn't journalism. Nope. It's not. But television news is a business and no matter how much the purists squeal about "journalism," the sad truth is viewers watch folks who look good. This is a business about ratings and more attractive people pull in more viewers. Depressing, but true.

And the folks who do the hiring in this business are very well aware of this. One of the bigwigs at one of the cable networks actually used to watch resume reels with the sound down so he could just look at the person first. I saw him do it with my own eyes so I know it's true. Scary, huh? That's why you have to look good.

Don't get depressed if you aren't Cindy Crawford or George Clooney. That's not what I'm talking about here. You do not have to be movie star gorgeous. Nor do you have to be a hipster in your twenties to get a job in this business. I am simply saying that you must put your own best foot forward. Wear the up-to-date clothes that work well on-camera. Pay attention to your hair. Freshen your lipstick. Even men need to powder their shiny noses. It all matters in the end, especially on your tape. And there are unattractive folks who make big names for themselves in this industry, but each and every one compensates for looks by being brilliant in other areas such as writing.

Also remember, this tape is about you — not the anchor who throws to your piece. So don't put any anchor tosses on the tape. Only you and your stuff should be on this reel. Nor do you want any station IDs or show opens on the tape. Remember, a news director is really busy. They aren't interested in what cool graphics a station has. They're only interested in you. Don't get lost in a bunch of clutter.

Also, there's nothing more unprofessional than a tape that includes you talking to the camera about who you are. That's not what news directors want. They want reporters, not spokespeople. I truly believe one of the worst things you can do is sit down and talk to the camera as though you're having a conversation with your potential employer. That's a big no-no. Show them you can report, not talk.

Format

So what to put on the tape isn't hard. Of course, the tricky part is just how to edit that tape. There are many, many formulas for tapes and no one formula is better than another. What I describe below has worked for me and for other folks I know so I figure it's as good a formula as any.

The Montage

The first image is the most important and it should come near the head of the tape. Don't make folks wait 30 seconds after they pop the tape in for the first image to appear. News Directors are busy people who live and die by seconds. Thirty seconds is a long time to them. Heck, that's a whole commercial break! So don't put 30 seconds of black at the top of the tape. Five seconds is enough.

Remember, your first impression is really important so make it a strong one. It's kind of like walking into an interview looking like a million bucks ... or not. So, I don't care what you're doing, start with the image of yourself looking your best. Period. Again, this is a visual medium.

After that, you have about 30 seconds to hook 'em. There have been informal studies (don't ask me for footnotes on this one!) that show news directors watch resume tapes for about 30 seconds and, if they don't like what they see, they'll eject the tape. That's it. Thirty whopping seconds. So make it good.

The montage is kind of a tease. By tease, I mean, "Hey, Mr. News Director, look at all the different things I can do. Aren't you curious? Keep watching for more." Relating it back to dating, the montage is kind of like when you lock eyes with an interesting person across a crowded bar. They see you and suddenly want to get to know you better. That's the job of the montage.

Montages are easier to do the longer you've been in this business. That's simply because you have more material to include. It's best to use different material in the montage than you do in the body of the tape. The idea is to show the breadth of your experience — not the same thing over and over. In fact, if you don't have enough of your work to do both a montage and a body, then just do the body.

This is obviously tougher to do when you're just starting out. If this is your first intro tape, the same rule applies as above. Just go out there and tape a bunch of different stand-ups with the montage in mind. But don't forget, full disclosure is a must when you send out that first tape.

The style I've used starts with a 30-second music montage at the top. No sound from you. None. The music is up full and there's just image after image after image of you cut to the music. The more versatility you can show in that 30 seconds the better. There should be no special order here. Mix it up. Make it visual. But remember: You must look good in each and every image.

If you don't have a large enough body of work to do 30 seconds, then do 15 or even 10. But you should definitely jam pack it full of images. That's the idea. This is the age of MTV. We are now accustomed to a saturation of images. So saturate 'em, baby.

The music should be fast-paced and in accordance to what you do. I'm a feature reporter. My music is fun. And my images are quite varied and truly bizarre. By the end of watching my montage, you know exactly who I am. Obviously, a hard news reporter or an investigative reporter would use music with a completely different tone or none at all.

If you don't use music, still include a montage using a variety of stand-ups from you with your sound up full. This is a good option for people who want to do hard news or investigative reporting. If you go with this choice, include five different styles: hard news, breaking news, sports, feature, weather ... whatever. But show yourself in a variety of situations. Remember: You want this montage to show your versatility. And the same rule applies: You need to look great — and speak really well!

The Slate

Following your montage, dip to black for about three seconds. That's it. Don't wait longer than that or people might think the tape is over.

After three seconds, a slate should come up. It should have your name and contact information. If you have an agent, put your name and your agent's name and phone number. If you don't have an agent, just put your own name, address and phone number on the slate. The slate should not be too busy or bizarre looking. Make it simple and graphically pleasing. It's kind of like a billboard when you drive down the highway. If there's too much information on there, folks driving by won't get it all read. That's exactly the same thing with a slate. Simple is better.

Leave it up for about five seconds or so.

The Body

After the slate, dip to black for another three seconds. Now it's time to show the body of your work.

I personally believe it's best if you don't put entire stories on your tape. Remember, this tape is your first date with your potential employer. The idea is to leave them wanting more. Put some of your story on the tape up to a point where the viewer is hooked and then move on to the next story. And put the piece on as it broadcasts. Don't try to improve it for the tape. Others might disagree, but it seems unethical to me.

In between each story, put some kind of graphic effect with a sound effect. Something very quick ... maybe two seconds worth. This is simply a device to let them know that one story is over and we're moving to the next one. My graphic effect is simply a piece of tape shot when the camera was moving from one location to another very quickly — a kind of swish effect. Nothing in it is recognizable to the eye, but for the record, it's grass. It was shot by accident during one of my stories. The swish of grass worked really well for transitions on the tape.

Include a variety of stories that show off your versatility. This is your showcase and a news director needs to know you can do it all. They want to hire a reporter who is just as comfortable reporting on a fire as they are covering a lottery winner. You want to show breaking news and feature stories and everything in between. That's true unless you're after a particular type of job such as investigative reporting. Then your tape should concentrate on your investigative skills. I'm a feature reporter and my reel is primarily features, but the end of my reel includes a bunch of breaking news stories to show I can do hard news — just in case.

You don't always have to include your stand-up in each story though they certainly want to see you as well. But remember, they've gotten a good look at you in the montage. So use your discretion about using yourself every time. This section of the tape is also about showing off your writing and storytelling abilities.

Other Considerations

Tapes should be no more than ten minutes long, preferably five. I don't care if you're the best thing since Walter Cronkite, you do not want to make your tape longer than ten minutes. Leave them wanting more.

Show your tape to your friends and family. Do they like it? What don't they like about it? Generally, friends and family are television viewers. They're your target audience in many ways so their opinion is actually more valid than you might think. But choose friends who are honest and will tell you the truth instead of, "You're absolutely wonderful." That's not helpful. But remember to take everything they tell you with a grain of salt. After all, you are the television professional, not them. Trust your own gut.

Hopefully, you're getting to be a stronger reporter every day, so be willing to update your tape often. If you have time to make a special tape for each job application, please do. You can then research what that particular employer likes and include that on your tape. Or if you're up for a feature job rather than an investigative job, you can tailor your tape to show more feature work. But the general rule is that you want a tape that is versatile and can be sent out at a moment's notice, so generic is best.

Tapes should be cut and stored on Beta, digital or a nonlinear edit machine as they are better quality and last longer. Use originals to recut your tape every time. There is nothing worse than watching tape that has been taken down several generations. Bad-quality tape is annoying and distracting. Nothing should take away from you.

Tapes should be sent to potential employers on VHS. You also want to buy nice hard tape cases for the tapes. Everything you send out should be of the highest quality. Labels should include your name and contact information and should go on the spine and the face of the tape AND the tape case, both. So there are four labels necessary for every tape sent out. You can buy these labels at an office supply store and print them out on your computer. There is no sense in spending a ton of money.

Table of Contents

You also want to include a Table of Contents. This will include the name of the piece as well as the starting timecode for each element. Make it clean and easy to read, for example:

- ❖ :00 Montage
- ❖ :35 Apartment fire (breaking news)
- ❖ 2:00 Man wins lottery
- ❖ 3:30 Tiger eats child
- ❖ 5:00 Mama Jan turns 100

The Table of Contents should not be attached to the actual tape itself. How can anybody follow along if they can't read it because the Table of Contents is stuck on the tape that's in the machine? I print my Table of Contents on another label and stick it on the inside of the tape box.

The Follow-up Tape

I know. Making a tape is a pain in the neck. Now you want me to make TWO tapes. Yes, I do.

Your first tape was your first date. You left them wanting more. Now, be prepared to give them more.

This second tape is your follow-up tape, available upon request. This tape is composed of full pieces and nothing else. No montage. No talking to the camera. No stations IDs or anchor tosses. Just include your top full stories. They could be full-length versions of the stories you put on your first tape. To truly wow them, make the second tape different stories. But again, include only your very best work. It's better to repeat strong pieces than include marginal ones.

In other words, put a slate at the top, dip to black for three seconds and then follow it with your three to five strongest whole pieces. Each should be well written and show off your looks.

What Do Others Think?

I decided not to leave this chapter solely to my own opinion. True, I've made a zillion reels for myself. And when I was a producer and did some casting, I saw a zillion more. Still and so, other opinions help.

So, first I called a hard news network correspondent. We kind of do the opposite types of stories, but our reels are not that different. He also puts a montage at the top because, as he puts it, news directors know they can work with your writing or your storytelling abilities, but they can't change who you are. They want to see you right off, not listen to track in a story and wait and wait to get a glimpse of you. So he puts four or five stand-ups of himself in completely different situations: one breaking news, one hard news, one feature, one sports — you get the idea. He does not use music, but rather you can hear his voice the entire time. He follows his montage with four full pieces. So — the format is the same, just executed a little differently.

I also called my agent. After all, few folks in the business see as many tapes as agents do. She told me that the first three minutes really have to grab her and that she often turns down the volume to see if the tape can keep her attention without the sound.

But the person she wants to represent has more than just looks because looks are no longer as important as they used to be. So she's not just watching with the sound down solely for appearance, but mannerisms and facial expressions. On top of just being capable, the person has to be likable even if that person is presenting a hard news story. In the end, she wants somebody credible, accessible and authentic.

She wants to see more than just a person reading news. Good-looking news readers are a dime a dozen. She is looking for somebody who is not like everybody else — somebody special — somebody who could break out and be a star. She likes to see people interviewing other people whether it's a man-on-the-street kind of interview or one that takes place on the set. These little interviews give her more insight as to what the person is really like and whether or not they're really authentic people.

Authentic is a big thing with her. Heck, it's a big thing with everybody. What does that mean exactly? Hmmm ... that's a tough one to pin down. But basically, I take it to mean somebody who is not pretending to be a reporter, but who IS a reporter. People don't want somebody who has a fake voice or who is really full of himself. Agents and news directors alike know that a reporter's job is to make people at home want to be your friend. A reporter's job is to say, "Hey come with me through that television set of yours and look at this cool thing I found." An anchor's job, on the other hand, is "Let me come sit at your kitchen table with you and tell you about today's news." And viewers won't take that journey with you unless they like you, trust you and think they could be friends with you. And that's true no matter what kind of story you're telling.

When my agent watches the packages included on a reel, she's looking to see how unique you are. How is your storytelling different from everybody else's? What makes you stand out? Do you have a gimmick or a specialty? What will make her job of selling you to a station easy?

Okay, the Tape Is Done, but Now What?

As I said before, getting a job in television is really tough. You have to dedicate time to the search every single day. Looking for a job is a full-time job in and of itself.

Branding Yourself

The key is to think of yourself as a product to market.

You will need to brand that product. Every single thing that you send out attached to your name should include the same look or logo. My resume has a little, brightly colored television in the upper left hand corner. So does my cover letter. So does my tape case and tape. So do my freelance business cards. If I'd been able to do so, I would have made my slate on my reel match as well. Everything should match. If it does, you have now become a brand.

Don't make the brand fancy or too odd. I can use a brightly colored TV because I'm a feature reporter. If your style is more serious, use a more serious brand. Perhaps it's only your monogram in a unique typeface. But whatever it is, it belongs to you.

You don't have to spend money on a brand. Mine was included in some software that came on my computer. If it's simply your monogram, you can design that on your computer, as well.

You'll definitely want something you can do yourself. And you'll want a place you can print this out yourself. Putting together a marketing kit is time-consuming and will need updating. Here's where the passion part comes in. Make it your job to look for a job. It'll pay off in the end.

There are three other very important things that should go in this marketing kit. You'll need a headshot, a resume and a cover letter.

Don't skimp on the headshot. It's an expensive process, but worth it. You can't get a job without getting your tape seen and if you don't look good in your headshot, a news director may never even put your tape into a machine. News directors are buried in tapes so any excuse not to watch is a welcome one. Don't give him an excuse with your headshot.

There are a zillion books on how to write a resume out there so I'm not going to go into that here. All I will say is make it easy to read and concise. Do not make it more than one page. I've been in this business for 15 years and was freelance for much of it. If I can whittle my resume down to one page, so can you.

Cover Letter

The cover letter is the tricky part. The idea is to get the attention of the news director. Why the heck should somebody watch your tape? Well, first off, your logo will help just get your letter read. But what they read is really important.

Good writing is obviously a must. But beyond that, you need to wow them. Do a little research. Find out about the station or the news director himself. Don't break any laws or make the guy feel like you're a stalker, but hey, you want to be a reporter ... do a little digging. Tailor each and every letter to a specific situation. The tape is hard to update. The letter is not. Do not be lazy about this.

And, of course, you have to sell yourself in this cover letter. Why in the world should they hire you? Come up with a reason. It's almost a sell line or slogan of sorts. Every product has one. You're a product. What makes you unique?

Be direct. Be blunt. Be cocky — but not overly. Writing a cover letter is a true art though I find the less time I sweat over them, the better they turn out. There are also many books on writing cover letters so read them and learn. And, hopefully, you're a good writer or you wouldn't want to be a journalist.

Sending Out Your Reel

Okay, so you've got this great reel and marketing kit. Who gets it? That, of course, depends where you are in your career. I'll address this to folks just starting out. Again, this takes a few of your investigative skills. Find out about stations that need reporters. Look at the back of trade publications.

Research, Research, Research

Most of the time, your television career starts out in a small town and then you move to a bigger town and after several steps, you finally end up in a big market. It's a process. I was lucky in that I started out in a fairly big market, but that's because I had produced for many years before I went in front of the camera. My producing experience helped me tremendously.

When you're looking at smaller markets, think about where those markets are located. Are they feeder markets for bigger cities?

Are they vacation spots where big network executives might see you on vacation? Are they states that have lots of big news stories? If you want to be a sports reporter, do they have a strong sports team in town? These are the kinds of things you want to consider. It's better to hold out for a job in a market like these than to take one in a town you can't escape. Really think about where you send your reel.

You can also consider moving to a big market and working in production first. That experience will help your reporting. And it will also give you many contacts you can call upon after you've learned the ropes.

But here's the thing — don't ask your blue chip contact to look at your reel until you're really ready for a big job. It's one thing to ask for advice and get a mentor, but you do not want to put a sour taste in somebody's mouth. Hold out calling that big name person until you're ready to call in that favor.

Meanwhile, talk to everybody you've ever known in your entire life and not just while you're hunting for a job, but in between the hunt, too. In a sense, you're always looking for a job in this business. And connections are everything. This is such a business about who you know — but not always.

I'll give you my examples from my own life. My first reporter job was at News 12 New Jersey. I didn't know a soul there, but I got a job. How? Well, I pushed and pushed and pushed. First, I called the assistant news director and told her on her voicemail who I was and that I'd be sending my reel, to please watch for it. And I told her it'd be the package with the little television on it.

Then, I sent the reel with my marketing kit. A few days later, I called to tell her I had sent it and was just calling to make sure she got it. I explained I felt certain she probably hadn't had time to look at it yet, but that I wanted to be sure it had arrived. Again, I left this message on her voicemail.

About a week later, I called again only this time I didn't leave a message. I called her until I reached her in person. And I was mindful of her own schedule calling after newscasts rather than right before or during.

I introduced myself and reminded her I was the girl with the little television. She said, "I haven't had time to watch your tape yet," to which I responded, "No problem, I know how busy you must be. So I'm not a pest, why don't you give me a date I should call back." She did. I called as requested and then pushed for an interview.

When I finally met her, she said, "But why should I hire you? You've never reported before in your life." I said, "I'll be able to get the interviews others can't. For example, how many folks send you their reel? How many do you actually see in person? If I can talk you into meeting me, imagine what I can do with potential news stories." That opened her mind and I was able to then sell myself. She let me come in as a freelancer and, eventually, I ended up as the station's live morning reporter.

A great resource with tips on how to get in the door is Harvey Mackay, a CEO and author who has great advice for how to get ahead in the business world. Remember: Television is a business so everything he says really does apply.

But my one pointer is follow-up. That's the key to everything.

My second reporting job was at WB11 in New York City. The assistant news director there had interviewed me to be a writer many years before. At the time, he wouldn't hire me because my writing skills were "too strong." He knew that I was also writing for the local CBS affiliate and that they paid better. He figured they'd want to use me a lot and he didn't want to take the time to train me and then never be able to use me. He said at the time, "But be sure to call me when there's a better job."

So I did. The WB was launching a new morning show in New York. I'd been the live feature morning reporter for News 12 New Jersey. So I called the same fella at the WB and reminded him that he'd told me to call when there was a bigger job. We kept in touch for several months as they began prepping for the show.

Eventually, I landed a job there as the helicopter reporter who also did feature stories. I'd never imagined that being a chopper reporter would be a good thing for me, but it was a very visible position. And they let me do a lot of fun stuff. I also covered breaking news including September 11. So ... my reel after this job was pretty strong.

Good thing, too, because I was ready when opportunity knocked. My big network break actually came through somebody I'd met 17 years earlier. That's right, 17 years. Nancy Reardon was my on-camera coach way back then. Her husband was a producer at CBS at the time and was very encouraging. He told me I had a certain spark and that I should pursue an on-camera career. I got sidetracked for a while working in sales, then producing. But when I had a chance to be on-camera years later, Nancy's coaching kicked in.

After September 11, I worked on a book about the event. It was a snapshot of the day told through the eyes of journalists who had covered the story. One of the contributors was Nancy's husband, Tom. He was curious about what I was doing and asked for my reel. He passed it on to the bigwigs at CBS.

One thing led to another and I eventually snagged a network job. Of course, Tom got me in the door, but I had to sell myself once I was there. Still, it was his connection that got my tape viewed and that's more than half the battle.

But I didn't take his introduction for granted. Before my first interview, I wrote a proposal about why they needed a feature reporter on the national morning show and why that reporter should be me. I left nothing to chance. And I didn't just let my reel do all the talking — or my interview. I wrote a second proposal after the interview about how we could implement the job I was proposing. I just kept hammering them. And, in the end, it paid off.

So as I said, this business is really all about who you know. You can certainly get a job based on your merits and ability, but having an inside connection can make a huge difference. When you're trying to land a job, call everybody you know. Hang out at the local joints where the people doing the hiring hang.

Network, network, network.

It's the key to employment. But you can't just let who you know be enough. You still have to earn the job.

Once You Get a Job

Congratulations! You're a reporter! You've reached your goal. Wahoo!!

But your journey is not over. A career in television is just that, a career. Every job you have leads to the next. It's a career of stepping-stones — and that does not mean stepping on other people to get ahead.

I truly believe with everything in me that your reputation has as much to do with getting a job as your talent does. By that I mean if a news director has a choice between two candidates who are equally talented, he'll choose the one who has a reputation as being the kindest and the hardest working. Nobody wants a whiner on the staff. Nobody wants a diva. Nobody wants a slacker.

So when you report, work hard. Don't cut corners. Do your own work and give credit where credit is due. If your photographer had a great idea that made your piece better, be sure other people know it. You recognized it as a good idea so that makes you smart, too. The photographer will appreciate you crediting him and will work harder for you next time. That's true of everybody on your team — bookers, producers, satellite truck operators, editors. Be kind. And you'll build a reputation as a person others want to work with. And, even better, you'll make friends.

Television is a team effort. A television piece cannot get done without the photographer and the editor, too. Eventually, you'll also have a producer and an audio person as well. And no matter what, you can't do a piece without ALL of you. Just because you're the one in front of the camera doesn't make you IT. In fact, I recently taped a piece about lobstering. The photographer was very sick while we were on the boat and it reminded me that the piece could be shot without me, but not him.

In fact, I find two minds are better than one. There have been many times when the most unlikely people have given me fabulous ideas. I took them — and credited those people and my piece was far the better for it.

And remember, the technical folks are carrying around all that equipment. You're just talking for a living. Yes, yes. You have to be smart. You have to investigate. You have to write. You have to have the personality. You have to work hard, too. But a photographer is also an artist and it takes both strong words and strong pictures to tell a story. So be considerate. If you are asking the photographer to shoot for eight hours off the shoulder (without a tripod), then be sure to give him a few breaks to rest his shoulder. Offer to buy him water and feed him. If you have a bigger crew, offer to get them water, too. A little kindness goes a long way.

You'll also catch more flies with honey than vinegar. That's an old Southern expression that basically means people will be willing to do more for you if you are kind to them than if you yell at them. And there will be times that you really have to be a cheerleader and encourage your team to work hard. I've had times when I've had to really sweet talk crews into going above and beyond the call of duty — like climbing 137 steps of a bell tower in 104-degree weather. Ugh. They did it because they were professionals. But they did it without whining because I was nice about the whole thing.

What will happen in the end is that you'll build a reputation as somebody people like. People will want to work with you. People will try harder for you. People will go the extra mile to make your piece sing. And you can never underestimate the joy of that.

And perhaps most important, your reputation will get you the next job. There will be a day when some news director at some bigger station will call for recommendations and what people say about you will make or break you.

That's not to say there won't be times when people let you down. A photographer may come back with video that's all blue. Or perhaps the audio guy forgot to record audio. It happens. It's television, not brain surgery. Remain calm and talk to them — just like you'd talk to a friend who let you down. Don't scream. Don't freak out. Just talk to them and let them know you're disappointed. That's usually enough. Trust me, they're already beating themselves up without you doing it, too. And think about what you'd like your boss to say to you if you screwed up. I guess it's the Golden Rule, "Do unto others as you would have them do unto you."

Try not to get caught up in office politics or become competitive with the other reporters. Sure, you want the top assignments, but it doesn't hurt you to say to another reporter, "Your piece today was great." You are not competing with them. You are only competing with yourself to be the best that you can be.

And if you are, you'll go a long way in this business.

A Final Thought

Bob Scheiffer, Dan Rather, Diane Sawyer, Jane Pauley, Katie Couric, Jay Leno, Anderson Cooper, Jon Stewart, Paula Zahn and Oprah Winfrey did not start off in their careers as smart, or as relaxed or as knowledgeable as they are today. Nobody did. Nobody does. It takes a long time to look and sound the way they do.

They didn't begin their careers on national television. They started working at small stations. But by the time they arrived at the network or as the hosts of their own syndicated shows, they had plenty of experience. They all made gaffs along the way. They all took risks. They were passionate, curious and ambitious, and worked very hard to get where they are now.

Perhaps most important, they all loved what they did and do. They loved the whole process, not just the fame and the money. They got to the top jobs by putting in the work and the necessary preparation.

It is the journey that is important. Never forget that. Then you will relish and be able to handle everything that comes your way in this difficult and competitive business.

NANCY'S
RULES

Don't stop honing your craft.
Never lose your passion or your inquisitive nature.
Be polite, humble and respectful of those around you.
Believe in your talent and trust your individuality and you will
  be a success.

Kimberly Dozier was the war correspondent in Iraq for CBS
News. She is a driven and passionate reporter who wants to leap
into such dangerous areas that sometimes her crew has to stop her.
Her spirit to tell the story is legendary. It is sad to report that she
was severely wounded on assignment north of Baghdad and her crew
killed.

She and her crew are not the only brave and dedicated journalists. Not only have correspondents and anchors risked their lives
in wartime, but there are also many who have had the courge
to confront powerful people in the corportate and governmental
worlds. They represent another threat in the course of a journalist's job. I know that many of the people who read this book will
keep these flames burning. It has been so from Lincoln Stefans to
Woodward and Bernstein, to Kimberly and all of those brave men
and women who still seek out the inside stories today. Sometimes
they are attacked, wounded, or jailed, yet they continue to search
out the truth.

To all of you who will dare in the future—you add glory to the
entire profession.

Index